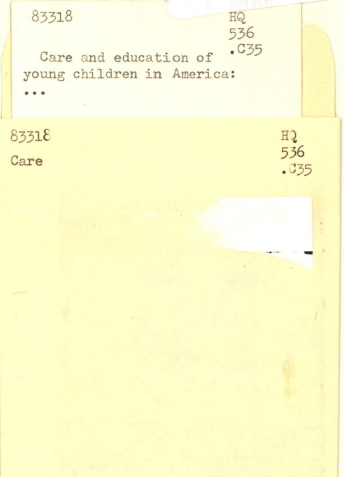

CARE AND EDUCATION OF YOUNG CHILDREN IN AMERICA

Policy, Politics, and Social Science

RON HASKINS
JAMES J. GALLAGHER

editors

ABLEX Publishing Corporation
Norwood, New Jersey 07648

Library of Congress Cataloging in Publication Data
Main entry under title:

Care and education of young children in America.

"Papers . . . originally presented in a colloquium series
at the University of North Carolina at Chapel Hill. The
series was sponsored by the Bush Institute for Child and
Family Policy at UNC."
   Includes bibliographical references and index.
   1. Family policy—United States—Congress. 2.
Children's rights—United States—Congresses. 3. Education and state—United States—Congresses. 4. Federal
aid to education—United States—Congresses. 5. Children—Care and hygiene—Congresses. I. Haskins, Ron,
1943- II. Gallagher, James John, 1926- III. Bush
Institute for Child and Family Policy.
HG536.C35   362.7'0973   80-11788
ISBN   0-89391-040-6

ABLEX Publishing Corporation
355 Chestnut Street
Norwood, New Jersey

Contents

This book is the first product of an enterprise undertaken by a group of social scientists, physicians, and lawyers at the University of North Carolina at Chapel Hill. All of us have been involved to varying degrees in research, service delivery, and policy formulation at the state or federal level. Like many other people involved in these and similar activities designed to increase the general welfare of children and families, we have often felt uneasy about the interrelations between discovery, policy decisions, and services to children and families.

Surely the fit between these elements could be improved, and surely those who claim to have and to generate knowledge should play a role in the fitting. But how best to proceed? The traditional methods have shown only limited—some would say nonexistent—usefulness. Commissions of experts provide policy-makers with long lists of programs that, if enacted, would exhaust the federal treasury, and if implemented, might not be very useful. Congressional testimony or public speeches by child development experts have by now made some people realize that research expertise is not a license for policy pronouncements.

What is needed, then, is an approach to policy formulation that goes well beyond social science research and the boundaries of any particular discipline. This volume is intended to be a small, but certain, step in that direction. The papers assembled here were originally presented in a colloquium series at the University of North Carolina at Chapel Hill. The series was sponsored by the

Preface

University's Bush Institute for Child and Family Policy which was created to function both as an interdisciplinary training program in policy analysis and an umbrella organization that would provide the resources and opportunities for faculty and students to define and refine methods of developing or improving public policies that affect children and their families. The institute invited a group of social scientists and policymakers to present papers on the theme "Care and Education of Young Children in America." The invited guests represented a variety of disciplines; most of them have been involved in both research in their discipline and policy applications of social science knowledge.

In short, the people whose papers appear in this book were able to call on a background of experience in advising policymakers, influencing government decisions, or actually devising or implementing child and family policy. A brief survey of the papers and authors will give prospective readers a notion of the objectives for which the work was undertaken.

After an introductory chapter that outlines and illustrates the model of policy analysis used at our institute, Bettye Caldwell of the University of Arkansas traces the historical development of children's rights, parents' rights, and the role of society in arbitrating potential conflicts between children's and parents' rights. Caldwell concludes her very thoughtful paper by outlining various mechanisms through which society can avoid, or at least ameliorate, this potential clash between the rights of children and parents.

Irving Lazar of Cornell University follows with a paper which examines factors that have prevented the successful application of social science knowledge to the formulation of public policy. Lazar, who has had extensive experience advising government agencies on preschool programs for poor children, demonstrates that, although a select group of social science studies has been able to influence policy, the vast majority of research has accumulated in abstruse journals read only by specialists. Henry Levin, an educational economist who heads the Institute for Research on Educational Finance and Governance at Stanford, provides detailed examination of educational vouchers, a school-financing mechanism that has often been proposed as a solution to many problems that beset public education. Levin's analysis of this policy alternative, by careful attention to the probable effects of vouchers, shows that unintended consequences of policy initiatives can often be predicted even before the policy is implemented.

If Levin concerns himself with exposing the weaknesses of an untried policy currently in vogue as a solution to problems faced by our public schools, James Comer, a child psychiatrist whose clinic is the inner-city school, describes an educational program that has actually achieved many of the objectives for which vouchers were designed. Based on eight years of direct involvement in ghetto schools of the type that many educators and policymakers regard as hopelessly buried by financial problems, despair, and vandalism, Comer offers a model of intervention that has galvanized a poor and previously powerless community, taught poor black children to read and write at grade level, and reduced the absenteeism that plagues so many of our nation's ghetto schools. From this unique and tested model of educational intervention, Comer proceeds to draw a number of principles that should guide the formulation of educational policy.

No less pressing than the educational problems of America's poor children are health problems that threaten their futures if not their very lives. Mortality among infants from low-income families, for example, is a national scandal—especially since the technology of preventive medicine has proved its effectiveness among the fortunate children of middle-class families who can afford private, preventive care. But the distribution of health services, like the distribution of income, is extremely uneven in America of the 1970s. Examining European countries in which health services are often advanced well beyond those of the United States, George Silver of Yale, formerly a health official in the Johnson administration, argues that the elements of a national health policy for children already exist in this country. What is needed now is the imagination and political organization to bring a unified American health system for children into existence.

The final two papers were written by activists with more than a decade of experience working in Washington to influence federal policy that affects children and families. Both Martha Phillips, Assistant Minority Counsel of the House Ways and Means Committee, and Ellen Hoffman, Director of Government Affairs for the Children's Defense Fund, bring a sobering tone to the consideration of policy analysis. Hoffman describes the complex forces that produce federal policy, as well as the equally complex forces that currently impede progress toward a federal policy for children and families. After a careful description of the congressional budget process, which must be of central concern to anyone interested in affecting federal programs, Hoffman turns to a series of concrete proposals that would move us toward a national family policy.

Hoffman's concern with constraints on the creation of a national policy for children and families becomes the central focus of Martha Phillips' paper. Paramount among these constraints is the Proposition 13 mentality and fiscal restraint. But Phillips also detects in these and similar developments a conservative trend in the national mood. The underlying cause of this trend is excessive government activity in nearly every phase of national life, and even more particularly, government activity that often seems to undercut initiative and reward profligacy. Turning to the central item on the liberal agenda, Phillips states flatly that an income redistribution program is out of the question for the foreseeable future. Further, she questions the philosophical assumptions on which income redistribution is based.

Each of these seven papers is followed by two brief reactions by Bush faculty members, other faculty members at UNC or Duke University, or officials in the North Carolina state government. Reactions focus on one or two central issues raised by the respective authors. These reactions have been included in this volume both because they present a second and third view of major policy issues and because they indicate the uncertainty and lack of solid agreement on policy matters—even among people who have worked for, and with, children for much of their professional lives.

A colloquium series and a volume like this one are based on the efforts of many people and organizations. Primary recognition, however, must go to Stan Shepard and Humphrey Doermann of the Bush Foundation who not only provided the money to conduct this series, but also have given our institute the freedom to use resources from the Bush Foundation with great flexibility. We also acknowledge Anthony Jenzano and UNC's Morehead Planetarium, as well as Betsy Pritchett and the Morehead Foundation, for making their superb facilities available to us during the colloquium series. Sheila White, Susann Hutaff, Paul Hirschbiel, Ruth Kirkendall, and Chris Houghton also provided assistance too diverse to enumerate in planning and conducting the colloquium series. Florine Purdie, Sherree Payne, and Marie Butts typed and retyped each of the papers and comments. We wish to express special thanks to Jennifer Ferguson who provided us with excellent editorial advice on each of the papers. Finally, we frankly admit our indebtedness to members of the Bush faculty at UNC and to our doctoral students and professional fellows. The possibility of adapting social science knowledge and techniques to promote the welfare of children and families has generated vast enthusiasm among all of us. Thus, we have full confidence that this volume represents the first among many tangible products that will bring us closer to a goal shared by all citizens—strong families capable of ensuring the development of all their members.

RON HASKINS received his Ph.D. in developmental psychology from the University of North Carolina at Chapel Hill. He is currently Associate Director of the Bush Institute for Child and Family Policy and Assistant Director of Longitudinal Research at the Frank Porter Graham Child Development Center at the University of North Carolina. Dr. Haskins's research concerns the development of children from low-income families and the effects of acute illness on the behavior of children and their caregivers.

Introduction— A Model for Analyzing Social Policies

As recent experience with comprehensive child-care legislation demonstrates, America faces a substantial dilemma in creating a national policy for children and families. At the heart of this dilemma is a conflict as old as the American Constitution. Where does private responsibility end and public responsibility begin? It is only somewhat simplistic to argue that many politicians, much of the electorate, and the establishment of people concerned with research about and services to children and families can be divided into two camps on this issue. On one side are those who believe that our nation does not provide well for its children, that the family is in serious trouble, and that comprehensive government programs for children and families are needed. On the opposing side are those who support the traditional view that the family is private and that government intervention is justified only in cases such as abuse, delinquency, poverty, and physical, mental, or emotional handicap. And even in these cases, the courts have made it clear that intervention in the family is justified only under extreme circumstances.

The conflict between these two views has sharpened in the 15 years since the inception of the Great Society programs. This period has seen an increase in the number of federal programs to help children and families: day care, public assistance, Supplemental Security Income, aid to public education, school lunch, Medicaid, and others. By functional category in the 1977 federal budget, such programs spent $18.2 billion on education, $7.2 billion on training and employment, $46 billion on health, and $177 billion on income security. In 1977, domestic transfer payments alone were equal to 8.9 percent of the Gross National Product, as compared with 5.1 percent for defense spending. By contrast, in 1947 defense expenditures were 4.3 percent of the federal budget and domestic transfer payments were 3.5 percent (Office of Management and Budget, undated).

Despite these increases in expenditures on social programs, there is an uneasy feeling among both citizens and professionals that these programs do not have their intended effect. Indeed, commission after commission cites declining SAT scores, increased crime rates, increased divorce rates, growing numbers of teenage pregnancies, and a host of other statistics to argue that children and families are now worse off than ever.

The current feeling of unease is complicated further by America's economic difficulties. The energy crisis plays a substantial role in these difficulties, but more fundamental is the continuing high rate of inflation. The upshot has been renewed emphasis on a balanced federal budget. Not only have the President and Congress attempted to avoid large new expenditures that would increase the federal deficit, but serious social thinkers have proposed a constitutional amendment that would require a balanced federal budget.

Gone–but not forever one suspects–are the days of large new expenditures on social programs. The repeated failures to revamp our welfare system, to legislate some type of income maintenance program, and to pass a child development bill are all signs that political reality has changed. Though some choose to interpret these and similar debacles of the children's cause as evidence that America's funding priorities do not adequately recognize the needs of children and families, others see a picture that is not totally grim. Indeed, in recent years the Congress has passed a number of moderate programs for children and families: a law requiring the education of handicapped children; Supplemental Security Income; Early and Periodic Screening, Diagnosis, and Treatment; increases in Head Start funding; child abuse legislation; and a number of others.

It seems wise to assume, as both Hoffman and Phillips argue, that only such incremental and small-scale programs are to be expected for the next decade or so. Given this assumption, how should advocates, child development experts, educators, and others interested in children respond?

One answer that has become increasingly popular in recent years is the use of something called *policy analysis*. Though policy analysis is not a new field (MacRae, 1976; Nagel, 1977), the application of policy analysis tools to social problems is, if not new, at least a growing concern among psychologists, educators, and other social scientists. As the papers in this volume demonstrate, the large and somewhat disparate group of researchers and other professionals who focus on children and their families has begun to pay explicit attention to the public policy implications of their work. The purpose of this introductory chapter is to outline a particular approach to the examination of problems dealt with by social policy.

MacRae and Wilde (1979) have defined policy analysis as "the use of reason and evidence to choose the best policy among a number of alternatives" (p. 4). This definition, like many others (Gil, 1973; Rein, 1976; Titmuss, 1974), emphasizes the application of reason and evidence to policy alternatives. In these respects, policy analysis has much in common with social science. The use of reason implies that decisions will be based on some explicit set of criteria that are themselves defended as appropriate for the case at hand. Whim, personal prejudice, and political belief, then, must be minimized and subjugated to the rules of logic and inference.

An important element in attempts to subdue whim and prejudice while emphasizing logic is the application of evidence to selection among policy alternatives. Though social science research constitutes an important type of evidence, it is by no means the only type that the analyst can use. The history of a social problem often supplies evidence that should be taken into account, as does demographic information. Nor can the analyst afford to be bounded by the confines of a favored academic discipline. Indeed, there is no current problem of social policy—health care, day care, income maintenance, education—for which one discipline can supply all the relevant evidence.

To take child care as an example, any moderately complete analysis of the problem and its potential solutions would consider the history of child care in the United States, provide an economic description of the current child care market, and examine the sociological and psychological effects of various types of child care on children and families. Such an analysis is, of necessity, interdisciplinary. *Interdisciplinary,* another term much in vogue refers to nothing more than an activity which uses the information and techniques from more than one discipline. The term rolls easily off many tongues, but when developmentalists begin to deal with benefit-cost analysis, trade-offs, and externalities, while economists begin to consider early experience, the development of aggression, and the complexities of gene-environment interaction, interdisciplinary activities take on a concrete meaning, and professionals quickly realize the depth and importance of evidence and techniques about which they have received little formal training. But if evidence refuses to recognize the artificial boundaries of the scientific disciplines, analysts have no choice but to expand their perspective and overcome the prejudices of their own disciplines.

A MODEL OF POLICY ANALYSIS

Having defined policy analysis, I would like now to outline a specific approach to analysis that promises some reasonable possibility of successfully attacking social problems. Although the sketch offered here must be brief, I mean to provide a concrete set of proposals that, taken together, constitute a concise but comprehensive method for analyzing social problems, selecting a solution, and communicating that solution to those who can cause it to be enacted and implemented.

This model consists of five distinct steps: analyzing the problem situation, specifying the analysis criteria, generating alternative strategies, synthesizing information to select a policy alternative, and examining the feasibility of the policy alternative selected. In expanding somewhat on each of these five steps of the analysis model, examples will be drawn from day-care policy. Although examples might have been taken from any of various policy problems, day care was chosen because of its timeliness and because it provides particularly clear and rich illustrations of steps in the model.

Before proceeding further, I wish to acknowledge that this model has been developed over the past two years by faculty members and fellows of the Bush Institute for Child and Family Policy at the University of North Carolina. The particular version offered here varies in some respects from other models we have discussed, but on the whole I cannot claim ownership of the ideas embodied in this model.

Analysis of the Problem Situation

Most problem situations arise because of changes in demographic features of society, the breakdown of traditional patterns of behavior, the gradual evolution of new values and attitudes, or technological innovation. The outcome of these forces is that some group sees an opportunity for advancement, believes that its current situation is threatened, or perceives an unfulfilled need.

In this stage of analysis, an historical perspective is often helpful. In fact, one might argue that understanding the problem situation is impossible without examining the problem's origin and, if appropriate, previous attempts to deal with the problem. History informs the present and, in so doing, offers important insights to both the nature of a policy problem and its potential solutions.

Analysis of the problem situation must also include a review of groups that want to implement a particular policy and groups that may be affected by a policy. This review will show that often the groups most concerned see a threatened value or an opportunity to promote an important value.

For many policy problems, defining the problem situation should also include an examination of current state and federal policies that influence the situation. Almost every problem that affects children and families has been dealt with in some way by state or federal laws. Previous and current government activity, then, is an integral part of the problem situation and must be taken into account if the analyst is to avoid creating policies that actually oppose one another. Further, as will be argued later, examining the outcomes of current policies can yield important insights for devising new policies.

Finally, an important product of a thorough analysis of the problem situation should be a clear and comprehensive statement of the problem which the analysis aims to attack. This statement may well differ from that held by the analyst when review of the problem situation began. Indeed, one particularly important justification for analysis of the problem situation is that thorough analysis often changes the analyst's understanding of the problem, its causes, and its potential solutions. Such changes constitute a restatement of the problem in a form more consonant with historical facts and more comprehensive in its understanding of which groups are interested in, and affected by, the policy.

The current interest in day-care policy can be used to illustrate a number of these points about analyzing the problem situation. To begin with historical background, it should be emphasized that day care has a long history in the United States (Steinfels, 1973; Steiner, 1976; Woolsey, 1977). Not only have centers for young children operated in this country for over a century, but the federal government has also played an increasingly important role in the day-care market. During the depression and again during World War II, federal funds were appropriated for the operation of day-care centers. The latter example of federal involvement in day care was contained in the Lanham Act (1941) which had the specific purpose of facilitating female participation in war industry. Though federal support of day care ended with the war, President Kennedy again put day care on the public agenda with the Social Security Act amendments of 1962. Kennedy's intent was to help welfare mothers obtain jobs and thereby escape welfare dependency. Three years later, in 1965, Head Start brought day care to widespread public attention by introducing the proposition that day care could be used to promote optimum development, especially among children from poor families. More recently, a number of bills have proposed universal day care that would be available to nearly all preschool children, with a substantial portion of costs paid by the federal government. Indeed, in 1971, Congress actually passed the Brademas-Mondale comprehensive child care legislation which, among other things, would have provided federal money for day-care services. President Nixon, however, vetoed the bill.

This brief historical survey demonstrates that day care is not a new issue for Americans or for the federal government. More important, it reveals the long-standing existence of many justifications for day care and the demographic groups and values that underlie these justifications. To take only the most obvious examples, day care supported by the Lanham Act was designed to support labor force participation by women. Though this objective has a very modern ring, the underlying value was not the independence fostered by earning one's own living, but the need for women's labor during a time of labor shortage created by a national emergency. By contrast, a different value was involved in Head Start; namely, the promotion of optimum development of children from low-income families. This particular value was—and still is—associated with the assumption, made frequently by social scientists, that the early years of life are extremely important for adequate development.

Implicit in this historical overview is a partial roster of the groups most concerned with day care. Given the recent increases in divorce and single mothers (National Academy of Sciences, 1976), working women constitute perhaps the largest demographic group in need of child care. But this is certainly not a monolithic population with a single need. On the contrary. It contains welfare mothers who need very cheap care, often at unusual hours, to make their work profitable. It also includes professional women who want quality care even at relatively high prices. Nor are the primary motives for wanting day care identical for all families. Mothers on welfare and single mothers often work out of absolute necessity. Women with working-class husbands want child care because their earnings can enable the family to enjoy some of the material benefits accorded the middle class. And many middle-class and professional women need child care because they seek self-fulfillment through work. Thus, although working women constitute the largest demographic group seeking child care, the analyst must be aware that very different needs and values underlie the desire for child care by various groups of women. It follows that specific policy questions, such as cost of day care, hours of operation, and curriculum content, may receive very different answers from these rather disparate groups of working mothers.

Nor are working women the only important group supporting day care. The analyst must consider at least three other groups, and the value they hope to maximize through day care. First, many politicians are willing to support day care as a means of getting welfare mothers trained, into the labor force, and off welfare. Second, child-care professionals believe that day care is a means of promoting development of children—especially poor children. Third, and a group of fairly recent entry into the picture, public school teachers and their unions support child care as a means of relieving the economic plight of teachers left without jobs by decreasing public school enrollments (Levine, 1978).

In the case of day care, analysis of the problem situation should also include a description of the current day-care market. Many people seem to assume that most nonmaternal care is provided by day-care centers. This assumption is false. Indeed, as shown in Table 1, American families seem to prefer care by a family member or relative. Table 1 does not show that roughly 50 percent of the day care used by American families, whether provided by relatives or nonrelatives, is provided in the family's own home. This contrasts sharply with the fact that only about 10 percent of the families needing care place their child in a center.

Whatever the exact figures for child-care arrangements might be, federal policy must be based on the realization that a large majority of Americans who need child care use informal and nonmarket forms of care. Both increased federal expenditures and federal regulation of licensed centers and homes will fail to help the majority of families with preschool children or the children themselves.

Turning now to the federal role in the day-care market, it should be noted immediately that the federal government spends over $2.5 billion on programs for preschool children. More than 90 percent of these funds are spent on six programs: Title XX of the Social Security Act, Head Start, Child Care Food Service Program, Title I of the Elementary and Secondary Education Act (ESEA), Aid to Families with Dependent Children (AFDC), and the Work Incentive Program (WIN). Each is unique in the policy setting in which it originated, its intended purpose, and its area of major focus. Table 2 compares the cost, number of children served, federal cost per child, and the federal agency or department responsible for administration of the program (adapted from Rivlin, 1978). Perusal of the information summarized in Table 2 indicates the diversity of child care programs supported by federal funds. Despite this diversity, federal involvement in the day-care market can be summarized in three points. First, most

Table 1 Some Estimates of Percentage of Children Receiving Various Types of Child Care

Source	Year of Data Collection	Number of Families Sampled	Brief Description of Sample	Percentage of Families Using		
				Center	Family or Relative	Nonrelative with Pay
Low and Spindler	1965	35,000	National Probability Sample; mothers worked at least 6 months in the previous year; at least one child less than 14.	2	44	17
Kurz, Robins, & Spiegelman[a]	1972	1,183	Employed female heads of families participating in Seattle and Denver Income Maintenance Experiments; at least one child less than 13; low- and moderate-income families.	7	38	46
Duncan & Hill	1973	511	National Probability Sample; both parents work; one or more children under 12; use at least 10 hours care per week.	12	48	37
Unco[b]	1975	4,609	National Probability Sample; all households with at least one child less than 14.	14	49	37

SOURCES: Low & Spindler, 1968; Kurz et al., 1975; Duncan & Hill, 1975; Unco, 1976.
[a]Figures were computed by averaging the data in Kurz et al., 1975, table 4, p. 11; table 5, p. 12.
[b]Data based on total hours of care.

Table 2 Cost and Number of Children Served by Six Primary
Federal Child-Care Programs (1977)

Program	Cost (millions)	Number of Children Served (thousands)	Cost per Child	Administering Agency
Title XX	$899	799	$1013	HEW
Head Start	448	349	1284	HEW
ESEA Title I	136	367	371	HEW
Child-Care Food Service	120	580	207	USDA
AFDC	84	145	579	HEW
Work Incentive Program	57	85	671	HEW

support for low-income families requires that children be placed in day-care centers. Second, there is relatively little day-care assistance for working-class and middle-class families. Third, federal day-care efforts are characterized by fragmentation of program and administering agencies. Each of these conclusions must be considered by the analyst attempting to revise or reform current federal day-care policy.

Specifying Valuative Criteria

As Quade (1975) and others point out, policy analysis grew out of systems research, operations research, and public administration. Many of the problems to which these analytic methods have been applied were technological—building highways, conducting war, sending men into space. As various groups and individuals now apply these methods to social problems, and especially to child and family policy, it becomes increasingly clear that difficulties abound. A basic cause of these difficulties is that the solution of human social problems involves the *synthesis of values*. By this I mean simply that various groups enter the policy arena with competing needs, interests, claims, and rights.

How are these incommensurables to be resolved? As I shall argue, analysts of social policy can answer this question by using analysis criteria. The important point to be made here is that values necessarily play a powerful—even pre-eminent role—in the analysis of child and family policies. Thus, a primary characteristic of analysis models for social policy must be some means of making values explicit and, where necessary, choosing among competing values. If, as MacRae and Wilde (1979) argue, policy analysis is the process of using "reason and evidence to choose the best policy" (p. 4), valuative criteria are the heart of policy analysis because they are the yardstick by which we judge the worth of policy alternatives.

A number of these valuative criteria are universal; i.e., they can and should be considered in the analysis of most social policies. Four examples of these universal criteria are vertical equity, efficiency, preference satisfaction, and stigma.

Vertical equity. Vertical equity involves the unequal treatment of unequal individuals and groups. To satisfy the criterion of vertical equity, a policy must result in redistribution of resources in such a way as to provide greater benefits to the poor than to the rich. Much of current child and family policy, particularly that originating from the War on Poverty, was designed to use resources to benefit the poor. Whether these policies always achieved such a criterion might be questioned (Haveman, 1977), but the intent of the health, housing, employment, and education programs passed during the early years of the Johnson administration was to place greater economic and political resources in the hands of poor people.

The criterion of vertical equity, like most valuative criteria, is not accepted as a primary objective of social policy by all political groups. Liberals and conservatives agree that a society should have some fairly substantial difference in financial reward across job categories in order to maintain incentives for increasing productivity. Further, as Plattner (1979) has argued recently, American society has never sanctioned the government's right to redistribute income. Even in the case of the graduated income tax, which in fact has a substantial redistributive impact, the original justification was not that money should be taken from the rich and given to the poor. Rather, the justification was that the rich could better afford to carry a heavy tax burden.

On the other hand, a persistent charactertistic of liberal and reform movements in Western countries has been desire to help the poor and, more recently, their children. This tendency is evident, not only in socialist thought but in popular movements, such as the labor movement in Great Britain and the Populist tradition in the United States.

The important point is that vertical equity is not a right, a law, or a firm principle of democratic society. It is a value that some accept and some do not. Or more properly, it is a value held with various degrees of strength by various citizens and groups. The analysts' role is to state clearly the degree to which their analysis will be influenced by the attempt to maximize this value.

Efficiency. A second important valuation criterion, not completely separable from vertical equity, is efficiency. *Efficiency* is defined as that use of resources which will produce the maximum benefit. By this criterion, a policy is less desirable if another policy would produce, on the whole, greater benefits. Needless to say, the word "benefits" does not have clear meaning in these definitions. What is a benefit? Who receives the benefit? In what units can it be measured?

Economists have devised a method that provides a partial answer to these questions. Benefit-cost analysis has the potential to maximize efficiency by expressing both the benefits and costs of a program in dollars. Except for a few complications, such as opportunity costs (MacRae & Wilde, 1979), the measurement of program costs is usually straightforward. Thus, we can usually measure in dollars what expenditures were made, or are planned or estimated, for a given social program. But measuring the benefits of a social program is often more difficult. In what units can we measure the value of a ten-point IQ gain produced by a preschool program? Of 1,000 single women placed in jobs by a training program? Of 10,000 children from poor families receiving a balanced lunch? Of a 10 percent reduction in infant mortality?

The answers to these questions are neither simple nor, in the few cases in which bold analysts have actually affixed a dollar value to such program benefits, widely accepted (see discussion of Weber, Foster, & Weikart, 1978). Nonetheless, attempts to devise methods for measuring program benefits in dollars may be well worth the effort. For if such methods can be devised, the analyst will be able to directly compare the benefit-cost ratios of various strategies intended to produce valued social objectives. Further, benefit-cost analysis holds the possibility of comparing the value of expenditures on very diverse programs. Theoretically, for example, if it were possible to achieve consensus on the dollar value of military security and of early detection of handicapping conditions, benefit-cost analysis would enable policymakers to spend public money on programs where the general welfare—and efficiency—would be maximized.

Although there is probably good reason to despair of ever achieving such consensus, the kind of thinking that underlies benefit-cost analysis can still be of assistance to the analyst. Thus, we might at least be able to make estimates of the benefits produced by a given program, measured in whatever units are practical or available, and thereby permit comparison among programs costing various amounts of money.

In other cases, the logic of benefit-cost analysis may lead to better policy decisions in a rather straightforward way. To take just one example, if the average cost of center-based day care is $1,630 per year (Coelen, Glantz, & Calore, 1978), a government training program designed to place welfare mothers in jobs that paid only the minimum wage would be of questionable efficiency for women having three or more children. Accepting such a mother's annual income of $6,032 as a measure of the social benefits produced by her labor, we find that the day-care cost of $6,520 for four children is greater than the value of her labor. Such a policy, then, would be inefficient.

The criterion of efficiency should play a primary role in all policy decisions. Since everyone gains in the long run when public funds are spent efficiently, there would seem to be little reason for anyone to quarrel with this criterion. It must be admitted, however, that the intended outcome of many social policies cannot be easily measured; this problem limits ability to apply the efficiency criterion.

Preference satisfaction. In a society that values freedom and often avoids government intervention on the grounds that it limits individual choice, preference satisfaction must be considered a fundamental criterion in that individuals are better off when policy helps them satisfy their own preferences. As with the case of efficiency, few will disagree that this criterion is important.

At least two complications, however, make this criterion quite difficult to maximize. First preferences can best be satisfied when individuals are able to buy the goods and services they prefer. But many individuals and families in our society do not have enough money to satisfy basic preferences. Even worse, many parents do not have enough money to satisfy their children's basic preferences. As a result, government programs, such as Aid to Families with Dependent Children (AFDC), have been designed to help parents support their children. Yet such programs often minimize the criterion of preference satisfaction because decisions about the goods and services to be purchased have already been made by the government. Thus, especially in categorical programs, the government will provide the poor with food, housing, health, training, or education. But such categorical programs do not allow the poor to spend an equivalent amount of money on the goods or services they would prefer for themselves and their children. Further, it might be argued that by making choices for people, the government increases dependency. In the long run, continued dependency may have a cumulative eroding effect on people's ability to make choices for themselves. Thus, such policies may not only minimize preference satisfaction in the case at hand, but reduce future possibilities for maximizing preference satisfaction.

Second, it is obvious that not everyone has the same preferences and that the preferences of some individuals and groups may be in conflict. This problem is especially important for policies affecting children because parents make many decisions for their children and in this way serve as a proxy in helping children satisfy their preferences. Professionals and policymakers, however, often seem to be in conflict with parents about what is best for their children. A striking example of this conflict is the expenditure of federal money on day-care programs—such as Title XX day care—for preschool children from poor families. One assumption underlying these programs seems to be that low-income parents provide an environment for their preschool children that does not adequately support their intellectual growth and does not prepare them for school (Haskins, Finkelstein, & Stedman, 1978). Thus, it follows that if preschool children are to have an adequate chance to achieve preference satisfaction at some future time, government must intervene to promote the children's development. Similarly, federal day-care policy works in such a way as virtually to require low-income parents to place their children in day-care centers—a mode of child care they do not seem to prefer (Kurz *et al.,* 1975; Larson, 1975; Shaw, 1976)—while allowing middle-income families to claim the child-care tax credit regardless of the type of care used (Haskins, 1979). In such cases, federal policy restricts the preference satisfaction of poor families while promoting that of wealthier families.

Stigma. As used here, *stigma* means that a policy results in recipients being labeled as different in some negative way from citizens not affected by the policy. The value underlying this criterion is that all citizens have a right to benefit from government programs without their fellow citizens attributing deficits, weaknesses, or pathology to the participants' characters.

Many federal and state policies intended to help children and families do so at the cost of stigmatizing program recipients. Public housing brings large numbers of the poor into a central, and conspicuous, location. Anyone living there is automatically known to be poor by other citizens. Food stamps also stigmatize beneficiaries by requiring the use of coupons that must be shown publicly when food is purchased. And day care sometimes stigmatizes because centers receiving federal funds tend to be segregated by race and income of parents (Coelen *et al.,* 1978), thereby making it easy for people to assume that all children in such centers are poor and receive federal support.

As these examples suggest, it seems wise to minimize stigma, not just because it violates the privacy of families, but because it may contribute to prolonging the very conditions a given policy aims to ameliorate. Although persuasive evidence is not available, it seems reasonable to argue that when parents or children are constantly reminded of their inferior status and dependence on public largesse, they may come to resent such treatment, to have their self-esteem damaged, and to develop a sense of hopelessness (see, for example, Rainwater, 1970). In any case, it seems unwise to risk these effects of policy where they can be avoided.

It might be pointed out that, in general, universal policies and cash, as opposed to in-kind, programs are least likely to have a stigmatizing effect. In the former case, all citizens would be eligible for public programs, and there would be no requirement that participants demonstrate their eligibility by proving their need. An extreme example of a universal program that would have virtually no stigma is Gil's (1973) recommendation that all mothers receive a cash allowance based on the number of children they bear. Since every mother would receive this allowance, there would be no stigma attached to recipients (of course, one might question this policy as a violation of the criteria of efficiency and vertical equity). Cash programs, such as Supplemental Security Income and Social Security, also minimize stigma by sending people a check and allowing them to spend the money as they choose; i.e., as if it were earned income.

Policy-specific criteria. In addition to the universal criteria just discussed, every policy problem will have idiosyncratic criteria appropriate to that particular problem. These criteria are typically ones that concern the specific objectives of a given policy and that allow comparison of particular strategies or alternative programs designed to address the problem.

Referring again to day-care policy in order to illustrate this type of criteria, we can identify a number of important dimensions along which day-care policies might be compared. Two general types of criteria, each having a number of more specific criteria, are effects of child care on children's development and effects on the family. Regarding the former, the analyst should consider the effects on intellectual development, social development, and health. Regarding the latter, the analyst might consider effects on the mother-child relation, on employment of mothers, on marital satisfaction, and on the mother's sense of accomplishment and fulfillment. These, of course, are not the only possible criteria for assessing the effects of day care, but they illustrate the point that the analysis should include criteria tailored specifically to the policy problem at hand.

In addition to universal and policy-specific criteria, one other criterion merits attention. Nearly every policy has effects that were neither planned nor anticipated. These consequences associated with the policy may be either positive or negative. In either case, the experienced analyst may be able to anticipate them and thereby avoid or capitalize on these associated effects.

Turning again to day care, we can illustrate both positive and negative associated effects. Regarding the former, Golden (undated) has shown that infants and children attending day-care centers, as compared with those attending family day-care homes, consume significantly less nonnutritious and significantly more nutritious food. Although the programs participating in this study were designed primarily to provide stimulating child care, an easily overlooked consequence of center-based care was that children in these programs ate more nutritious foods than children in family day-care homes. Thus, policies designed to encourage use of centers to promote intellectual and social development, or to enable greater numbers of mothers to work, may have the felicitous effect of improving children's nutrition. This outcome in turn may lead to improved physical development and health status. Such outcomes, of course, can be considered a benefit of center-based care and should therefore constitute an argument in its favor.

By contrast, center-based care may also have the perverse associated effect of weakening family networks among low-income families. As Stack (1974) has shown, child care is one of the shared obligations that serve to bind relatives together and strengthen kinship bonds—especially among low-income, Black families. Removing children from this network by placing them in day-care centers may therefore have the perverse effect of weakening kinship bonds. This effect, of course, must be considered a cost of center-based care.

Generating Policy Alternatives

Having surveyed the problem situation and established the analysis criteria, the analyst is now in position to generate alternative strategies. The objective of this stage of analysis is to identify an extensive list of potential policies addressed to the problem situation and then to eliminate alternatives that seem clearly infeasible.

There are at least four sources of ideas for identifying policy alternatives. One of the most important of these is history. As indicated previously, the historical background of a policy problem will often suggest a number of policy alternatives. Some of these may actually have been attempted at some level of government; others will have been proposed by particular individuals or groups but never enacted; still others will occur to the analyst who is familiar with the policy problem and its background. A second source of ideas of policy alternatives is the practices and policies of other countries. Particularly with regard to social programs, such as child care, income supports, and health, many European countries have a long history of progressive and effective policies (Kamerman & Kahn, 1978). Indeed, as Silver demonstrates in Chapter 4, European health policies and practices are a potent source of ideas for American policy.

Social sciences research may also provide suggestions for policy alternatives. Especially significant in this regard are the income maintenance experiments (New Jersey, Gary, Iowa/North Carolina, and Seattle/Denver) which have provided massive information on the effects of a guaranteed income. Various papers published from these studies concern the use of child care by working mothers, the use of social services, school achievement of children, the consumption of health care, and so on. This type of information can be used to evaluate the effects of income maintenance—a strategy that has been advocated as a basic solution to many social problems (Keniston, 1977; National Academy of Sciences, 1976)—on each of these policy concerns. Further, careful reading of these reports will both demonstrate some problems with current policy and suggest alternative policies that may be more effective [see, for example, the paper on day care by Kurz *et al.* (1975)].

The fourth source an analyst should examine in generating policy alternatives is the particular strategies favored by interest groups, prominent research or policy organizations, and powerful public figures, including politicians. Policy alternatives supported by individuals or groups may be spelled out in particular detail in a public speech, written report, or pamphlet. Recent examples of such detailed policy proposals are Senator Kennedy's national health insurance proposal and the recommendation for some type of income maintenance program by the National Academy of Sciences (1976) and the Carnegie Council on Children (Keniston, 1977).

Once these policy alternatives have been identified, the analyst may want to eliminate some because they are too costly, too impractical, or too strongly opposed by powerful individuals or groups. In any case, the final list of policy alternatives is now subjected to the critical stage of policy selection.

Policy Selection: The Synthesis of Information

As shown in Table 3, the various policy alternatives can now be compared by estimating their effects as measured by each of the criteria. The analyst uses social science research, historical information, and best guesses to make these estimates.

Of course, quantitative estimates are preferable, but given the present state of knowledge, it is often impossible to reach such estimates with any degree of precision. Hence, one often must use techniques that have not been traditional in social science. An example of such a technique is the Delphi procedure (Linstone & Turoff, 1975). In this procedure, experts are asked to estimate the quantitative value of a particular policy's effect on some variable. The experts' individual estimates are shared with the entire group of experts, and they are then asked to make a second quantitative estimate. Obviously, this procedure attempts to encourage agreement between experts—the underlying assumption being that convergence among experts is the best way to estimate the value of a variable that is not well understood.

A more traditional approach to estimating policy effects is for the analyst to use available research information to predict outcomes. In conducting this search for information, the analyst usually examines social science research, previous similar policies implemented in the United States, and similar or identical policies implemented in other countries.

We can refer to the decision matrix in Table 3 for examples of analyzing policy alternatives. The first policy alternative is to maintain the *status quo*. MacRae and Wilde (1979) recommend that this alternative, which they refer to as *do nothing*, be included in all analyses to serve as a kind of baseline against which to compare the effects of other policies. Of course, we should keep in mind that for virtually any policy problem that affects children and families, the option of maintaining the *status quo* does not refer to a situation free of government intervention. In fact, many levels of government are already involved in most problems that affect children and families. Thus, the *status quo* alternative means that current government policy will continue to operate.

The second policy option listed in Table 3, and the one on which I will focus for illustration, is increased direct support to day-care centers. This option more or less accurately describes current federal policy, and is the primary funding mechanism recommended by most of the comprehensive child-care proposals of the last eight years. As shown in Table 2, most current federal expenditures on day care are spent on six programs, and the great majority of money spent by these programs goes to day-care centers (Haskins, 1979; Rivlin, 1978). Should this emphasis on support of center-based care be extended?

As measured by the criterion of vertical equity, center-based care is moderately effective. This outcome, of course, is not the result of supporting center care itself, but the result of the way federal guidelines were written.

Table 3 A Decision Matrix: Effects of Alternative Day-Care Policies on Six Criteria

			Criteria			
Policy Alternative	Vertical Equity	Preference Satisfaction	Stigma	Child Development	Efficiency	Perverse Associated Effects
Status Quo	Low	Low	Low	Low	Moderate	High
Direct Support to Centers	Moderate	Low	High	High	Moderate	High
Vouchers	High	High	Low	Moderate	Moderate	Low
Income Maintenance	High	High	Low	Moderate	Moderate	High
Information	Low	Moderate	Low	Low	Moderate	Low
Tax Deduction	High	High	Low	Low	Moderate	Low

NOTE: Many of the effects estimated above depend on the particular way in which the various policy alternatives are implemented.

Nearly all the programs—Head Start, Title XX, Work Incentive, AFDC—enroll primarily children from low-income families. Since the money for these programs is taken from general revenues, one would think that such programs promote vertical equity.

Recent data indicate, however, that centers receiving federal financial participation (FFP centers) have more highly trained staff than non-FFP centers (Coelen *et al.*, 1978). Although a well-trained staff may be good for other reasons, well-trained teachers tend to be from the middle class. Therefore, a large proportion of federal expenditures on center-based care supports middle-class families. Low-income people may get the service, but middle-class people get the jobs. By contrast, federal support of care by relatives and neighbors would result in both the service and the jobs benefitting low-income families. Primarily for this reason, direct support of day-care centers cannot be rated as high on the criterion of vertical equity.

Turning to the criterion of preference satisfaction, we must rate the policy of direct support to centers as low. First, as indicated by data already presented, not more than 10 percent of families using child care take their children to a center. Second, a number of surveys have indicated that most people are satisfied with their current, noncenter-based child-care arrangement, and would not like to change (for review, see Larson, 1975). Third, in two studies in which families were offered subsidized center-based care, participation rates were low— apparently because families preferred to make their own, more informal, arrangements (Kurz *et al.*, 1975; Shaw, 1976).

Nor does center-based care seem very desirable as judged by the criterion of stigma. Children in FFP centers are identifiable both by race and social class (Coelen *et al.*, 1978, tables 55, 61); hence children attending these centers are known to be poor by the staff and by other residents in the community.

In considering the effects of center-based care on child development, we are presented with an excellent example of applying social science research to policy decisions. Indeed, a very substantial body of research, some of very high quality, has been conducted and published on the effects of center-based care on child development—particularly intellectual development. This literature has been reviewed extensively by a number of authors (Bronfenbrenner, 1975; Cicirelli, 1969; Haskins *et al.*, 1978; White, 1973). Two primary conclusions seem to be widely accepted. First, center-based programs produce IQ gains on the order of 8-10 points in children from low-income families, but have no measurable effect on IQ of children from middle-class families. Second, within two or three years after school entry, there are no achievement test or IQ test differences between children from low-income families who attended day care and control children who did not. These outcomes seem to give only moderate justification for federal policy that encourages attendance at centers by poor children.

An exception to this conclusion has been provided by results recently published by Lazar's Consortium on preschool programs (Lazar *et al.*, 1977). By assembling a group of 12 investigators who conducted preschool programs during the early 1960s, Lazar was able to coordinate efforts to find former program participants and their controls when they were in junior and senior high. Although there were no IQ or achievement test differences between children who had attended and those who had not attended preschool programs, a surprising and provocative finding, as Lazar points out in Chapter 3, was that children who had attended preschool managed to avoid special educational placements and grade failure significantly more than control children.

As impressive as these findings might be, they are marked by a shortcoming that characterizes much social science research and prevents its easy application to policy problems. It is a reasonable inference that the investigators assembled by Lazar are an astute and careful group of social scientists who conducted preschool programs of high quality. Thus, whether the results obtained by these programs could be duplicated by ordinary day-care programs conducted in cities and counties across the country is another question altogether. Unfortunately, social scientists interested in child care, with the single exception of Golden (undated), have not produced information on this very important question.

This assessment of day-care effects on intellectual development leads nicely to consideration of the efficiency criterion. It will be remembered that this criterion calls for the use of resources in such a way as to produce the maximum effect for the minimum investment. The effect of center-based care on intellectual development provides an excellent illustration of the efficiency criterion.

One of the day-care programs participating in the Lazar Consortium used three approaches to conduct a benefit-cost analysis of program effects (Weber *et al.*, 1978). First, by equating time spent in special education with census figures of average earnings of people with varying years of education, Weber and his colleagues projected a $305,731 (1958 dollars) surplus in lifetime earnings by the 58 experimental as compared with 65 control children. These authors also calculated the marginal benefit of Weikart's program by comparing the cost of educating experimental and control children once they entered public school. The formula used took into account the cost of special education and grade retention. This calculation indicated that about 62 percent of the costs of Weikart's two-year program, and about 105 percent of the cost of his one-year program were recovered by savings realized because children attending preschool were less expensive to educate in the public schools. Finally, the internal rate of return for investment on the entire project was calculated as 9.5 percent for the one-year program and 3.7 percent for the two-year program.

One might question some of the assumptions upon which Weber's analysis is based, and as mentioned previously, it is not clear that results from a high-quality, carefully monitored program like Weikart's would generalize to other day-care centers. Nonetheless, this analysis demonstrates that under some conditions center-based care is indeed cost effective, and therefore represents a wise expenditure of public funds.

Turning finally to associated effects of this policy, substantial evidence can be cited to indicate that two perverse consequences may result from expansion of direct federal support to day-care centers. First, as mentioned previously, centers are partially segregated by race and income, with FFP centers enrolling disproportionate numbers of Black and low-income children. In effect, then, federal policy supports segregation of preschool children by race and class. There is no need to belabor the point that this outcome is in direct conflict with federal programs designed to promote integration in other institutions in our society.

Second, federal intervention in day care tends to limit the choices of poor people. Thus, to take advantage of the various federal programs outlined earlier, in most cases poor families must place their children in day-care centers. This seems particularly unfortunate since there is good evidence, much of which has been reviewed, that low-income families prefer informal and nonmarket forms of care. An increase in federal support of centers would expand this somewhat coercive policy. By contrast, current policy allows middle-class citizens who pay taxes to claim a child-care tax credit, regardless of the form of care used. This difference in policy toward middle-class and low-income families implies that the federal government has determined that low-income families should place their children in centers whereas middle-class families may use whatever form of care they prefer.

Feasibility

Feasibility—or the probability that a policy will actually be carried out—has already played a role at the stage of generating policy alternatives. In that case, it was recommended that after generating an exhaustive set of policy options, the analyst could save considerable time and trouble by eliminating from further consideration any policies that were clearly infeasible.

After selecting the policy of choice, feasibility again becomes a primary consideration. Indeed, as MacRae and Wilde (1979) note, when the policy option has been selected, much work remains to be done. In particular, it is now necessary to devise a plan for enactment and a plan for implementation of the policy.

Enactment. Having selected the best policy option, the analyst must now consider ways in which the policy of choice can actually receive legislative support. In so doing, as Gallagher points out in Chapter 9, the analyst may in some cases adopt more of an advocacy role. Of course, whether an advocacy role is appropriate depends in large measure on the analyst's position—the citizen o academic analyst is usually free to become an advocate; an analyst employed by a private firm or the government may not be free to play this role.

In any case, the problem is still the same—to achieve the legislative or administrative action that will translate the selected policy alternative into law or administrative regulation. Of the many requirements demanded by this task, only three will be mentioned here. First, the analyst must communicate to key policymakers both his policy choice and its justification. This usually requires both written and oral presentations that are characterized by clear reasoning and simple, nontechnical language. And brevity is usually an asset. Not all social scientists have these skills; therefore, they must be learned.

Second, the analyst may wish to become allied with powerful groups or individuals who will help enact the policy. Unfortunately, as Steiner (1976) points out with regard to the 1971 comprehensive child-care legislation, co-operation between diverse individuals and groups is often quite difficult. Again to use day care as an example, many interest groups and professional organizations could unite behind the banner of "expanded federal child-care programs." However, as the particular legislation became more specific on crucial issues, the coalition of interest groups began to break down. Few child development professionals would ever agree to legislation supporting complete parental choice of unregulated child care as in a voucher system. Rather, professionals would insist on some federal regulation of staff/child ratios, training of staff, and so on. By contrast, groups of private day-care providers would be more interested in keeping staff/child ratios and staff training high in order to increase profits. Similarly, public school teachers and their unions, especially the American Federation of Teachers, could not be expected to support any day-care proposal that failed to give a favored place to the public schools and to require a staff of trained teachers. But many child development professionals would refuse to permit a favored place for the public schools on the grounds that schools currently fail to educate some children over age five—so why should schools be given an opportunity to educate children under age five (Steiner, 1976)? Needless to say, private providers would not support any day-care proposal that granted a pre-eminent position to the public schools.

It must be concluded as a fact of political life, then, that coalitions are usually necessary to enact legislation, but that specific legislative proposals often drive coalition members apart. This is a problem for which there is no easy solution.

Third, as Hoffman suggests in Chapter 7, the process of enacting and funding a federal program is extremely complex, and passing legislation in most state legislatures is also quite complex. This means not only that the analyst must be familiar with the legislative process, but that patience is often as important as careful policy analysis. Indeed, many good policy ideas take years or even decades before a bill is actually passed that translates the idea into law. Negative income tax, reform of the welfare system, and comprehensive child-care legislation are only three current examples of policy ideas that have received widespread attention and support, but as yet have not become law.

Implementation. Even if a policy is enacted, its actual effect on children and families cannot be assumed until the policy has been implemented. Excellent policy ideas and sufficient funding can be foiled at a number of points between the federal or state level and the site of service delivery—as demonstrated by recent experience with Title I of the Elementary and Secondary Education Act (Wargo, 1972) and the War on Poverty job training programs (Levin, 1977). At least four factors can be cited to account for the problems often encountered in trying to implement social legislation.

First, and perhaps most important, is the way legislative directives are translated into actual policy by the writing of administrative regulations and guidelines. These guidelines will determine to a large degree how funds are distributed, reports are written, and services are delivered. Thus, the analyst must pay careful attention to the way these guidelines are written and be prepared to offer assistance where possible and to protest obvious flaws in the guidelines where necessary.

Closely related to the problem of guidelines is the administering agency selected to implement the policy. In some cases, the administering agency will have played an important role in writing the legislation, but even in such cases the agency may write and enforce guidelines in such a way as to give its staff maximum flexibility in policy implementation. Thus, it is not surprising that an agency which is hostile to a given policy can often subvert the intent of the legislation. Indeed, a favored device of presidents and high administrative officials for killing a policy they oppose is to assign it to an agency that also opposes the policy. President Nixon's approach to dismantling the Office of Economic Opportunity is an excellent example of this technique. A possible solution to this problem of implementation is for the analyst to recommend that program administration be assigned to a particular agency that favors the policy and to attempt to have this recommendation written into the legislation. Further, it will be necessary to ensure continuous monitoring as the legislation is implemented. In this regard, a congressional oversight committee may be somewhat helpful.

A third serious problem with implementation is that individuals or groups hostile to the policy but with insufficient political strength to block the legislation may be able to subvert implementation. Techniques that can be applied to this end are legion—including both techniques just outlined. In addition, congressional foes may be able to delay implementation by blocking either the appropriation or authorization of the policy's funding. Further, opponents of the policy may be able to subvert implementation at the local level by influencing the appointment of key administrators or the local regulations that guide expenditures.

Fourth, a number of policies fail at the level of implementation because the technology or knowledge needed to ensure success is not available. A careful reading of Haveman's (1977) collection of papers evaluating a decade of War on Poverty programs yields many illustrations of this problem. The clear impression left by these papers is that many programs failed–or at least failed to be as successful as originally hoped–not only because of political opposition and inadequate funding, but because the knowledge needed to implement the programs was not available. One might argue that social scientists bear some of the responsibility for this problem as their testimony before Congress in the early 1960s was not always modest or balanced. In particular, one might single out job training programs and child development programs as examples of policy that were not successfully implemented because the requisite knowledge base concerning human behavior or development was inadequate. Hopefully, careful analysis of potential policies using techniques such as those discussed earlier can minimize this problem.

A final word is in order about program implementation. Information about the effects of any policy can be of immense help in subsequent modifications of program implementation. Thus, as part of the implementation plan, the analyst should always include provisions for data collection that will provide the knowledge base needed to improve the policy in the future. This plan should specify what information is to be collected, who is responsible for collecting the information, and what use will be made of the information.

SUMMARY

The hallmarks of policy analysis, as I have argued in this paper, are reason and evidence. The analysis model outlined and illustrated here is simply one among many possible approaches to systematic analysis. Nonetheless, this model, perhaps adapted slightly, could be applied to the analysis of many social problems–poverty, health, child abuse, and so forth.

It must be recognized, however, that in the American system of making social decisions, analysis will always play a limited role. Political decisions are often–perhaps usually–determined by forces that have little or nothing to do with analysis. The current fiscal crisis, as both Hoffman and Phillips argue in their papers, makes it clear that all policy problems and their potential solutions are conditioned by forces beyond the analysts' control. Further, once political decisions are made at the federal, state, and local level, a wide range of forces influences implementation. Many of these forces–the quality and training of professionals who implement the policy, the response of citizens affected by the policy, and the willingness of bureaucrats and professionals at all levels of service delivery systems to adapt to changing social forces and local conditions–are also beyond the analyst's ability to influence or even predict. In short, the cloak of humility is not ill suited to the analyst.

Yet, to recognize the limits of analysis is not to demean its importance or potential social contribution. As economists since Ricardo have known well, scarcity is a permanent part of the human condition. In a world of finite resources, systematic policy analysis, grounded in reason and evidence, can play an important albeit limited role in promoting the general welfare.

REFERENCES

Bronfenbrenner, U. Is early intervention effective? In M. Guttentag & E. Struening (Eds.), *Handbook of evaluation research* (Vol. 2). Beverly Hills, Calif.: Sage, 1975.

Cicirelli, V. *The impact of Head Start: An evaluation of the effects of Head Start on children's cognitive and affective development.* Athens, Ohio: Westinghouse Learning Corporation, 1969.

Coelen, C., Glantz, F., & Calore, D. *Day care centers in the U.S.: A national profile 1976-1977 (Prepublication Copy, Vol. 3).* Cambridge, Mass.: Abt Associates, 1978.

Duncan, G., & Hill, C. R. Modal choice in child care arrangements. In G. Duncan & J N. Morgan (Eds.), *Five thousand American families: Patterns of economic progress* (Vol. 3). Ann Arbor, Mich.: Institute for Social Research, 1975.

Gil, D. G. *Unravelling social policy: Theory, analysis, and political action towards social equality.* Cambridge, Mass.: Schenkamn, 1973.

Golden, M., *et al. The New York City infant day care study.* New York: Medical and Health Research Association of New York City, undated.

Haskins, R. Day care and public policy. *Urban & Social Change Review,* 1979, *12,* 3-10.

Haskins, R., Finkelstein, N. W., & Stedman, D. J. Infant-stimulation programs and their effects. *Pediatric Annals,* 1978, *7,* 123-143.

Haveman, R. H. (Ed.). *A decade of federal antipoverty programs: Achievements, failures, and lessons.* New York: Academic Press, 1977.

Kamerman, S. B., & Kahn, A. J. (Eds.). *Family policy: Government and families in fourteen countries.* New York: Columbia University Press, 1978.

Keniston, K. *All our children: The American family under pressure.* New York: Harcourt Brace Jovanovich, 1977.

Kurz, M., Robins, P., & Spiegelman, R. *A study of the demand for child care by working mothers.* Menlo Park, Calif.: Stanford Research Institute, 1975. (Research Memorandum 27.)

Larson, M. A. *Federal policy for preschool services: Assumptions and evidence.* Menlo Park, Calif.: Stanford Research Institute, 1975. (Research Memorandum EPRC 2158-24.)

Lazar, I., Hubbell, V., Murray, H., Rosche, M., & Royce, J. *The persistence of preschool effects: A long term follow-up of fourteen infant and preschool experiments.* (Final Report for ACYF Grant No. 18-76-07843). Ithaca, N.Y.: Cornell University, Community Service Laboratory, September 1977.

Levin, H. A. A decade of policy developments in improving education and training for low-income populations. In R. H. Haveman (Ed.), *A decade of federal antipoverty programs: Achievements, failures, and lessons.* New York: Academic Press, 1977.

Levine, J. A. *Day care and the public schools: Profile of five communities.* Newton, Mass.: Education Development Center, 1978.

Linstone, H. A., & Turoff, M. (Eds.). *The Delphi method: Techniques and applications.* Reading, Mass.: Addison-Wesley, 1975.

Low, S., & Spindler, P. G. *Child care arrangements of working mothers in the United States,* (Children's Bureau and Women's Bureau Publication). Washington, D.C.: U.S. Government Printing Office, 1968.

MacRae, D. *The social function of social science.* New Haven: Yale University Press, 1976.

MacRae, D., & Wilde, J. A. *Policy analysis for public decisions.* North Scituate, Mass.: Duxbury Press, 1979.

Nagel, S. S. (Ed.). *Policy studies review annual* (Vol 1). Beverly Hills, Calif.: Sage, 1977.

National Academy of Sciences. *Toward a national policy for children and families.* Washington, D.C.: Author, 1976.

Office of Management and Budget. *Special analyses: Budget of the United States government, fiscal year 1977.* Washington, D.C.: U.S. Government Printing Office, undated.

Plattner, M. F. The welfare state vs. the redistributive state. *Public Interest,* 1979, *55,* 28-48.

Quade, E. S. *Analysis for public decisions.* New York: Elsevier, 1975.

Rainwater, L. *Behind ghetto walls: Black families in a federal slum.* Chicago: Aldine, 1970.

Rein, M. *Social science and public policy.* New York: Penguin, 1976.

Rivlin, A. *Child care and preschool: Options for federal support* (Congressional Budget Office Publication). Washington, D.C.: U.S. Government Printing Office, 1978.

Shaw, L. B. *The subsidized child-care program.* Indiana University Northwest; 1976. (Gary Income Maintenance Experiment.) (Available from Mathematica Policy Research, P. O. Box 2393, Princeton, N.J. 08540.)

Stack, C. *All our kin: Strategies for survival in a Black community.* New York: Harper & Row, 1974.

Steiner, G. *The children's cause.* Washington, D.C.: Brookings, 1976.

Steinfels, M. *Who's minding the children? The history and politics of day care in America.* New York: Simon and Schuster, 1973.

Titmuss, R. M. *Social policy: An introduction.* New York: Pantheon Books, 1974.

Unco, Inc. *National child care consumer study: 1975* (4 vols.). Washington, D.C.: Office of Child Development, 1976.

Wargo, M. J. *ESEA Title I: A reanalysis and synthesis of evaluation data from fiscal year 1965 through 1970.* Palo Alto, Calif.: American Institutes for Research, 1972.

Weber, C. U., Foster, P. W., & Weikart, D. P. *An economic analysis of the Ypsilanti Perry Preschool Project.* Ypsilanti, Mich.: High/Scope, 1978.

White, S. H., *et al. Federal programs for young children: Review and recommendations* (4 vols.). Washington, D.C.: U.S. Government Printing Office, 1973.

Woolsey, S. H. Pied piper politics and the child-care debate. *Daedalus,* 1977, *106,* 127-145.

BETTYE M. CALDWELL is Donaghey Distinguished Professor of Education and Director of the Center for Child Development and Education at the University of Arkansas at Little Rock. Prior to her present position, she was principal of Kramer Elementary School in Little Rock, Arkansas, forum member of the 1970 White House Conference on Children, the editor of *Child Development,* and a member of the Arkansas Governor's Commission on the Status of Women. In 1976 Dr. Caldwell was selected as Woman of the Year in the category of Humanitarian and Community Service by the *Ladies' Home Journal.* Among her numerous research and scholarly accomplishments, Dr. Caldwell is perhaps best known for her studies on the effects of early intervention programs and of factors that influence the development of preschool children.

2

Balancing Children's Rights and Parents' Rights

Those among us who happen to be parents have perhaps never been so fortunate as we are today—at least not in terms of the rhetoric with which we are surrounded. We hear a great deal about parent power and parent involvement and many extol the virtues and importance of parent participation in decision making and program operation. Parental wisdom is exalted in contrast to the seemingly hollow and valueless knowledge possessed by professionals. The school, the church, and the clinic have been dethroned as environments of great importance in the lives of children, and professionals who transmit whatever influence those environments might offer have been recast as auxiliary personnel whose function is merely to support parents. "Parenting Is Primary," to quote a slogan that served as the title of a recent conference in Little Rock, Arkansas. Furthermore, in what must be considered an interesting paradox, parents are cautioned in a deluge of articles and films prepared by professionals to be wary of professional advice and instead to trust their own instincts about what to do with, for, and about, their children. In short, we are generally exalting parenthood, proclaiming its power, prestige, and privileges. In the business world this might be described as engaging in a massive advertising campaign to sell parenthood. Big Mama and Big Daddy are the human counterparts of the Big Mac.

Yet, at precisely the same point in history when it is apparently so great to be a parent, it appears distressingly difficult to be a child. "The family is in trouble" proclaims the slogan. And essentially, the slogan seems to mean that functions traditionally carried out by parents on behalf of children have been so adversely affected by modern conditions that the well-being of children is in jeopardy.

THE FATE OF CHILDREN AS FAMILIES CHANGE

The generalized apprehension about the welfare of today's children is buttressed by an alarming array of statistics produced by every census or obtained when any sample of families is studied. Thus, we note in such statistics the decrease in the proportion of *traditional* families—those in which there are two parents, a single breadwinner, and one or more children—and an increase in *nontraditional* families; i.e., those in which both parents work and the care of children is provided outside the immediate family, those in which there is only one parent, or those which are experimenting with some different style of family life, such as social contract matings or communal living. The average duration of marriage is now approximately seven years, and one out of three new marriages will end in divorce. More and more children can expect to grow up in sequential families living with one set of parents and siblings for a time, moving (usually with one parent) into another family setting for another time with a different set of siblings and half-siblings, living later still in a third family. Close to one million children per year are now born to mothers in their teens, most of whom are unmarried and without adequate emotional and financial support for their parenting task. Table 1, adapted from Ramey (1978), presents a reasonably up-to-date picture of the proportions of families that fall into these various non-traditional categories.

Perhaps more alarming than these demographic indicators of change in family structure, which it is feared bode ill for children, are certain descriptions of family life. One that immediately comes to mind is the highly publicized incidence of child abuse (DeFrancis, 1977; Friedman, Cardiff, Sandler & Friedman, 1978). Of course, whether the high incidence of child abuse represents an increase or merely the acceptability and even legal necessity of reporting is a moot question. Nonetheless, there is more than a touch of absurdity in a national popular literature about family life which exalts the beneficence and wisdom of parents and, at the same time, refers to the incidence figures of child abuse as a national disgrace.

Quite apart from statistics about child abuse, there are quieter but perhaps more significant indicators that many parents do not view their task—or their performances—through rose-colored lenses. For example, at the risk of appearing naive about the greater likelihood of responding to a survey if one has an ax to grind, I would cite Ann Lander's assertion that 70 percent of the parents who responded to her questionnaire about family life indicated that, if they had it to do over again, they would choose not to have children. In a similar vein, one can

Table 1   Percentage of Adults Living in Various Family Forms
in United States, 1975

Family Form	Percentage
Heading single-parent families	16
Other single, widowed, separated, or divorced persons	21
Living in childfree or post-child-rearing marriages	23
Living in dual-breadwinner nuclear families	16
Living in single-breadwinner nuclear families	13
Living in no-breadwinner nuclear families	1
Living in extended families	6
Living in experimental families or cohabiting	4

Note: Adapted from Ramey (1978).

cite the increasing numbers of young adults who choose, now that such choice is truly available in most parts of the world, not to have children. Also worthy of mention here is some of the language of the women's movement—of which I consider myself very much a part. For twenty years now some of the more articulate representatives of the movement have implied that parenting may be a less than enchanting role and that it does not allow the self-fulfillment and gratification associated, at least in fantasy, with a career.

It is important to understand that these changes are not viewed with alarm by citizens and policymakers because they represent a threat to the well-being of the adults whose actions are producing the demographic changes. In fact, many of the recent changes, such as divorce, remarriage, and early sexual activity resulting in pregnancy, would not have occurred if they did not bring gratification to adults. Rather, recent trends in family life are sources of national concern because they seem to threaten the welfare of children who are swept along but who do not themselves initiate such changes.

A favorite rhetorical question asked these days is whether the family is "here to stay" (Bane, 1976) or whether it "can be saved" (Vaughan & Brazelton, 1976). I feel entirely comfortable in predicting that the family as a social institution is in no danger whatsoever. The interdependence of human beings involved in the processes of social living and the creation of new life requires the continued existence of some kind of family structure—or, as we say, a reasonable facsimile thereof. But the increasing diversity of family styles makes equally secure the prediction that the term *family* will soon be used in the singular only to refer to a specific family unit. When we refer to the manifestation of the social institution, we will tend to use the term in the plural. The change in name for the 1980 White House Conference from the "White House Conference on the Family" to the "White House Conference on Families" succinctly but eloquently validates this prediction.

THE DOMAIN OF HUMAN RIGHTS

Implicit in concern about the impact of changes in family structure is the fear that such new structures will not adequately meet the needs of children whose rights will thereby be violated. Likewise, there is a comparable level of concern that rights which we customarily associate with the parental role will either be threatened or else be inapplicable. Some of this vague concern is perhaps based on our rarely being explicit about exactly what we mean by such terms as *parents' rights* and *children's rights*. According to Hafen (1977), some of this ambiguity can be traced to a document justly famous for its articulation of other rights, the U.S. Constitution:

> Few themes have been more fully treated in legal literature than the tradition
> of individual liberty. The "family tradition," however, has been such an
> obvious presupposition of our culture that it has not been well articulated, let

alone explained or justified. The absence of explicit mention of minority status or parental roles in the Constitution or early laws of the Republic may be among the most potent of the "great silences" in our jurisprudence (p. 1383).

Parental Rights as Historically Conferred

This "great silence" of the Constitution has not been copied by other historical and legal documents, in many of which we find fervor and eloquence about the domain of parental rights. In the earliest recorded set of social regulations—the Code of Hammurabi written around 2100 B.C.—the father was assigned total control over the welfare of his children and total authority to discipline and even dispose of them if they were considered unsatisfactory. Nonetheless, the code communicated the expectation that, if the child paid his duty of respect, the father in turn had to provide minimal care for the child (Fraser, 1976). The Hebrew code, estimated to date from around 800 B.C., is similarly stern. The modern reader may be shocked at reading verses 15 and 17 of Exodus 21: "Whosoever strikes his mother or his father shall be put to death"; and "Whosoever curses his mother or his father shall be put to death." According to Fraser, Greek law became a little more humane in its treatment of children, but with the decline of Greek civilization there was a return to harsher attitudes toward, and treatment of, children.

Roman law was both harsh and unambiguous about the unilateral and total authority of the father. Not only was the father's authority total, but it was also never-ending, for there was no concept of the attainment of majority status. Adult women and female children were of no consequence, as a family consisted of all direct male descendants of the oldest living ancestor.

According to Fraser, early English law, from which many of the concepts of the American codes were drawn, was based primarily on Roman law. English writers concerned with parental rights drew a parallel between the family and the kingdom and asserted the father's right of sovereignty over all subjects within the family. In *Leviathan,* originally published in 1651, Hobbes (1945) declared that "a great Family if it be not part of some Common-wealth, is of it self, as to the Rights of Soveraignty, a little Monarchy . . . . wherein the Father or Master is the Soveraign." Only about 50 years after Hobbes, John Locke (1952), philosophically more concerned with human freedom, advanced the position that this "soveraignty" was not absolute but contained within it a natural check and balance in the form of parental benevolence. Although asserting the obligation of children to honor and serve their parents, Locke recognized that this obligation in no way gave "parents a power of command over their children, or an authority to make laws and dispose as they please of their lives and liberties" (p. 150). Thus, Locke thought of children as having certain "natural," if not legal, rights, and assumed further that these rights would be protected because what was good for parents was also good for children.

An important legal concept introduced by the English tradition was the doctrine of *parens patriae,* which translates literally as "father of his country." Formulation of this doctrine represented the first recognition that the sovereign of a country had certain "paternal rights" which could be extended to the protection of minor children whose interests were occasionally jeopardized by persons responsible for their welfare. Originally advanced during the fifteenth century, the doctrine of *parens patriae* was not firmly entrenched in the British legal machinery until early in the nineteenth century. As Fraser summarizes:

> The relationship between the parent and the child was a trust. The right was endowed by the crown as a trust because it was assumed that the parent would discharge it faithfully on behalf of his child. If the trust were not faithfully discharged, it would be incumbent upon the crown to intervene and to protect the child's interest. . . . The doctrine of *parens patriae* simply interjected a third party into conflict between the child and his parents: the State. The State would act as a guarantor of the trust (Fraser, 1976, p. 322).

The assortment of public documents compiled by Bremner (1970) as a means of chronicling the evolution of American public policy relating to children and youth contains many fascinating examples of the conferring upon parents of authority over the lives of children. From earliest Colonial times, however, parental authority was generally considered finite and in some danger of being forfeited if duties were not carried out properly. This threat of forfeiture is perhaps the most surprising aspect of the American historical documents. For example, as early as 1648 Massachusetts selectmen were ordered to enforce laws pertaining to training children within the family:

> Forasmuch as the good education of children is of singular behoof and benefit to any commonwealth, and whereas many parents and masters are too indulgent and negligent of their duty in that kind: It is therefore ordered that the selectmen of every town, in the several precincts and quarters where they dwell, shall have a vigilant eye over their brethren and neighbors to see, first, that none of them shall suffer so much barbarism in any of their families as not to endeavor to teach by themselves, or others, their children and apprentices so much learning as may enable them perfectly to read the English tongue and knowledge of the capital laws, upon penalty of twenty shillings for each neglect therein (cited in Bremner, 1970, p. 40).

At about the same time, the office of "tithingman" was established. The tithingman's job was to inspect 10 or 12 families to make certain they discharged their duties to their children. Apparently, such regulations developed less out of concern for any rights of children than out of fear that, without training by parents, children would grow up unfit for the society in which they lived. Nonetheless, the willingness to monitor parental behavior to ensure compliance is, to us at least, surprising if not shocking.

Almost 200 years later, in the early years of the Republic, a prominent New York jurist, James Kent, expressed even more strongly the restrictions inherent in the exercise of parental rights. He also gave recognition to what might be considered a psychological law as the foundation for legal arrangements:

> The wants and weaknesses of children render it necessary that some person maintain them, and the voice of nature has pointed out the parent as the most fit and proper person. The laws and customs of all nations have enforced this plain precept of universal law. . . . *The obligation of parental duty is so well secured by the strength of natural affection, that it seldom requires to be enforced by human laws.* . . . The rights of parents result from their duties. As they are bound to maintain and educate their children, the law has given them a right to such authority; and in the support of that authority, a right to the exercise of such discipline as may be requisite for the discharge of their sacred trust. . . . But the courts of justice may, in their sound discretion, and when the morals, or safety, or interests of the children strongly require it, withdraw the infants from the custody of the father or mother, and place the care and custody of them elsewhere (quoted in Bremner, 1970, pp. 363-364; italics added).

My own reaction to these historical writings was one of amazement—which perhaps merely shows how little I know about the history of the family and the evolution of modern concepts concerning family governance and inviolacy. In this age of nonjudgmentalism, of aversion to labeling or monitoring of any sort, I found my mind conjuring up an image of the look on the face of the Massachusetts tithingman (again, never a woman) when he went back to report to the magistrate or commissioner about the

> . . . single persons that live from under family government, stubborn and disorderly children and servants, night-walkers, tipplers, Sabbath breakers by night or day, and such as absent themselves from the public worship of God on the Lord's days, or whatever else course or practice of any person or persons whatsoever tending to debauchery, irreligion, profaneness, and atheism amongst us, whether by omission of family government, nurture, and religious duties, (or) instruction of children and servants, or idle, profligate, uncivil or rude practices of any sort. . . . [With apologies to William Faulkner; the foregoing is only a brief segment of the sentence (Bremner, 1970, p. 42) which describes the duties of the tithingman].

One gets the feeling that, over the past 300 years, the concept of individual adult autonomy has so overpowered the concept of parental duties referred to by Kent that we tend to think of parents' rights as having stronger basis in family and legal history than is actually the case. From the beginning of American common law, and to some extent from the legal and philosophical sources upon which it drew, the power of parents over their children was apparently always regarded as finite and bounded.

This brief historical summary should make it obvious that when we speak of *children's rights,* we are speaking more from a moral and philosophical than from a legal viewpoint. Yet the concept of *parens patriae,* if nothing else, at least casts a legal shadow over the discussion. But moral or legal, what are children's rights?

A number of lists of putative children's rights have been published, and apart from slight differences in wording related to geographical or historical context, all have been fairly similar. I shall choose as an example the list of rights adopted by the United Nations in 1959:

- The right to affection, love, and understanding.
- The right to adequate nutrition and medical care.
- The right to free education.
- The right to full opportunity for play and recreation.
- The right to a name and nationality.
- The right to special care, if handicapped.
- The right to be among the first to receive relief in times of disaster.
- The right to learn to be a useful member of society and to develop individual abilities.
- The right to be brought up in a spirit of peace and universal brotherhood.
- The right to enjoy these rights, regardless of race, color, sex, religion, national, or social origin.

One finds little to disagree with in such a list, and upon first thought, little basis for a potential struggle with parents for an equitable division of rights.

A similar list of children's rights was proposed by the 1970 White House Conference on Children. The last "right" on this list, however, contained wording perhaps more appropriate for a Colonial Massachusetts tithingman than a contemporary parent advocate, to wit:

- The right to *societal mechanisms* to enforce the foregoing rights (italics mine).

The use of the verb "enforce" makes clear that someone in the White House Conference deliberations recognized that the rights of children might not be automatically forthcoming through normal channels (i.e., through parents, in the exercise of their duties) and that some type of third-party arbitration ("societal mechanism") might occasionally be necessary.

Protection Rights and Choice Rights

Most rights contained in the United Nations list could be described as relating to the need for certain growth-fostering conditions (e.g., love and affection, health care, education) considered essential to the full flowering of children's capacities to learn and be well-integrated socially and emotionally. That is, the rights essentially refer to the availability of present conditions, most or all of which are to some extent mediated by parents, which assure future capabilities. Thus, the rights accorded children might be described as protecting their developmental potential. Protection is needed because children presumably lack the experience and competence to forecast for themselves the abilities and traits they will need in later life and thus know how to conduct their lives during the formative years. Adult rights, in contrast, refer to present and continuing perquisites and privileges.

Recognizing the unique aspects of children's rights, Hafen (1977) distinguishes between "rights of protection" and "rights of choice" and suggests that failure to withhold choice rights from children temporarily will mean greater deprivation in the long run:

> Some forms of discrimination are wise and appropriate, precisely because they lead ultimately to greater individual liberty for those temporarily subject to the discrimination. There is no better illustration of this truth than the way in which a preparatory and protective period of minority within the walls of family life provides the essential educational opportunity that is prerequisite to meaningful participation in a democratic society. It would be an irony of tragic proportions if, in our egalitarian zeal, we abandoned our children to their "rights" in a way that seriously undermined their claim to protection and developmental opportunity (p. 1387).

In any discussion of children's rights, this concept of the rights of protection appears essential if we are to keep the issue in perspective. *Rights of choice* refer to such things as entering legally binding contracts and being held legally responsible for one's actions. One of the very reasons for withholding choice rights from children is to allow them the luxury of being free from such long-term accountability; i.e., of affording them a protective right. To offer a simple example, there is probably no infant alive who, having once experienced the needle but lacking knowledge of the disease thereby being prevented, would choose to take the second or third in a series of immunizations. Benevolent parents withhold the choice right in order to allow the protection right to have prepotency. To quote Hafen (1977) further:

> The denial of choice rights during minority is a form of protection against a minor's own immaturity and his vulnerability to exploitation by those having no responsibility for his welfare. The conferring of the full range of the choice rights—essentially, adult legal status—requires a dissolution of the protection rights of childhood. One cannot have the freedom to live where and as one chooses and still demand parental support; one may not deliberately enter into contracts and yet insist that they be voidable. The lifelong effects of binding, childish choices can cause permanent damage far more detrimental than the temporary limitations on personal freedom inherent in minority status. To be protected against that risk requires a restriction on the range of choice rights (pp. 1387-1388).

Although choice rights for children, especially adolescents, represent a legitimate area of concern addressed by a number of persons identified with the children's rights movement (e.g., Fraser, 1976), in this paper I shall be concerned entirely with rights of protection. It is in the area of protection rights that we find the greatest potential for a legitimate conflict of interests and the most pressing need for arbitration. With choice rights, the most important decision is that of designating the age at which adult rights can be conferred. For example, does a sixteen-year-old who has the biological maturity to become pregnant have the legal right to decide about abortion; i.e., to assume a full adult right? If the choice right is withheld, there is surely some protection involved, as the adolescent may need protection from the consequences of an injudicious decision (and certainly the unborn child does). Even so, this situation is quite different from one in which a three-year-old is not adequately fed and is subject to chronic emotional and physical abuse. In the latter instance, the type of protection needed involves arranging conditions, either through the parents or through other resources, that can be sustained long enough to allow judgment and maturity to develop in the child. In the former example, societal arbitration, in the form of court action, is likely to be fairly quick and easy, if not necessarily correct. By contrast, arbitration in protection conflicts is rarely quick and never easy.

A TRIADIC MODEL OF RECIPROCAL RIGHTS AND RESPONSIBILITIES

In my earlier discussion of the historical antecedents of today's concern with balancing rights between generations, I pointed out that the role of the state as *parens patriae* has been gradually strengthened as the necessity for some type of arbitration became evident and socially acceptable. Although any time we deal with statutory arbitration we are concerned with the state, the entire network of private institutions that affect family living also plays a role in arbitration. Thus, I prefer to speak of the third party as "society" rather than "the state."

As suggested in an earlier paper (Caldwell, 1979), it is helpful to think of Child(ren), Parent(s),[1] and Society as representing three companies of a triadic reciprocal system, each component of which influences and receives influences from the other two. Furthermore, all three components may be conceptualized as having both rights and responsibilities, as indicated in Figure 1. Only if each component adequately fulfills its responsibilities can the other two achieve their rights. Thus, if parents are loving and nurturant, if they protect children from the usual hazards of life (such as accidents and avoidable diseases), and if they provide the sort of education and training necessary to equip children for the future assumption of full adult roles, then the children's rights are adequately protected. Similarly, if children are loving and respectful to their parents, and if they carry out the behaviors and acquire the competencies expected of them

---

[1] It is difficult to know whether to use the singular or plural designations here. Although frequently the *dramatis personae* in any rights confrontation are plural on both sides, our legal decisions and actions always eventually translate into action on behalf of individuals.

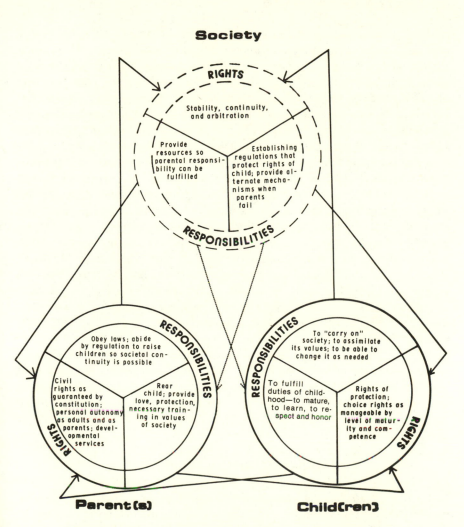

Figure 1. A triadic model of the rights and responsibilities of children, parents, and society.

by their parents (and indirectly by society, from which the parents received their standards and norms), then parents can gradually diminish the frequency and intensity of their parenting behaviors and resume the broader array of roles allowed adults within the society.

The reciprocal nature of the relationship between society and either parents or children might be a little more difficult to accept because we do not often think of society or the state as having rights. Although no constitution specifies the rights of society, we can infer that all functioning societies assume their rights to a stable existence and to continuity. Existence of any society will depend on the extent to which it can meet with contemporary needs of adults;

37

continuity will depend on the extent to which it can protect the rights of children and assure their effective functioning as eventual adults. As a result, society, with a divided allegiance to both the present and the future, needs to assert a third right—that of arbitration between the rights of parents and children. This societal arbitration is often described as the *protection* of rights; at the program level it manifests itself in the provision of services which allow representatives of both generations to fulfill their responsibilities to one another and in monitoring the extent to which these responsibilities are fulfilled.

In its responsibilities to children, society needs to make certain that conditions exist which will protect the rights of children until they are mature enough to claim their choice rights. Furthermore, society has a responsibility to monitor parental performance, even if only sketchily or demographically (much less exhaustively than a Massachusetts tithingman), and in the event of some breakdown in the assumption of parental responsibility, to provide alternative mechanisms which protect the child. The child, in turn, has the responsibility to assimilate the value of society and, somewhat paradoxically, to develop in such a way as to be able to change the society if it ceases to provide the necessary conditions either for meeting the contemporary needs of adults or protecting the future rights of children. Parents, in turn, have the responsibility of obeying laws established by the society, including laws that pertain to the care and nurture of children. Reciprocally, the society owes parents a distribution of resources and the provision of services which will allow parents to fulfill their responsibilities to children. Only when all three components of the system function adequately are the rights of all protected; breakdown in any part leads to trouble in the other two.

IMBALANCES WITHIN THE SYSTEM

In Figure 1, I divided the domain of rights and responsibilities for each component of the triad into three equal parts, with no consideration of whether the assumption of equality was justified. Certainly it is not if we are concerned about choice rights because, as already mentioned, children have virtually none. Yet if we are willing to consider protection rights of equal value, and if indeed these rights are guarded by parents and society, then the proportion of rights allocated to children is not trivial. It is in the impotence of children to obtain these rights for themselves and their need to rely on parents and society that we find the potential for imbalance. Viewed in this perspective, parents have a disproportionately large share of rights; viewed in another perspective, parents have more responsibility.

Let me examine the premise that children depend on parents and society to secure their rights by presenting again the list of children's rights proposed in the UN declarations. In Figure 2, I have regrouped the list of rights into three

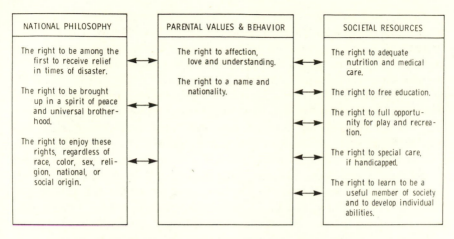

NATIONAL PHILOSOPHY	PARENTAL VALUES & BEHAVIOR	SOCIETAL RESOURCES
The right to be among the first to receive relief in times of disaster.	The right to affection, love and understanding.	The right to adequate nutrition and medical care.
The right to be brought up in a spirit of peace and universal brotherhood.	The right to a name and nationality.	The right to free education.
		The right to full opportunity for play and recreation.
The right to enjoy these rights, regardless of race, color, sex, religion, national, or social origin.		The right to special care, if handicapped.
		The right to learn to be a useful member of society and to develop individual abilities.

Figure 2. Three sources of support for children's rights.

major categories. At least three of the rights (and possibly a fourth—the right to a name and nationality) can be described as contingent upon a kind of national philosophy. These are rights pertaining to what might be considered universal moral and spiritual values. In the second column we find those rights relating to love and nurture and family identity that must be directly supplied by parents (or by persons filling the parental role). In the last column are listed those rights which can be directly tied to the availability of resources within a given society—food, health care, education and training, recreation, special services. When one looks at this division quantitatively, parents appear to have relatively less responsibility for ensuring children's rights than does society, in the form either of value transmission or the provision of services. But when we reflect on the mechanisms through which values are transmitted and services delivered, we realize that the responsibility for providing conditions necessary to secure children's rights flows through parents, even if it does not reside directly with them.

The formal and legal structure of a society may value children and formally eschew any sort of discrimination based on race, sex, religion, or national origin. If such values are flouted within the family, however, there is little likelihood that children will grow up to exemplify these values in their own life. Likewise, a given society may be rich in food supplies, have a superb health care and educational system, including special facilities for the handicapped, and have an abundance of splendid recreational opportunities; yet some children in that society may be denied access to these resources because their parents do not, or cannot, take advantage of them. A sick child could live in the shadow of a great medical facility and die for lack of treatment unless taken there by his or her parents. When I was an elementary school principal, I had more than a few families stroll into the office in November or December to enroll their children for the school year which had begun in September. If I asked the parents why they had waited so long, I would get an answer something like: "He had a cold," or "I knew I was going to move and just waited," or "I wasn't sure when it started." The right to a free education meant nothing for these children in spite of the resource being readily available. Thus, even when society has established the conditions necessary to ensure children's rights, responsible action by parents is usually necessary for the rights to actually be fulfilled. The need for such mediation by parents is indicated by the lateral arrows in Figure 2.

On the other hand, the most conscientious parents cannot fulfill their responsibilities without help from the society. It is difficult for parents to teach brotherly love in a racist society; likewise, it is impossible for parents to provide good nutrition and obtain adequate medical care for their children in a society that does not produce enough food or have any dependable health care system. Thus again, from the vantage point of children and their rights, a synergistic relationship between parents and society is necessary. The society must provide resources, but parents must avail themselves of such resources and make certain that their children actually receive them. Rights cannot be secured without resources, and resources are irrelevant if not utilized.

RESOURCE ALLOCATION AND UTILIZATION

Regardless of the necessity for mediation by parents, even a cursory examination of Figure 2 reveals that it is fatuous to talk about children's rights without being equally concerned with resources and services, which must be deployed if such rights are to be achieved. Mary Kohler, who chaired the forum on Children's Rights in the 1970 White House Conference on Children, has cautioned against the creation of a "tyranny of services" in which the availability of a service becomes a mandate for its utilization. She feels that most services are inadequate because

> ... service delivery arrangements are geared more to professional and field needs than to those of children; we deal with crises more than prevention; we reach only a fraction of the population in need and, all too often, with too little, too late; we know that problems often begin in infancy, yet we develop programs that intervene after this critical period (Kohler, 1971, p. 229).

Kohler's criticisms appear to be entirely justified by an examination of services available in most communities. There can be no question that service availability and utilization are closely linked. If a city has a big foster care system and virtually no facilities for parent education or counseling, then in a conflict situation the child is likely to be placed in a foster home (or worse). And certainly crises get our attention, whereas pre-crisis trouble signs frequently go unattended. A mother who goes to a mental health clinic with the hesitantly announced fear that she may physically harm her children may well be put on a six-month waiting list; the same mother will get instant attention (if not help), and her child will get some sort of protection, if serious injury actually occurs. Those of us who are convinced that the roots of mutual parent-child satisfaction and support begin in infancy, and can be modified only with great difficulty and effort in later years, deplore the lack of services geared to the critical developmental period. Thus, it is clear that new ways of conceptualizing, designing, and delivering services are needed if both parental rights and children's rights are to be protected.

Parent-Enabling Services Allocation

In view of the extra burden placed on parents in securing rights for their children, it would appear that the simplest and most direct way to help protect children's rights is to provide services which enable parents to fulfill their responsibilities more effectively. Although I do not wish to go on record as implying that any services we now have are unnecessary, or are overrepresented in most parts of the country, I do agree strongly with Kohler that we need to shift the direction of our service efforts from crisis toward prevention and that we need more services to help parents during the prenatal and infancy period of their children's lives. Historically in our country we have been reluctant to fund preventive services, and we are almost phobic about intervening in family life in any way during a child's early years. The estimated cost for the stay of a premature infant in an intensive care unit is $85,000. How many nutrition and parent education programs, reaching how many prospective mothers, could be funded for the cost of such care to one infant? Similarly, the cost of residential care for a child-mother unit receiving treatment after an episode of child abuse is quite exorbitant. Long-term professional and paraprofessional assistance is often required to help the mother and child establish a bond to one another; and such efforts cannot succeed without allocation of significant financial resources to the therapeutic program. On a cost basis alone, quite apart from humanitarian considerations, offering preventive education on the importance of bonding to prospective parents might be justified.

It is of interest to me, a worker in the day-care field for about fifteen years, that we now have statutes in all fifty states relating to child abuse and neglect, and yet have failed repeatedly to pass a national Child Development Act. The former statutes are established to deal with crises which often lead to family dissolution; the services called for in the latter (chiefly family-oriented day-care services) are preventive and family-strengthening. Yet we pass the former and refuse to legislate the latter. This is a clear example of a trend away from service development and expansion which would be considered parent-enabling.

Clearly not all parent-enabling services fall into the categories of educational, social, or psychological. Many services would relate to economic indicators, such as level of family income, access to adequate housing, and security about the family's ability to cope with the developmental tasks of childhood and adolescence. In fact, many social critics assert that the most effective way to fulfill the rights of both parents and children would be simply to make enough money available to families through some type of income maintenance program. This seems to be the conclusion arrived at by Keniston (1977) in the report of the Carnegie Council on Children. And yet this appears to me to be an unwarranted conclusion, as the types of problems referred to in the beginning of this paper occur now in all strata of social and economic life. As Frankel (1976) has suggested, a highly significant development with respect to family functioning is that norms of family structure have changed; hence family styles considered pathological in an earlier era are now accepted as merely representative of the diversity of modern life.

In a brilliant analysis of services available in seven countries (Federal Republic of Germany, France, Israel, Poland, the United Kingdom, Canada, and the USA), Kahn and Kamerman (1976) conclude that what they call "personal social services" are needed at all income levels and under all varieties of social and political systems. The need for such services is not eliminated by any economic or political system nor by any level of personal or family financial achievement. Nor is the need for them likely to disappear any time soon. As Kahn and Kamerman (1976) state:

> In historical perspectives, these programs which buttress daily living take over what family, village, or primary group may once have done. They are social inventions to fit our era and not, as once thought, temporary, second-best substitutes until the old "basic" institutions of family and church are restored. This latter type of thinking would be akin to the view that public education could be foregone once the family updated its capacity to teach (p. 7).

One of my fervent hopes is that some of the current zeal to see a strengthening of children's rights will translate into action to achieve more services—preparation for parenthood, nonstigmatizing family counseling, developmental day care, family planning, business- and industry-related family perquisites, universally available parental and well-child care, and so on—which will result in parent enablement. This appears to be the surest way to guarantee that children's protection rights will not be disregarded.

Mechanisms for Encouraging Service Utilization

The best and most complete array of services in the world will accomplish nothing for children unless their parents can be persuaded to take advantage of those services. Indeed, there is hardly a "right" in the UN list that draws on societal resources to which a child can have direct access—except under drastic or emergency conditions. For example, a seriously injured child will generally be given emergency medical care without authorization from an unavailable parent, but even this sort of service is not given without some discomfort on the part of service providers lest the child's parents disapprove and hold them liable for any error. Service providers are often more willing to be guilty of nonfeasance than of malfeasance or misfeasance. Thus, an important activity for advocates of children's rights is that of encouraging parents to use whatever growth-fostering services might be available to help them in their parenting task.

In 1973 I made a fascinating trip to the People's Republic of China with a group of early childhood specialists. At that time, the Chinese were not prone to confess their shortcomings publicly—a characteristic which seems undiminished today. Whenever they discussed parental involvement in the kindergartens (day-care programs) or elementary schools, they made it sound as though every parent was present for every activity. Likewise, no child ever missed a well-baby checkup because parents always brought their baby to the clinic. Whenever one of us would ask how it was that they had achieved this remarkable cooperation from parents, one of the Chinese would say something that came out in translation as, "We persuade them." The Americans would look knowingly at one another upon hearing this word "persuade," for to us it conjures up images of brainwashing and torture. Yet one evening when we were joking about the word (the actual Chinese antecedent of which we did not know, for none of us, in good American style, spoke the language), a member of our group spoke up and said, "That's what's wrong with our service delivery system; we don't persuade parents to use it."

Certainly we do not persuade in a systematic way, and perhaps we should. In an earlier paper (Caldwell, 1979), I suggested that we have at least three techniques to encourage parents to use whatever growth-fostering services are available for their children. These techniques may be described as lying along a continuum ranging from noncoercive toward coercive. Or, phrased another way, they range from those which maximally protect parental autonomy to those which threaten to subordinate that autonomy to the task of protecting children. All three mechanisms grant the parents some degree of autonomy, and all represent a way of deploying resources to enable parents to assume the major responsibility for protecting their children's rights without direct intervention by society.

Education. The least coercive type of resource which should be available to help parents protect their children's rights is education, or consciousness-raising. Such education needs to be directed not only at parenting as a process; i.e., how to accomplish what parents wish to accomplish, but at parents' understanding that theirs is a vitally important role. Our language is full of words and phrases that demean the importance of parenting—such phrases as the pejorative "*just* a housewife and mother" or the incredibly inaccurate designation baby-*sitter*. Within the past five years, better preparation for parenthood for all young people has become something of a *cause celebre*, and many school districts, family service agencies, prenatal and postnatal clinics, and the like, now offer some kind of educational service for parents-to-be—especially very young parents.

Earlier in this paper, I mentioned the Parenting is Primary Conference held in Arkansas in 1978. The more than 1,000 participants at that conference formulated a set of parenting goals for the state. The one that received the largest number of votes as being most important was: "Parenting education for all children, kindergarten through college, offered through the public schools." A task force organized during the conference is currently working toward the implementation of that goal. One of the interesting things about the work of the task force (of which I am a member) is the minimal resistance we have encountered to the idea. Similar efforts in which I was involved even as recently as three years ago met with serious opposition.

Thus, perhaps the *zeitgeist* is right for getting preparation for parenthood into our schools, our churches, our service organizations, our unions, our business and professional organizations. Certainly, if parents move into their parenting role better informed about the processes of child growth and development, more appreciative of the importance of their role, and more aware of community services that can help them in their task, then they should be better able to fulfill their responsibilities to their children. Education is the first and most vital step in the hierarchy of parent-enablement services.

Rewards or incentives. A second technique which should be used as a means of encouraging parents to protect their children's rights is rewards and incentives offered to parents who take positive steps toward meeting their children's needs. In a culture such as ours, dominated by the work ethic, we look with horror upon any suggestion that involves some sort of payment or bonus for work that should be done anyway. Parents ought to take care of their children, and we certainly should not do anything to make it easier for them! This attitude is strong even though our culture rewards virtue and hard work through an incentive system involving wages and benefits. Few indeed among us could or would work at our professions without compensation. Nonetheless, we are loathe to offer bonuses for meritorious parental service to children.

Poor people would probably benefit most from a bonus system. As pointed out repeatedly in the Keniston (1977) volume, poverty is the biggest deterrent to an adequate job of parenting; the single mother trying to rear several children on Aid to Families with Dependent Children (AFDC) has to be so concerned with substance that she has little time or energy left over for such luxuries as fun and games with the kids. Technically, AFDC represents, in the language of Figure 1, efforts on the part of the society to ensure the protection rights of children (the broken line in Figure 1) by helping parents carry out their responsibilities to children.

Parents who receive income supports are in contact with various social agencies, each of which oversees some kind of personal or family function. For example, a single mother receiving AFDC may be enrolled in a job training program and have two of her preschool children enrolled in a Title XX day-care center. Personnel in the center may have noted that the mother consistently attends parent meetings, always has her children at the center on time, responds to notes sent home, and so on. Similarly, records at the neighborhood health center used by this family might indicate that the children are always brought in for appointments, and that treatment programs worked out for the children when they are ill are always carried out. Would it not seem consistent with our work ethic and, at the same time, likely to reinforce this mother's tendency to utilize existing services, if her AFDC allowance were to be increased in recognition of the efforts she is making toward the fulfillment of her children's needs. Records are available in each of the service agencies she has utilized, but only rarely does such information get brought together in the same folder. Perhaps in our fear that a person or family might be stigmatized by the accumulation of negative information, we might have denied parents functioning responsibly on behalf of their children the opportunity to let such evidence identify them as worthy of some reward. Whenever a network of public services is received by the same family, some simple type of monitoring in the form of notation on a card should be sufficient (e.g., initials from a health center physician indicating that the child had been brought in for an appointment).

Although it is perhaps easier to think of examples that fit needy families, bonuses for "good" parenting need not be limited to families with low incomes; nor do they all have to involve additional income transfer. For example, many public facilities used by parents and children have operating costs not directly tied to the number of people who use them. "Free" admission to such facilities as zoos, amusement parks, camping facilities, and museums could be offered as rewards to parents who offer evidence that they have successfully carried out some responsibility—such as the completion of an immunization program—which protects a right of their child. Although such benefits are not technically without cost, certainly the additional costs they represent are minimal.

Contingent benefits. The third step in this hierarchy of mechanisms designed to encourage parents to utilize services for their children simply carries the reinforcement process one step further. This procedure involves the specification of certain actions which the parents must take on behalf of their children as necessary preconditions for the release of certain expected benefits. Such a mechanism would, of course, be used only if the less coercive ones had failed to produce results. To stay with examples given in the previous section, evidence would have to be presented that certain actions had been taken (immunizations completed, nutrition status as assessed by weight improved, attendance at day-care center verified) before an AFDC check is authorized. Most of us recoil in horror at the thought of using such a mechanism. In doing so, however, we demonstrate greater concern for the choice rights of parents than the protection rights of children.

This example fits only situations in which parents lack financial resources, and thus may prompt the accusation that contingent benefits would be used only with poor parents. Perhaps this may be true for parent-child situations, but the mechanism works well to guarantee that adults will perform actions that are good for the total society. Everyday examples can be found in the inspections required for automobiles or the blood test required before marriage. It is unlikely that this type of inspection ever caused a car to be kept off the highway or a marriage to go unconsummated. When we really think a protective service is important, we have no qualms about linking utilization of the service to a valued benefit. In some situations, this type of linkage may be necessary to "persuade" parents to use available societal resources in fulfilling their responsibilities to children.

For these parent-enablement mechanisms to work for the benefit of all—parents, children, and the total society—some sort of monitoring of service utilization by parents is necessary. Any mention of monitoring conjures up images of a "Big Brother" government, and most of us are frightened at that prospect. Yet we are already monitored for a great variety of activities all the time. My name, address, and zip code seem to be known to hundreds of catalogue companies, which obviously have some sort of information about my family's buying habits. And, should my Visa account be over-extended, it is amazing how quickly that information gets out across the network! But we have tended to keep what we do as parents behind closed doors and assume that it is nobody else's business. Kempe (1975) has for some time advocated the use of lay health visitors similar to those used in Scotland to go into the homes of young children in order to make certain they are receiving appropriate health care. He feels this type of relatively inexpensive outreach would prevent the disappearance from the health care system of children most in need of service. The Feshbachs, who are perhaps less concerned about service delivery than they are about minimizing the physical abuse of children, have also advocated more openness in child rearing. They state:

> A major barrier in the education and communication to parents of effective and psychologically sound socialization practices is the secrecy that surrounds this area of interaction . . . . We believe that how a parent rears a child should be an open matter, available for discussion, help, and inquiry (Feshbach & Feshbach, 1976, p. 164).

The Feshbachs go on to say that they are not advocating any true dilution of parental authority and that they feel the most effective "opening up" of the parenting process is through education and other service programs needed by parents. They feel, as I have expressed in this paper, that parents have the right to expect services from the community and that, if these are available, the rights of children will be protected in the process.

ARBITRATION VIA PREEMPTION OF POLICY

Fortunately, in most situations it appears possible to enable parents to be such successful advocates for their children that their children's rights are adequately protected. But occasionally rights will collide, and society will have to assume its "right" of arbitration specified in Figure 1. It is generally assumed that societal preemption of parental rights will be temporary and that, once certain supports have been deployed and utilized, the parent or parents will redress the imbalance and resume their parental duties. Thus, societal preemption of parental rights and responsibilities could have been listed as a fourth mechanism for encouraging parental utilization of services that would help in the parenting task. It was not so classified because parent enablement is perhaps only secondary in such action; direct protection of the child is the primary motivation. In addition, action is mandated rather than encouraged; autonomy is no longer an option.

The clearest example of such a mechanism occurs when there is evidence of child abuse or neglect. (We also see it occasionally when a child's life is threatened because parents have withheld permission for an emergency medical procedure.) Child abuse and neglect laws make it clear that our society sanctions complete usurpation of parental rights when the threat to the child is tangible and serious. Even in such situations, however, it is not done lightly and without a great deal of conflict on the part of the professionals who represent "society." As indicated by Friedman and his colleagues (1978), the mandate to report abuse specified by the laws of most states presents a serious dilemma for the professional who may, by taking such legal action, close out any opportunity to help the family.

Once parents cross an ill-defined threshold in dereliction of parental duties and societal preemption occurs, there appears to be little reluctance to set into motion all kinds of mechanisms to mandate service utilization. Any early court action will most likely involve specification of contingent benefits ("You may regain custody of your child *if* and *when* some service such as therapy or counseling is obtained"). Subsequent action will involve a reward or incentive mechanism ("As you have enrolled in the parent class at the high school, we're going to try having the child at home with you again for a while"), and the entire arbitration process will involve consciousness-raising about the importance of parenthood. It is interesting to speculate on why we are willing to use such services only after a child's rights have been flagrantly violated.

When rights collide, societal preemption of responsibility is essential, but it probably does little in the long run to redress any imbalance between the generations. Arbitration by court action represents the activation of an essential mechanism for dealing with a crisis, but it may well have little to do with the maintenance of an optimal balance among the components of this triadic reciprocating system—child, parents, and society. This long-term balancing process requires not emergency court action but rather a comprehensive social policy attuned toward both present and future, toward adults and children, toward individuals and the society of which they are a part. This kind of policy does not appear overnight, and in a nation which prides itself on diversity it evolves only after great travail. According to Kahn (1969), our society does not like to plan, and without planning we cannot have policy. Yet it does appear that we are on the threshold of planning efforts that will balance parents' rights and children's rights through the formulation of enlightened policy rather than through court action. The establishment of this Bush Institute for Child and Family Policy is certainly a step in the right direction. We are being encouraged to think of the family as a unit rather than as a collection of individuals. Although this is undoubtedly a good thing in terms of community planning and service design, unless the needs of all are met to a reasonably satisfactory extent, we may still be creating the kind of situation in which a clash of rights can occur. Only by preventing the clash can we achieve an effective balance.

SUMMARY

In this paper I have tried to highlight some of the main concepts needed to formulate social policies for families that will enable members of both generations to have their needs met and their rights protected. I have of necessity approached my assignment from the point of view of a child development professional rather than that of a lawyer; any naiveté in my approach I hope can be forgiven by those more broadly informed about the subject. Actually I have tried to think and write as a citizen, for as is the case with war and generals, the question of children's rights is too important to be left to any one professional group.

This is a propitious time in history for us to be concerned about children's rights. Such rights have historically been met within the context of the family, and the family is now changing rapidly and reappearing in new and as yet unnormed manifestations. Children's rights do not represent a new set of freedoms to be gained by yet another subgroup of the total population, despite some of the current rhetoric that proclaims them to be an oppressed minority. Rather, children's rights represent a fair share of the domain of basic human rights already enjoyed by citizens of our society. Historically, the children's share was small and perilously maintained, as the parents (the father) had all the authority and relatively little responsibility according to our modern perception. But with the advent of the concept of *parens patriae,* on the scene for over six centuries and firmly entrenched for the last century, society or state has come to represent a third claimant for a share of the rights domain. Each member of this triad has responsibilities to the other two, and only if these responsibilities are carried out satisfactorily can the other two achieve their rights. For young children, protection rights (those which guarantee that the child will be able to reach adulthood with maximal development of potentialities) are more crucial than choice rights, and the parents' responsibilities for providing sustained protection of the child provide the greatest potential for conflict.

The responsibilities carried by parents are so diverse and extensive that few parents can be expected to protect their children's rights without help from society. Thus, a major responsibility of society is to provide an array of services that will help parents in their task. To speak of rights without services is tantamount to talking about faith without works. Although society provides services, parents control access to them for their children. Therefore, the best leverage we have in making certain that children's protection rights are accorded them is to make certain that parents are enabled to carry out their functions effectively. Several mechanisms, representing a hierarchy ranging from noncoercive toward coercive, for encouraging parents to take advantage of services that would enable them to do their jobs better were outlined. Specifically mentioned were education, rewards, and contingent benefits. Reserved as a last step in this process was societal preemption of parental rights, which is necessary only in extreme conditions. However, this step is hopefully only temporary in most instances, and its success rate is not very encouraging. Thus, the establishment of a network of pre-crisis services and use of the techniques outlined above for encouraging service utilization should be given top priority. A primary goal should be the formulation of social policy which will help protect the rights of members of both generations rather than settle arbitration through the courts.

As a final thought, I should like to suggest that perhaps the most effective way of keeping parents' and children's rights in balance is to do everything we can to make Locke's assumption of almost 300 years ago—that parental benevolence is sufficient to ensure the protection of children's rights—a reality. One of my fears is that we will let our respect for adult rights so immoblize us that we shun our responsibility to develop a network of services designed to facilitate good parenting and thereby ensure the protection of our children's rights. My fervent hope is that our concern for children will intensify to the degree that we will not allow this to happen.

REFERENCES

Bane, M. J. *Here to stay*. New York: Basic Books, 1976.

Bremner, R. H. (Ed.). *Children and youth in America* (Vol. 1). Cambridge, Mass.: Harvard University Press, 1970.

Caldwell, B. M. Parents' rights versus children's rights—avoiding the confrontation. In T. B. Brazelton & V. C. Vaughan (Eds.). *The family: Setting priorities*. New York: Science and Medicine, 1979.

DeFrancis, V. Highlights of national study for 1975. In *Child Abuse and Neglect Reports*. Washington, D.C.: National Center on Child Abuse and Neglect, 1977.

Feshbach, N. D., & Feshbach, S. Punishment: Parent rites versus children's rights. In G. P. Koocher (Ed.), *Children's rights and the mental health professions*. New York: Wiley, 1976.

Frankel, C. The impact of changing values on the family. *Social Casework*, 1976, *57*, 355-365.

Fraser, B. B. The child and his parents: A delicate balance of rights. In R. E. Helfer and C. H. Kempe (Eds.), *Child abuse and neglect: The family and the community*. New York: Ballinger, 1976.

Friedman, A. S., Cardiff, M. F., Sandler, A. P., & Friedman, D. B. Dilemmas in child abuse and neglect. In J. Mearig (Ed.), *Working for children: Issues beyond federal guidelines*. San Francisco: Jossey-Bass, 1978.

Hafen, B. C. Puberty, privacy, and protection: The risks of children's rights. *American Bar Association Journal*, 1977, *63*, 1383-1388.

Hobbes, T. *Leviathan*. (Molesworth Edition, Vol. 3). London: J. Bohn, 1945.

Kahn, A. J. *Theory and practice in social planning*. New York: Russell Sage Foundation, 1969.

Kahn, A. J., & Kamerman, S. B. *Social services in intellectual perspective: The emergence of the sixth system* (SRS T6-05704). Washington, D.C.: U.S. Department of Health, Education, and Welfare, 1976.

Kempe, C. H. Family intervention: The right of all children. *Pediatrics*, 1975, *56*, 693-694.

Keniston, K. *All our children: The American family under pressure*. New York: Harcourt Brace Jovanovich, 1977.

Kohler, M. The rights of children—An unexplored constituency. *Social Policy*, 1971, *2*, 36-43.

Locke, J. *The second treatise of government*. New York: Bobbs Merrill, 1952.

Ramey, J. Experimental family forms—The family of the future. *Marriage and Family Review*, 1978, *1*, 3-9.

Vaughan, V. C. III, & Brazelton, T. B. (Eds.). *The family—Can it be saved?* Chicago: Year Book Medical Publishers, 1976.

Comments on Caldwell's Paper

CAROL B. STACK is Associate Professor of Anthropology and Director of the Center for the Study of the Family and the State at Duke University.

Discussions of liberalism and the rights of individuals rarely consider individual freedom as a cultural or social class issue. Although a particular policy may have a very different impact on poor and middle-class children and their families, the issue of parents' vs. children's rights has often been debated as an abstraction, without regard to issues of class and culture. Finding a suitable balance between children's rights and family independence is not just a philosophical issue; it is also embedded in legal, cultural, and political concerns. Dr. Caldwell's concern is that we will let our respect for adults' rights weaken our ability to protect the rights of children. As a result, she has proposed that parental behavior be monitored—especially with respect to how low-income parents use protective services for their children. In my brief response, I question whether implementing this proposition will improve the well-being of all children and families, or whether it will contribute to the creation of a dual system of children's rights—a system that creates differences in the rights of poor and non-poor children and families.

Whenever the rights of parents and the rights of children have been in conflict, our society has traditionally risen to protect the rights of parents—if the parents are affluent or middle class. There is no question that we endeavor to protect the autonomy of middle-class families. By contrast, our society has long thought that interventions or intrusions were appropriate if the families come from poor or "deprived" backgrounds. In fact, we have created an elaborate court system to protect the rights of children from poor families. This tendency to protect the rights of poor children by intervening in their lives has led to what I would call a dual system of children's rights. It appears that poor parents have lost rights to their children in their children's so-called "best interests."

Two examples of policies which effectively create a dual system of children's rights are our systems for providing foster care and day care. Neither system is noted for its attempts to heed the preferences or needs of parents. Our foster-care system typically does not allow a child to remain in the kin group, or to be placed with relatives. Moreover, the foster-care system rarely opts to provide support and services to poor parents as an alternative to foster care, despite the fact that the former alternative would support the rights of low-income parents and would certainly be less expensive. Similarly, federal day-care policies, Title XX in particular, have not been designed with the preferences of parents in mind (Larson, 1975). The preference of most parents is to have their children cared for in community-based home care rather than in large institutional licensed day care. The rights of low-income parents, and the concerns they have for the well-being of their children, are not a priority among policymakers. Dr. Caldwell does not address the preferences and needs of low-income families with children. To the contrary, her comments indicate her rather low evaluation of the concerns and capabilities of low-income parents.

It is my observation that in most low-income communities, parents and surrogate parents take great pride in raising their children (Stack, 1974). Raising children involves using cherished skills that are passed on from generation to generation. Parenting is a high status, rewarding activity. People, young and old, appear to derive self-confidence and feelings of adequacy from taking good care of their children. While many parents feel inadequate in relationship to their economic roles, they do feel competent as parents. They know how to love, nurture, and discipline their children, and how to teach them the skills they will realistically need in their lives. As I have written in *All Our Kin* (1974), children are very important to the poor. Most of the productive work of the kin group is organized around raising children, and child-rearing efforts are highly rewarded. Aunts and uncles, grandparents and cousins, siblings and friends all participate as caretakers who are responsible for the children in their extended kin network. Shared parental responsibilities are not only obligations of kinship, but constitute a highly cherished right. People assume these responsibilities because they are rewarded and because they derive a sense of success and competence from them. The skills necessary to rear children are taught by older kin to younger adults and children within family and community settings. Older women and men who have raised several children find themselves in a position of high status within the community; their advice is respected and sought.

Child socialization could be described as the kingpin of family relationships in lower income Black communities. Federal and state programs must be weighed in terms of their potential effect on how people feel about themselves as parents. Programs that closely monitor parental behavior may indeed undermine the competence and self assurance of parents. Moreover, such programs target the consequences rather than the causes of poverty. Programs that tell parents "how to do it" undermine proven expertise within low-income families. Programs that dictate which services children need and when they should get them; programs that tell parents when to play with their children, and how to talk with them; or programs that "teach" parents how and when to give affection—all undermine the sense of competence that families have concerning their ability to raise children. Dr. Caldwell's recommendations to give "bonuses" for good parenting and to monitor parental behavior with respect to the utilization of services for children infer that low-income parents have already failed as managers of their children's needs. Such recommendations are targeted at those parents who have failed. These parents are in the minority, and there are alternative ways to find them—rich and poor. Any program that proposes to intrude on the autonomy of family life must be assessed in terms of whether the program supports parents as the primary caretakers of their children.

I believe that good family policy must place the issue of individual rights solidly within a cultural context. Our American tradition has evolved from a political system that fiercely protects the rights of individuals. There are instances, however, in which such notions are in conflict with the cooperative and communal values of Afro-Americans in the U.S. This cultural conflict is most apparent when we focus on individual rights versus the rights of children. Among many working-class and low-income Black communities, we find not just individual but shared rights and responsibilities in children. Extended family groups have high regard for children. They hold shared rights in children of the kin group and shared responsibilities toward them. These rights have, as mentioned previously, been entirely overlooked by our current foster-care and day-care systems. This cultural oversight has failed to protect the rights of natural parents and the rights of other members of the kin group.

Our policies in general are pro "children" if the child is from a poor or low-income community. Our policies are pro "family" when our attention is focused on middle-class parents. The question that remains is whether we can simultaneously protect both parents' rights and responsibilities as well as the rights of children. As we increase our expectations of parents as educators and nurturers of their children, we must develop policies that parallel these values. We need policies that support our highest expectations for parents, and that support their families as well. We need policies that protect the rights of parents to obtain decent jobs, with decent incomes. We need policies that provide health care in the form of national health insurance for all children. We need policies that do not tax married parents more than single individuals, and tax policies that offer higher deductions for families with children or other dependents. We need a system of income maintenance that offers a decent standard of living and eligibility criteria that do not splinter families or require fathers to leave their children. We need foster-care policies that hasten a child's return home, and child custody decisions that respect the abilities of both parents.

Our personal freedoms will be protected when we can be assured that poor families are afforded equal protection, not only through legislation, but through our practices, our programs, and our customs. We need to protect the rights of children without devaluing or undermining the capabilities of their parents.

REFERENCES

Larson, M. R. *Federal policy for preschool services: Assumptions and evidence* (SRI Project 2158). Menlo Park, Calif.: Educational Policy Research Center, Stanford Research Institute, May 1975.

Stack, C. B. *All our kin: Strategies for survival in a Black community.* New York: Harper & Row, 1974.

Comments on Caldwell's Paper[1]

EARL S. SCHAEFER is Professor of Maternal and Child Health, School of Public Health, University of North Carolina at Chapel Hill. In addition, Dr. Schaefer is a Senior Investigator at the Frank Porter Graham Child Development Center at UNC.

Dr. Caldwell's discussion of children's rights and parents' rights, and of the rights of society in mediating conflicts between children and parents, is a useful addition to the growing literature on the rights of children. Her focus is on the responsibilities of parent and child in their relationship with one another, with less discussion of the specific responsibilities of society, or professionals who are the agents of society. A critic of a statement on parental rights, a less frequent occupation than drafting statements on children's rights, stated that a defensible statement of rights should include a parallel statement of responsibilities. Thus, professionals in interaction with parents and children should have defined rights and responsibilities with parents as well as with children.

Dr. Caldwell's paper reflects awareness of the complexity of mediating the rights of children and parents. I question her focus on crisis intervention in which parents and children are adversaries, or in which deficiencies in parental care appear to require social intervention. As Caldwell points out, such a focus on parents and professionals as adversaries, with the professional engaged in law enforcement or in legal action to secure the child's rights, is suggested by the statement of children's rights drafted at the 1970 White House Conference on Children in which the last right of the child is "The right to have societal mechanisms to enforce the foregoing rights." If the verb were to "secure" or "ensure," other social means of strengthening and supporting parental care might appear more relevant. If parent and child are seen in conflict, with the professional intervening to enforce the child's rights, the probability of open communication and collaboration between the parent and professional is reduced. The lack of trust and confidence by low-income families in social workers who are seen as enforcers of the welfare laws should warn other professionals of the pitfalls in becoming policemen with a primary function of enforcing children's rights. Perceptions of professionals as allies of children and as adversaries of parents have contributed to a situation described as "Parents and Teachers: Natural Enemies."

The belief that professionals, rather than parents, are the primary advocates for children has often caused professionals to advocate increased funding

[1] This paper was written in response to an earlier version of Dr. Caldwell's paper.

for their own profession, institution, or program as the solution to children's problems. But who will mediate among the competing professions, each of which emphasizes its own contribution to child welfare? If professionals and parents were viewed as complementing one another and as collaborators in securing children's rights, together they might provide more effective advocacy and planning for children's needs.

The medical model of securing children's rights through monitoring development by screening or annual checkups would make a contribution within a comprehensive child and family development program. Yet, apart from children with severe biomedical defects that are less responsive to intervention, the child's future health and development can be better predicted from analysis of the child's family environment than from examination of the infant. Screening or annual checkups would provide diagnosis or treatment of problems after they occur. Thus, child-centered screening and treatment is not an effective way of securing the child's right to be nurtured by affectionate parents. Unless new family-centered approaches are developed, health services would provide professional treatment of the child after development of pathology rather than support for parental care that would foster health and development.

Emphasis on professional roles of enforcing children's rights or of treating children's problems implies that the professional is on the side of the child, rescuing the child from a pathological situation by supplementing or supplanting parental care. Such professional roles often lead to a perception of the parent as the problem rather than as a major component of the solution of meeting children's needs and of securing children's rights. The role of the professionals in strengthening, supporting, and enabling parents to provide for their children has been poorly implemented, despite Dr. Caldwell's claim that we provide a number of services to families that help them secure the protection rights of the children. Research on well-child services suggests that parents' questions about development of their children are often ignored and unanswered. Further, a majority of parents who perceive behavioral or development problems in their children have not received professional help in coping with these problems.

Policies concerning maternity services are an example of the need for a focus on the rights and responsibilities of both parents and professionals. Because hospitals often focus on the physical health of mothers and children, a mother is often separated from her infant soon after delivery—and fathers are usually excluded from labor and delivery altogether. Parents concerned with the goal of fostering maternal bonding and family cohesiveness often request provisions for maternal-infant contact after delivery, for rooming-in, and for the presence of the father. Often health professionals, in focusing on their responsibilities for maintaining physical health, may ignore the rights and responsibilities of parents, and deny professional responsibility for enhancing parental roles and family cohesiveness. This example shows the need to examine interactions among the rights and responsibilities of the child, the parent, and the professional. The current movement toward family-centered maternity care has been a response to consumer demands as well as to research and service initiatives of interested professionals. Recommended changes in maternity services and other services for children will be facilitated by collaboration between professionals and parents based on analyses of parental and professional rights and responsibilities.

Conflict between concern for children and belief in personal autonomy may be one basis for society's passivity in securing children's rights. However, lack of effective concern for all persons and inadequate commitment to social and economic equality may also be relevant. Perhaps concern for children is not translated into social action because concern for children cannot be separated from concern for their parents. The quality of life for children cannot be separated from the quality of life for parents unless the child is removed from the family. Parents without adequate strengths, skills, and supports confronted with major stresses, such as poverty and poor health, often cannot adequately provide for their children. In other cases, parents who fail to provide for the needs and rights of children are parents who did not themselves receive adequate care during childhood. As Caldwell recognizes, legal enforcement of the child's rights or removing the child from the family may be counterproductive. But despite our society's weak and inadequate commitment to increasing the quality of life for parents, professionals nonetheless resort to sanctions against parents when they fail or attempt to supplement or supplement rather than strengthen and support parental care. Yet, in the case of *Shelton v. Tucker,* 364 U.S. 479 (1960), while establishing the doctrine of the "least restrictive alternative," the Supreme Court held: ". . . though the governmental purpose be legitimate and substantial, that purpose cannot be pursued by means that broadly stifle fundamental personal liberties when the end can be more narrowly achieved." Although the purpose of providing for the rights and needs of children is legitimate and substantial, the solution implied by the least restrictive alternative doctrine would seem to be the provision of parent education and supports that reduce the need for legal intervention.

A U.S. Comptroller General's (1979) analysis found: "Research shows the most effective child development programs have been family-oriented programs that have meaningfully involved parents in educating their children" (p. 10) and recommended additional funding for such programs. Yet many professions and institutions provide direct services to the isolated child after parenting failures and after behavioral or biomedical problems have developed. Perhaps a new paradigm is needed that would lead to original solutions to the problem of securing children's rights and needs.

Professional paradigms determine their definition of a problem and the range of solutions to be considered. Questions about the legal and medical models for intervention suggest the need to develop models that stress development of health, education, and well-being of parents as well as children. Such attempts would require substituting a socioecological paradigm of fostering family and community relationships for the individualistic paradigm of providing services to the isolated individual child. Emphasis would be placed on strengthening and supporting family care of the child rather than on supplanting or supplementing family care. A major component of a new paradigm that would emphasize the well-being of parent and child is a developmental perspective of fostering health, welfare, education, and development as contrasted to the pathological perspective of screening, diagnosis, and treatment of pathology in the child or of distortions and deficiencies in parental care of the child.

Professionals have a choice of enforcing children's rights by monitoring and using sanctions against parents or by parent education and supports for parenting. I agree with Caldwell's emphasis on parents' rights and the need to develop a system of family supports to secure children's rights. Further analyses of the reciprocal rights and responsibilities of children, parents, and professionals—the agents of society—can contribute to more effective collaboration between parents and professionals and to the goal of securing children's rights.

REFERENCES

Comptroller General. *Early childhood and family development programs improve the quality of life for low-income families* (HRD-79-40). Washington, D.C.: General Accounting Office, February 1979.

IRVING LAZAR, who received his Ph.D. in Child Development from Columbia University, is Professor and Chairman of the Department of Human Service Studies at Cornell University. He also serves as chairman of the Consortium for Longitudinal Studies in which position he coordinates analysis of data from 14 longitudinal studies on the effect of early education on later learning in low-income children. He is past director of child development programs for the Appalachian Regional Commission in Washington, D.C. The author of numerous publications on day care and parent programs, Lazar serves as consultant to such organizations and government agencies as the Administration for Children, Youth, and Families, The National Institute of Education, and The National Institute of Mental Health. He is currently a Fellow with the Committee on Labor and Human Resources of the U.S. Senate.

3

Social Research
and Social Policy —
Reflections on Relationships

There is no doubt among many people in social science that their research, and the beliefs they derive from their research, should have special weight in the formation of public policy. Indeed, where social scientists do not see a linear relation between research findings and political decisions, they are likely to point to the disjuncture as a "proof" of the ineptitude of policymakers. Since there are very few examples of research directly influencing policy, one is amazed at the durability of this conceit.

With few exceptions, which will be reviewed later, quite the reverse seems to hold true for the relation of research to policy in America today. As I examine the behavior of my fellow social scientists, I am forced to conclude that policy affects research more clearly than the reverse—current public policies determine the problems to be supported and the research investments to be made. Investigators propose what the government says it wants to support. In short, research follows the buck—and government is supplying both the bucks and the specifications which support and define our research agendas.

The growth industry of child development studies dates from large-scale federal interest. The current spate of studies in day care and child abuse, for example, is a direct outgrowth of federal support for these topics. Similarly, the sudden interest among psychologists in family policy is correlated with earlier rhetoric by Presidents Nixon, Ford, and Carter. Let a new priority area be announced tomorrow, and within weeks, distinguished social scientists will suddenly discover that the new area falls within their interests, if not their competence.

HOW SOCIAL SCIENCE RESEARCH INFLUENCES POLICY

Although it is rare that social research directly affects a policy or program decision, it is not rare to find social research being used and being useful, in the advocacy efforts that lead up to policy change. Studies by Caplan (1976) and Weiss (1977) suggest that a major use of research findings is to change the *zeitgeist*—to get new ideas or questions into the social atmosphere which policymakers breathe and so indirectly influence the way they look at problems. Certainly it is clear from Caplan's work that policymakers are rarely aware of using a specific study in making a specific decision. Indeed, Caplan argues that many lawyers look at social science research as merely a tool of advocacy for favored positions.

In addition, research findings may sway the undecided policymaker, particularly when the options available have low levels of emotional response or when the findings support existing policies or programs.

Limiting myself, in this paper, to studies of children and families, I can think of only three studies that directly changed policies and actions in major program areas.

One of these is Spitz's (1945) study of the short- and long-term effects of institutional care on infant development. Within two years, foundling homes were being closed, legislation to prohibit group care of infants was passed in many states; foster care programs were expanded, and "Tender Loving Care" became part of hospital jargon. Despite subsequent critiques and the demonstrations by Keister and Caldwell that group care arrangements, when properly staffed, can avoid harm, the Spitz study continued to influence child and infant care policy in America.

A second line of research with clear impact on public policy was the work of Clark and Clark (1952) concerning the emergence of racial differentiation in preschool children. These studies served as a key element of the Supreme Court decision in *Brown* vs. *the Board of Education of Topeka, Kansas.*

The third social science study which has had a direct effect on policy is the investigation concerning long-term effects of preschool programs recently conducted by the Consortium for Longitudinal Studies (1977, 1978). I shall describe this work in some detail before continuing my review of the interaction between policy and research.

The Consortium includes a substantial number of investigators in child development and several methodologists and statisticians. Although I organized, raised the money for, and served as executive officer of the Consortium, the research findings reviewed here represent the work of teams of investigators.

The principal investigators (Table 1) are Kuno Beller, Martin and Cynthia Deutsch, Susan Gray, Merle Karnes, Phyllis Levenstein, Louise Miller, Frank Palmer, David Weikart, Myron Woolman, Edward Zigler, and the late Ira Gordon. The principal methodologist in these studies is Richard Darlington.

Because this paper is concerned with the relation between policy and research, I want to describe the history of this study, rather than its more technical aspects which have been adequately described elsewhere (Consortium 1977, 1978). In 1975 I had an opportunity to examine the forward budget projections of the federal government. If rejected, the President planned to phase out all support for Head Start and the Bureau for the Education of the Handicapped. The justification for cutting these substantially financed programs was based on the Westinghouse-Ohio University 1969 evaluation of Head Start (Cicirelli, 1969) and the opinions of well-known social scientists, including

Table 1 Members of the Consortium for Longitudinal Studies

Kuno Beller
Psychology Department
Temple University
Philadelphia, PA 19122

Richard B. Darlington
Psychology Department
Cornell University
Ithaca, NY 14853

Martin & Cynthia Deutsch
Inst. for Developmental Studies
School of Education, Health, Nursing
    and Arts Professions
New York University
239 Greene Street
New York, NY 10003

Ira Gordon*
University of North Carolina
Chapel Hill, NC 27514

Susan Gray
George Peabody College
Box 151
Nashville, TN 37203

Merle Karnes
Colonel Wolfe Preschool
403 E. Healey
Champaign, IL 61820

Irving Lazar
N-135 MVR Hall
Cornell University
Ithaca, NY 14853

Phyllis Levenstein
Verbal Interaction Project
5 Broadway
Freeport, NY 11520

Louise Miller
Psychology Department
University of Louisville
Louisville, KY 40208

Francis Palmer
Merrill-Palmer Institute
71 E. Ferry
Detroit, MI 48202

David Weikart
High/Scope Foundation
600 N. River
Ypsilanti, MI 48197

Myron Woolman
Institute for Educational Research
4828 16th St.
Washington, DC 20011

Edward Zigler
Psychology Department
2 Hill House
Yale University
New Haven, CT 06520

*Deceased, September 1978. Address inquiries to:
    Robert Emile Jester
    417 N. E. 4th Ave.
    Gainesville, FL 32601

Jensen, Herrenstein, Burton White, and Bronfenbrenner, all of whom, for different reasons, said—or seemed to say—that programs like Head Start were not effective.

Note, however, that no one had appropriate data with which to make such a judgment. Further, we had available at least two kinds of indicators that suggested otherwise. Since the turn of the century, about half of middle- and upper-class children have been sent to nursery school by their parents. So middle-class families have apparently always believed there is some value in preschool education. Second, Head Start teachers who kept track of their students were reporting positive gains. What was needed were good data to indicate that graduates from preschool programs did do well in the public schools.

By 1975, enough time had elapsed for participants from the early childhood programs mentioned (see Table 1) to have gone through the elementary, and in some cases, the secondary school years. Since a direct evaluation of Head Start itself is not possible—there are no controls, no random assignment, no baseline measures, no recording of curricular inputs, and no immediate post-Head Start measures—a follow-up study of these earlier programs seemed both possible and, given the widespread attacks on early education, potentially of direct relevance to federal policy. Assuming that a follow-up of the experimental and control children in these studies would be subject to high attrition rates, I identified 15 studies that had enrolled 100 or more subjects who would meet Head Start eligibility requirements and whose curricula were neither exotic nor unusual in practice.

All but one of the original investigators agreed to collaborate in a joint effort that had the following conditions:

1. Reanalyses of old data and analyses of new data were to be done by a group at Cornell who had no connection with any of the original studies. These analyses would be independent of any other analyses conducted by the original investigators;

2. All existing raw data on original subjects were to be sent to Cornell for re-scoring, coding, formatting, and analysis;

3. New data would be collected by the original investigators using a common protocol developed by Consortium members;

4. All new data would also be sent to Cornell for analysis.

Getting support for this effort illustrates a point to which I return later in this paper. There were people convinced that we should not proceed—that our findings would result only in putting the final nails in Head Start's coffin.

After all, the conventional wisdom was that preschool effects were evanescent. Thus, a well-designed study of high-quality programs would only remove what little doubt still remained. Nonetheless, Edith Grotberg at Administration for Children, Youth, and Families (ACYF) finally assembled enough money for us to have a single session with each of the youngsters and their parents, and to collect school data. Each of our institutions waived its usual overhead, and senior investigators waived payment for their work; indeed, some sacrificed summer pay in order to participate.

We anticipated a probable recovery of 30 percent of the subjects, and budgeted for a possible 50 percent. In fact, we found over 80 percent of the original samples. Refusals amounted to less than 2 percent of those contacted. There were no significant differences in the baseline characteristics of the 80 percent who were found and those who were not found. In short, this study had neither general nor selective attrition problems.

Knowing that our findings would be carefully examined by those opposed to, and those sympathetic with, preschool education, we adopted a consistently conservative approach to data analyses. After all, if we found no experimental-control differences, the Head Start folks would string us up. If we found differences, the Boston Brahmins would go for our scalps.

One other thing concerned us. Although we would look at intelligence test scores, it was clear to us that IQ was a grossly inappropriate outcome measure— at least when used as the sole criterion of program outcome. The purpose of these programs, of course, was to enable poor children to meet the ordinary expectations of ordinary public schools. Thus, with the school records at hand, we didn't need a substitute measure, such as IQ. Instead, we selected three school outcomes to measure the long-term effects of preschool programs.

First, was the person placed in a special education class during schooling? We eliminated children with marked handicaps from this count. Placement in special education is an expensive decision for a school to make and means that the child could not function adequately in a regular class. This variable, then, would not only measure children's performance, but would allow assessment of possible financial benefits for local school systems attributable to early education.

Second, was the child left back a grade or more? Because so many schools have automatic promotion policies, we knew that this would be a less sensitive indicator. Nonetheless, like special education placement, grade retention would provide a measure of children's performance as well as a measure that could be subjected to cost-benefit analysis.

Third, did the youngster finish high school by age eighteen? For this indicator, we knew we would have to wait, although five of the studies had subjects older than eighteen, and we could look at those.

These three measures had the virtues of unambiguity, independence, and comprehensibility to citizens and legislators. On the other hand, they have the disadvantage of being dichotomous and thus limited our ability to distinguish between effective program characteristics except in a rather gross manner. Ed Zigler nicely labeled them *molar variables*.

Let me quickly summarize the findings. The percentage of controls who were assigned to special education classes far exceeded the percentage for youngsters who had attended the infant and preschool programs. Figure 1 displays these differences for the separate studies. The pooled significance across studies, 2-tailed, is $p < .0004$. The techniques for pooling consist of comparing each study's experimental and control groups, converting the F value of those differences to z scores, and then pooling the z scores so that each study receives the same weight (Consortium, 1977).

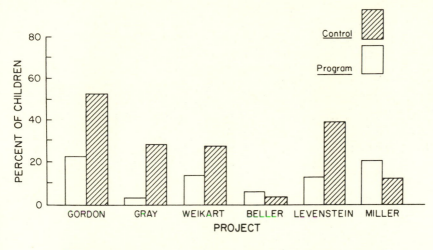

Figure 1. Percentage of program and control children in special education classes.

Figure 2 compares the number of experimental and control children who were held back a grade or more. Although not as striking as the data for special education placement, the pooled significance of the differences is still $p < .01$.

Since retention in grade and assignment to special classes can both be considered treatments for children who are not achieving at expected levels, we combined the two for an "underachiever" score for each study. Figure 3 displays the differences between experimental and control children on this combined measure. As Figure 3 suggests, the differences are significant at the $p < .0002$ level.

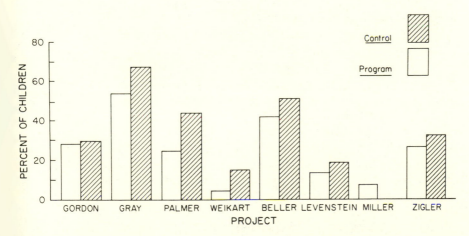

Figure 2. Percentage of program and control children held back a grade.

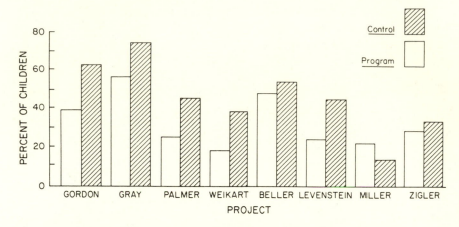

Figure 3. Percentage of program and control children who were underachieving.

Although we still have few data concerning high school completion, those we do have indicate experimental-control differences similar to those reported above.

These differences in special education placement and grade retention are so great as to be cost-effective. Indeed, the savings in special education costs alone would more than pay for the costs of universal preschool education, if we generalized from one of the most tightly designed of these studies—Weikart's Ypsilanti Perry Preschool Project. In a cost-benefit analysis of that study, there appears to be a benefit over costs in excess of 2500 current dollars per child (Weber, Foster, & Weikart, 1978).

We of course looked at other variables and, if we can finance it, hope to do another follow-up to focus on indicators of social and personal competence outside of school-related spheres. This summary is limited to these school-related findings, because it is these findings which made waves.

I will not dwell on the attacks by individuals and groups who greeted our findings with dismay. We were accused of going beyond our data by people who never examined the data and of having severe selective attrition problems before we even analyzed any data. One agency assigned a team to dismantle and discredit our findings. It failed to do so.

A funny thing happened along the way, however. The newly elected Carter administration asked for a $5 million increase in the Head Start budget, with the money to be earmarked for family-related research. Using our findings, Congress increased the Head Start budget by $150 million, and earmarked it for program expansion. Further, the General Accounting Office sent a team to evaluate our study. They examined raw data, sampled our calculations, ran cards, and then visited individual projects and other ongoing programs for young children. Their final report (Comptroller General, 1979) states that early intervention does indeed improve the later performance of low-income children and leads to an improvement in the quality of life for their families. In two years, then, the *zeitgeist* has changed completely, and Head Start and similar programs are, at least for now, going to continue to receive substantial public support. I noticed, with some satisfaction, that the President's 1980 budget proposal provides for further increases for Head Start while either cutting or freezing other components of the ACYF budget.

Now you should know that this response by Congress and the Administration did not occur by accident. Quite simply, instead of writing articles for professional journals, we briefed as many congressional staffs, governor's staffs, and state legislators as we could reach. Instead of talking to academic audiences, we talked to advocacy groups. Instead of a monograph for the profession, Frank Palmer wrote around the clock for the President's Commission on Mental Health. We did occasionally present material at professional meetings and continue to do so. But our first priority was to get the news to those who make decisions and not expect them to read about it in the *New York Times,* or even less likely, in *Child Development.*

We made an impact because it simply makes sense that if someone takes the trouble to teach children, they are likely to learn. We have some ideas as to how the effects lasted so long, but that's for another paper.

Notice that, although we pointed out the quality controls which distinguish these studies from many regular Head Start programs, the increase in Head Start funds did not carry with it a requirement to assure new quality-control measures.

THE MISUSE OF SOCIAL SCIENCE RESEARCH

This brings me to the more common fate of research findings, which is to be deliberately misused to support a policy already arrived at. Let me illustrate with three examples.

The first example is the Westinghouse-Ohio University evaluation of Head Start (Cicirelli, 1969). On the one hand, as I pointed out earlier, there is no way to conduct a sound evaluation of Head Start. When we asked Head Start, just last year, at least to collect baseline data on a random sample of the thousand new sites established by increased appropriations, ACYF refused to do it. So the Westinghouse-Ohio University group had a basic problem which was not solvable. They did the best they could and indeed collected a rich variety of data going far beyond mere IQ scores. But the reported washout of IQ data is what fit the administration's policy—and Dr. Moynihan, then in Nixon's White House, emphasized the IQ findings alone. The rest of the findings never caught up with this selective emphasis which had substantial effects on policy for a decade. Dr. Lois-ellin Datta (1976, in press) documented the history of these effects in recent papers.

Another example of the misuse of social science research happened to Moynihan himself. His paper, "The Negro Family" (1965), was grossly misrepresented by the news media. In fact, the attacks began before the paper was available by people who never even saw it. A complete account of how the media misrepresented the Moynihan Report has been assembled in an excellent book by Rainwater and Yancey (1967). The point I am emphasizing here is that important and widely discussed reports and studies by social scientists are often less read than discussed and interpreted. This says a great deal about the writing and reporting style of social scientists and our naiveté in dealing with the mass media.

A third example of misuse of social science research is provided by the Income Maintenance Studies (Watts & Rees, 1977). The positive finding that a guaranteed income increases the long-term purchasing power of the breadwinner by allowing him to take some risks is rarely reported. Nor is it widely mentioned that the greatest decrease in labor supply was found for mothers, probably because a guaranteed income allowed them to stay home with their children. Rather the big play is reserved for the finding from Seattle and Denver (Tuma, Groeneveld, & Hannan, 1976; Tuma, Hannan, & Groeneveld, 1977) in which increased marital dissolution was given almost exclusive attention by the press, Senator Moynihan, and others.

Strategies for Preventing Research from Affecting Policy

Caplan (1976) and Weiss (1977) report that decision makers emit proper sounds about how policy should build upon research, but the requirements for evaluation that Congress imposed on social programs have led to the development of a whole set of avoidance tactics whose sheer cleverness should reassure us of the intelligence of program managers. Let me list some of the more common tactics and strategies for preventing research from affecting policy.

First, program evaluations are usually controlled directly by the managers whose programs are being evaluated. Managers can thereby control access to information and prohibit release of information unfavorable to their program.

Second, the use of private consultant firms, which have a vested interest in getting new contracts from the same agencies, often assures that findings will look the way the agency wants them to look. I was once told by a commissioner that he would never give an evaluation contract to a university. "Why," he said, "you can never tell what an academic will publish. I'll stick to private firms who need me to butter their bread."

Third, not all consultant firms are equally talented at turning sows ears into silk purses, so a second tactic is deliberately to flaw the design of a demonstration program at the beginning. If the later evaluation findings are negative, the agency can then reject the findings on the grounds that they were produced by a flawed design! This, in Washington jargon, provides a basis for later deniability.

Fourth, a suicidal contractor will occasionally devise a way of getting around the design flaw and will provide clear and undeniable evidence that a program is miserable. I've seen three common solutions to this problem. The agency can simply suppress the original report and have a friendly consultant write a whitewash which is published as a "summary" of the original report. Another tactic is to select the three or four sites which look best and relabel them a "new" demonstration, with a new evaluation. In that way you can produce a winner without the fuss of figuring out why the other sites failed. In such cases, information about causes of failure, which may be even more valuable than information about the sites that were successful, is sacrificed to bureaucratic convenience. Finally, if a program manager does not dare risk getting real data, he can usually hire a big name to write a selective review of the literature which reaches conclusions favorable to the program and which can then be disseminated widely.

STRATEGIES FOR APPLYING RESEARCH DATA TO POLICY DECISIONS

What is to be done about all this? I share the hope that the link between policy and data could be more direct than through a change in the climate of opinion surrounding policymakers. Let me end by suggesting eight things that can make that link more direct.

First, agencies, organizations, or individuals responsible for evaluating public programs must be independent from the control of agencies sponsoring the programs. This principle of separation should apply also to the writing of requests for proposals and the judging of grant applications.

Second, we should support the passage and implementation of a strong sunset bill. Such a bill would automatically terminate programs at the end of five years unless an independent evaluation justified their continuation. I would have these evaluations carried out by a congressional agency rather than an executive agency.

Third, the social science community should challenge the big names when they make noise instead of science or distort findings to fit their fancies.

Fourth, we need to educate lawyers, who often see science as simply another form of advocacy. After all, it is lawyers who run government. If they are to appreciate the type of social science information that can inform policy decisions, they should be familiar with the rudiments of experimental design and methods of statistical analysis. Not only will this help lawyers distinguish between good and poor studies, it may also tend to diminish any worries they may feel when faced with the jargon of design and measurement.

Fifth, as social scientists, we need to be more politically adept. We need to know how to, and be willing to, reach decision makers. Further, we must be willing to set aside our own narcissistic needs when necessary to present a united, or at least less disparate, front to policymakers.

Sixth, we should take seriously the search for more effective ways to motivate the general public to take a more active role in policy and politics. An important step in this direction would be basic research concerning factors that influence group participation by young children.

Seventh, we must remind ourselves that although the beginning of wisdom is the knowledge of ignorance, there are useful things that we do know. Our frequent unwillingness to say clearly what the current state of knowledge suggests for action today abandons decision making to the ideologists who speak with the self-assurance that they have revealed truths.

Finally, I think it is essential that policy studies be tied to specific program designs and implementation. It is easy to design a new society, or new priorities in human behavior and motivation, or to muse philosophically about how our superior upper middle-class values would be good for everyone. But such blue-sky fantasies and imposition of values are not activities worthy of scholars. We don't make laws or run programs or face the realities of policy implementation. If we don't tie our policy concerns to practice, I'm afraid we'll never really be helpful—and so never really have very much influence on the course of events. Such practical concerns and limited goals may not satisfy the power goals of some who study policy, but perhaps we should counsel them to run for office and let the rest of us try to bring the fruits of science to a society seeking more sanity in its efforts to solve human problems.

REFERENCES

Caplan, N. Social research and national policy: What gets used, by whom, for what purposes, and with what effects? *International Social Science Journal,* 1976, *28,* 187-194.

Cicirelli, V. *The impact of Head Start: An evaluation of the effects of Head Start on children's cognitive and affective development.* Athens, Ohio: Westinghouse Learning Corporation, 1969.

Clark, K. B., & Clark, M. P. Racial identification and preference in Negro children. In G. E. Swanson, T. M. Newcomb, & E. R. Hartley (Eds.), *Readings in Social Psychology* (2nd ed.). New York: Holt, 1952.

Comptroller General. *Early childhood and family development programs improve the quality of life for low-income families* (HDR-79-40). Washington, D.C.: General Accounting Office, February 1979.

Consortium for Longitudinal Studies. *The persistence of preschool effects: A long-term follow-up of fourteen infant and preschool experiments* (Final Report for ACYF Grant No. 18-76-07843). Ithaca, N.Y.: Cornell University, Community Services Laboratory, September 1977.

Consortium for Longitudinal Studies. *Lasting effects after preschool* (Final Report for HEW Grant 90C-1311). Ithaca, N.Y.: Cornell University, Community Services Laboratory, October 1978.

Datta, L.-E. The impact of the Westinghouse/Ohio evaluation on the development of project Head Start: An examination of the immediate and longer-term effects and how they came about. In C. C. Abt (Ed.), *The evaluation of social programs.* Beverly Hills, Calif.: Sage, 1976.

Datta, L.-E. What has the impact of Head Start been?: Some findings from national evaluations of Head Start. In E. Zigler & J. Valentine (Eds.), *History of Head Start.* (In press.)

Moynihan, D. P. *The Negro family: The case for national action.* Washington, D. C.: U.S. Government Printing Office, 1965.

Rainwater, L., & Yancey, W. L. *The Moynihan Report and the politics of controversy.* Cambridge, Mass.: M.I.T. Press, 1967.

Spitz, R. A. Hospitalism. *Psychoanalytic Study of the Child,* 1945, *1,* 53-74.

Tuma, N. B., Groeneveld, L. P., & Hannan, M. T. *First dissolutions and marriages: Impacts in 24 months of the Seattle and Denver Income Maintenance Experiments* (Research Memorandum 35). Menlo Park, Calif.: Stanford Research Institute, August 1976.

Tuma, N. B., Hannan, M. T., & Groeneveld, L. P. *Variation over time in the impact of the Seattle and Denver Income Maintenance Experiments on the making and breaking of marriages* (Research Memorandum 43). Menlo Park, Calif.: Stanford Research Institute, February 1977.

Watts, H. W., & Rees, A. (Eds). *The New Jersey Income Maintenance Experiment* (Vols. 2 & 3). New York: Academic Press, 1977.

Weber, C. U., Foster, P. W., & Weikart, D. P. *An economic analysis of the Ypsilanti Perry Preschool Project.* Ypsilanti, Mich.: High/Scope, 1978.

Weiss, C. H. Research for policy's sake: The enlightenment function of social research. *Policy Analysis,* 1977, *3,* 531-545.

Comments on Lazar's Paper

CRAIG T. RAMEY is Associate Director and Director of Research at the Frank Porter Graham Child Development Center, University of North Carolina at Chapel Hill. Dr. Ramey is also Professor of Psychology and a faculty member of the Bush Institute for Child and Family Policy at UNC.

Much of what social scientists do has no *immediate* importance for public policies and programs concerning human development. I think we as social scientists should acknowledge this fact without guilt. The mission of the human sciences and especially the social sciences is a long-range one. Many different kinds of contributions are necessary and we only dimly perceive the well-ordered and creative social structures that we desire. However, when science and scientists *can* make significant immediate contributions to the general good, it is desirable that they do so. The work that Dr. Lazar has reported is an excellent demonstration of how social science techniques can be brought to bear on one of society's most fundamental issues; namely, can we significantly assist the development and accomplishments of children from disadvantaged families? I draw from Dr. Lazar's comments—and the Consortium's research findings— renewed hope and enthusiasm for the early childhood education community. I also have been stimulated by his paper to reflect upon the role of the social scientist at the synapse between science and public policy. I would like to discuss those reflections concerning the responsibilities of social scientists in policy matters before commenting more specifically on the findings from Lazar's Consortium.

Obviously, various publics need better and more education about the process of social science inquiry. Research scientists themselves could learn to communicate more effectively with their publics. All too frequently, I have heard social scientists express disdain for, and underestimate the scientific sophistication of, legislators and other public officials. It is also too frequently the case that social scientists use esoteric language that is publicly, and probably conceptually, unnecessary. This newspeak needlessly confuses and mystifies policymakers and the public alike. Thus, researchers sometimes contribute to their own cool and skeptical reception by lazy and parochial habits of reporting their ideas and findings. Further, it must be remembered that scholarly scientific journals are read mostly by one's scientific colleagues. Thus, supplementary avenues of communication must be used by researchers who choose to enter the policy forum effectively.

For policy-relevant statements, statistical significance should be only the starting point in reporting results. The difference between statistical significance and useful significance needs to be understood I think, both for our construction of theories as well as for the practical usefulness of our results. Too frequently, social scientists use statistics as conceptual camouflage to keep the lay public at bay.

In reporting scientific results to the general public, rarely are figures necessary beyond percentages, proportions, or frequencies of occurrence. A statement is needed about how confident we are in the accuracy of our results. We also need to make explicit statements about how important we think our results are, and why they are important.

There is a major danger in our country now that cost will be used as the sole determinant in deciding among alternative public policies. All things being equal, cost will prevail in the absence of other defensible criteria. Therefore, educators and psychologists must adopt, or create, criteria that are preferable to cost if they are to speak with the economist. I say this fully realizing that such a task is a large and difficult one. In addition to developing these alternative criteria, educators and psychologists also need to develop an appreciation for the economics of their recommendations. Recommendations such as those that came from the Joint Commission on Mental Health, in which programs were advocated with a cavalier disregard for costs, caused the proposers to be justly labeled naive and unaware of the realities of the public agenda.

It is my opinion that all social programs can and should receive adequate scientific evaluation on a periodic basis. Evaluation is particularly necessary when a program has not previously been shown to achieve its stated goals and to avoid undesirable side effects. In this context, evaluation is good science, good business, and good politics. I would argue that it is more expensive not to evaluate—more expensive because of the continuation of poor ineffective programs and because of missed opportunities for significant advancement.

Dr. Lazar has made the point that, for political reasons, scientists sometimes publish selective literature reviews or engage in biased evaluations. Scientists who are a party to deliberately misleading the public are unethical scientists, even if they are excellent politicians. In deliberately biasing the results, they have moved from one role to another with different rules. A clear separation of roles is essential if the public is to be prevented from becoming even more cynical about our major institutions, including the institutions of science. Because so much of social science can never be truly replicated in the sense that one can replicate a chemistry experiment, it is the special and inviolate trust of the public that social scientists must always maintain if they are to make continuous contributions. It would, however, be naive to expect that the scientist operate by the rules of science in all contexts. And one must realize that, when social scientists go public in the service of policy, their statements become part of the political process which is played by different rules than those governing the conduct of science. As a footnote, I would add that scientists should not expect universal adulation for their role in the policy arena.

Thus, they must learn not to feel hurt when unacademically sharp blows are the result of well-intentioned efforts.

As my final general point, I would like to argue that in policy-relevant research, as in theoretically relevant research, there is no substitute for well-designed and competently conducted work. Neither good intentions in the choice of significant social problems nor dedication to the long and arduous pursuit of ideas is a substitute, or an adequate apology, for inadequately designed or conducted studies. Adequately designed, and indeed pristine, research designs may not be successful in carrying the day from the social scientist's point of view when he speaks to a policy issue. However, in the absence of high-quality data which permit debate on the basis of rational ethics, currently powerful forces will continue to exercise their biases as policy unchecked by potential scientific contributions.

With these general points in mind, perhaps as a starting point in developing criteria by which to judge the performance of social scientists engaged in policy, I would like to make a few brief comments about the findings reported by the Consortium. Dr. Lazar and his colleagues in the Consortium are to be congratulated as effective administrators, dedicated scientists and practitioners, and major contributors to the process of establishing the public agenda concerning programs for disadvantaged children and their families. Dr. Lazar is to be particularly congratulated for his ability to entice, to cajole, or to use whatever means were necessary to bring 14 independent researchers from a diverse array of institutions and a diverse set of theoretical perspectives into a productively harmonious organization.

The methods of data collection and analysis used by Lazar and his colleagues are exemplary for early intervention research which has been characterized in general by weak research designs. Although the techniques for analyzing data may in some relatively minor incidences be debatable, I find them sound, thoughtful, and sophisticated beyond simple state-of-the-art status. In short, the study was well designed and conducted, given the limitations of the existing data.

The criteria by which the Consortium judged the program outcomes have face validity and are obviously of social importance. Who can seriously question that special education placement, grade retention, or graduating from high school are important potential outcomes? It is, however, necessary to know more about the processes and social mechanisms that underlie these outcomes if we are to benefit maximally from these early intervention experiments. Further, it is necessary to expand this important but somewhat molar set of measures with more and more refined measures of outcomes.

Finally, the Consortium's findings, and Dr. Lazar's advocacy in their behalf, have helped to bring the early education of disadvantaged children back to the public agenda in a constructive, creative, and exemplary manner. The results are clear and the task of educating disadvantaged children can proceed with renewed hope.

Comments on Lazar's Paper

QUENTIN W. LINDSEY is the Science Policy Advisor
to the Governor of the State of North Carolina.

In this paper, Irving Lazar is discussing a highly important set of issues: relationships between social research and social policy. He summarizes how research conducted by a consortium (of which he is a member) resulted in increased support to the Head Start Program by Congress and the Carter administration. He makes critical observations about other studies that have, and have not, been used properly and effectively in influencing social policy.

As a cogent, illuminating examination of the relationships between social research and social policy, however, this paper is on the order of a flickering candle in an arena where rays of sunlight are needed. If social scientists really want to influence policy, this paper reveals how much time they must spend in making research results clear to policymakers, rather than impressing one's peers with methodological sophistication. The paper also observes that social science research often follows the buck: announce a new policy objective, with funding, and a surprising number of social scientists will immediately find the objective to be consistent with their own most profound endeavors. The relationship between the policy and prior research, however, is, in Lazar's view, rather obtuse.

Lazar closes by listing several strategies for applying research data to policy decisions: Evaluation must be independent of program managers; sunset legislation should be enacted that would close down programs after five years if independent evaluations do not justify continuation; "big name" scientists should not be allowed to distort research to suit their fancies; social scientists should be more politically adept in reaching decision makers, in mobilizing the general public, and in educating lawyers; we should make better use of what we do know; and finally, we should tie our policy concerns to practice, face the hard realities of policy implementation.

My impression is that, in this paper, Lazar is floundering in the web of social research and social policy relationships. This impression stems, perhaps, from my conviction that these relationships are best examined within the context of the organizational structure of society. We have, within this structure, political entities of government. We also have economic, religious, and social entities—including families, communities, educational institutions, and other entities normally construed as the province of social scientists. In addition, we have academic institutions, with the multiple objectives of research, teaching, and sometimes, service. Within the structure of society, a policy decision guides the action of some individuals in relation to others. The admissions policy of an academic institution, for example, regulates who shall be taught by the faculty. A social policy of government may, as Lazar describes, govern the size and nature of a Head Start Program.

A policy decision by a governmental entity always has many dimensions: economic, political, cultural, social, religious, geographic, etc. The "mix" of these dimensions varies with the type of decision, with the people who formulate it, with the extent to which evidence accumulated through research is used, and with pressure from interest groups. But, existentially speaking, in making a decision the mix is fixed for the duration of the decision. Some may see it as a bad decision; others may see it as good.

Lazar fails to make clear that the process of policy formulation entails the exposure of the policymaking entity—e.g., Congress—to most of these dimensions of influence. The relationship between social research and social policy, in other words, is but one dimension of the process. Relations between Congress and the other dimensions are part of the web. There is no necessary reason why Congress or any other policymaking body should hold social science research in greater esteem than any other dimension that must be considered. This is especially so given the shortcomings of social scientists and social science research that Lazar describes.

Implicit in Lazar's reasoning is the assumption that social science research can somehow always improve a policy decision, and that policymakers ought to make use of social science research in formulating policy. True, he recognizes that some studies are flawed; they do not represent good science and hence would not improve decisions. He recognizes that some policymakers sort out only elements of research that coincide with their preconceived notions and ignore the rest. And he recognizes that some social scientists prostitute themselves by going after the bucks when a policy decision is announced.

But beneath it all, Lazar has faith in empirically based, social science research as being an important and meaningful ingredient in social policy formulation by government, particularly our federal government. He also holds it to be the duty of social scientists to carry their results to decision makers.

I agree with this position and am convinced that such faith and such awareness of the need for persuasive influence is required in policy formulation. I am also acutely aware that faith in one's cause and dedication to persuasion are the characteristics of a political zealot, of an influential lobbyist, or of a sincere, born-again Christian. The policymaker faces an existential choice as he formulates a policy; and the canons of science do not guarantee that a social scientist will provide him with a better basis for policy than anyone else.

Thus, I find Heisenberg's principle to be most revealing in expressing the relationship between social research and social policy, as well as in physics. Heisenberg recognizes that there is a distinct interaction between the observer and that which is observed. We do not devise scientific instruments, physical or social, and then observe phenomena with a clear, objective eye that reveals truth far superior to all other interpretations of reality. Objectivity in this sense, is merely a point of view; or in more poetic language, beauty is in the eye of the beholder.

Lazar seeks to report on (1) a good piece of research that had a strong influence on Head Start policy, and (2) relationships between social research and social policy. He does not do very well with either. His report of Head Start research and its impact is rather brief and sketchy; his examination of relationships lacks any meaningful theoretical structure.

Response to Lindsey's Critique

Implicit in Lindsey's critique is the notion that scientifically derived knowledge is simply another form of advocacy—no more valid than the beliefs of "a political zealot, . . . an influential lobbyist, or a sincere, born-again Christian." Studies of federal bureaucrats have found this attitude widespread, particularly among lawyers, for whom the search for truth sometimes seems to be an exercise in rhetoric—thus, the "public hearing" as the data base for decision making, and all the other substitutes for verifiable knowledge that many political folks prefer. Hard data, are, indeed, anathema to many politicians. They reduce options, interfere with the process of compromise, and make trading difficult. As long as a program choice is speculative, the politician can deal—and duck. If one concedes that a fact is known, then one must act. If it is a social fact, and requires expenditures for social programs in this period of recession, the need to deny its validity is indeed pressing to the politician. The promise of future savings means little to someone concerned with the next year's elections.

This, and other widespread misperceptions of the methods and meanings of science, is, of course, a reflection of our educational system. Those of us who teach the sciences need to do a lot better if intelligent people really believe that scientifically derived knowledge is no "better" than rhetoric.

Lindsey's misunderstanding of the uncertainty principle—which simply states that, whereas the behavior of a group is predictable, the behavior of particular individuals is not—reflects his apparent need to deny that anything is really knowable.

Of course, policy decisions in America are usually the product of competing interests and values. This paper did not address how policies are formed, but rather, how social research might make a more effective contribution to the decision process. I do plead guilty to holding firm to the belief that verifiable data are a better base for policy than superstition or "common sense."

IRVING LAZAR

GEORGE A. SILVER is a Professor of Public Health at Yale University's School of Medicine. He holds an M.D. degree from Jefferson Medical College and a Master's degree in public health from Johns Hopkins University. In addition to providing consultation on health policy to a number of national and international organizations, Dr. Silver helped formulate America's federal health policy for children during his tenure as Deputy Assistant Secretary for Health and Scientific Affairs in the early years of the Johnson administration. Dr. Silver's long concern with health policy is documented in over 70 articles and four books, the most recent of which is *Child Health: America's Future* (Aspen, 1978).

4

Child Health Services— A Basis for Structural Reform

Concern for the health of children is not new in American life; its expression goes back a long time, thus reflecting changing social and cultural pressures that contributed to the morbidity generating the initial concern. Early on, the critical issue was high death rates among infants and young children and what needed to be done to keep children alive. Private philanthropy contributed generously to early efforts aimed at ameliorating the shockingly high rates of infant mortality, and helped to generate public pressures that resulted in inauguration and extension of government action for improving the public's health. Agitation against economic exploitation of children resulted in child labor legislation and almost simultaneously culminated in establishment of the Children's Bureau and the decennial White House Conferences on Children and Youth. These gave national visibility to the expression of child health needs and stimulated programs for improvement of child health (Yale Health Policy Project, 1973).

Decade by decade, one can measure the level of concern for children's health by reviewing the agenda and discussions at successive White House Conferences. In 1930, for example, while Herbert Hoover was President, the famous "Children's Charter" was issued. Conference themes, as one might expect, reflected changing social attitudes and social values. Early conferences focused on the child as an individual; later conferences centered on system failures: the country as a whole had become system oriented, and system failures dominated the agenda, along with recommendations for system improvement. The emphasis soon shifted, however, to agitation for more and better health departments, more and better-trained personnel. Instead of pleas for services, the addresses promoted more consultation, planning, supervision, and evaluation—all professional goals.

By then services were more complex and demanding of professional skills, parents were shunted aside, professional roles were emphasized, and more people were found in headquarters than in the field. Paradoxically, as parents were seen as less competent in dealing with child care, fewer skilled professionals were available at the operating level because they were increasingly locked into official and administrative activities.

Recently, therefore, parents and professionals both have begun to feel uneasy. Strong statements of dissatisfaction with the *status quo* are heard from both professional and children's interest groups. Despite increasing legislative action, more money disbursed from the public purse, and increasingly specialized and complex medical care systems, the indicators of child health in the United States show little improvement. Certainly they have not caught up with or surpassed (as they should have) the standards of child health in countries less rich, less well endowed with both material and medical resources.

It isn't too difficult to show that the United States, resource rich and powerful, cannot measure up to the accomplishments of comparable technologically advanced industrial countries (Miller, 1975). We are twelfth in infant mortality (Department of Health, Education, and Welfare, 1978). This socio-medical indicator is commonly used, perhaps exaggerated in importance, because it reflects so many elements of those measures that symbolize health: nutrition, the status of women, and the availability and quality of, medical care, among others.

During a four-year period, a group of us with a variety of professional backgrounds—medicine, public health, sociology, political science, law, and education—sought to elucidate factors in the government health apparatus that might be the source of America's failure to provide effective medical care and health services for its children (Yale Health Policy Project, 1976). Eventually it became apparent that the term *medical care* included several different, though interrelated, program aspects. This realization helped not only to define the causative factors, but after some studies on European child health policies and programs, helped to define possible solutions as well.

Medical care for children, much more so than for adults, comprises three elements. First, there is social policy with regard to *protection* of children. This includes the protection of the fetus during pregnancy and at birth; and numbers, among other elements, such disparate factors as nutrition, welfare services, financial support to the family, legal protection, educational opportunities and programs—in a word, social consideration for the child. Then there is *prevention*. Under this heading can be included certain aspects of health supervision in institutional settings, such as day-care centers and schools; examination for discovery and treatment of handicapping conditions; immunizations against infectious disease; and psychological and social guidance to parents, children, and families. The third element is what is commonly called *medical care;* namely, diagnosis and treatment of illness.

In the United States, where protection, prevention, and medical care tend to be undifferentiated, these elements of health care become confused, and as a result, none of them is carried out properly. Some essential factors are ignored; others are delegated to untrained or unconcerned agencies which fail to accept or fulfill responsibility.

For example, although we have long known that the norms of pregnancy demand that a woman enter the pregnant state in good nutritional condition, little is done to assure suitable nutrition for young women during the inter-conceptional period. Further, the nutrition of children, particularly school children, is relegated to the vagaries of agricultural politics or welfare budgeting. There is no program specifically aimed at maintaining or improving the nutrition of young children.

In another important area where children could be uniformly protected, custom effectively blocks protection. Legal rights of children are bound up with traditional attitudes toward family responsibility so that mothers and fathers are dealt with—treated, punished, or rewarded—in the expectation that such techniques will influence the care received by children. Children themselves receive short shrift in social or judicial decisions about their care.

Specific preventive services are also insufficient in America's provisions for children. Well-baby clinics and preschool centers have given way to physician office care—where low-income families restrict "unnecessary" visits to a minimum; or hospital clinics—where the indignities, hustle, and irregular physician attendance offer little promise of solicitous preventive care. School health services seem to be a farce, with little if anything being done to make certain that illness, psychological disturbance, or handicapping conditions discovered in the school medical examination are treated—even in the not so common circumstances where school health examinations are carried out. In 1967 Congress passed legislation requiring that every child eligible for Medicaid should be examined for the presence of handicapping conditions. The law also required that, if found, such handicapping conditions should be treated. In the first five years of this program, called *Early and Periodic Screening, Diagnosis, and Treatment* (EPSDT), fewer than 8 percent of eligible children were so examined. There is no record of how many of that 8 percent were actually treated for whatever was found. The situation is better now, but uneven—few states look after the majority of eligible children (Foltz, 1975).

Among poor children, the proportion immunized against infectious diseases for which immunizations are available is generally less than 60 percent; for the country as a whole, only 70 percent of children in the eligible age groups are immunized (Office of the Assistant Secretary for Health, 1976).

Medical services for sick children are not uniformly available. Physicians are distributed unevenly in the country, and specialists, such as pediatricians, are even more unevenly distributed. In rural areas, poor communities, and inner city communities, physicians and particularly specialists are few. Hospital clinics, where they exist, are crowded, impersonal, and in many instances far from careful in examination or treatment. Even for the poor who are covered by Medicaid, the evidence seems to be that their children do not receive as many visits, or as much care as those in families with higher incomes. Worst off, of course, are the working poor, without sufficient funds to pay for their own care, often without health insurance, and ineligible for Medicaid (Davis, 1976).

Given these facts—lack of a social policy for the protection of children, lack of preventive services for children, and lack of universally available medical care services—much of the undistinguished public health record of American children is easily explainable. If one adds to this the fact that the United States lacks a comprehensive, universally available national health service or insurance to pay for medical care, it is apparent that many children for reasons of low income, geographic inaccessibility, or racial or cultural difference do not receive needed preventive health service or medical care. A great many studies and investigations bear testimony to the fact that poor minority children in the United States do not have the same access to medical services enjoyed by children from wealthier families (Davis, 1978).

In exploring the background for the failure of American society to recognize and come to terms with this pattern of neglect, the Yale Health Policy Project (1976) argued that blame could be apportioned among many levels of policymaking groups. Congress, for example, although legislating many kinds of programs for children and appropriating a great deal of money (over $2 billion in 1976) continues to draft laws in language sufficiently loose so as to allow recipient agencies to do more or less as they please in the name of carrying out health services for children. The states do, of course, use the money for child health or matters related to child health, but these actions have become increasingly bureaucratic and empire building, with diminished provision of actual services to children.

Part of the blame for this situation rests on the ambiguity of legislation and part on the laxity of congressional oversight. The federal/state relationship continues to be an uneasy one despite the growing approval of revenue sharing and block grants. States are still slyly trying to outmaneuver federal requirements in order to offset state matching with federal funds; intra-agency and interagency feuds are played out at federal and state levels; state legislatures are either unaware of, or unwilling to react to, federal demands. Congressional oversight rarely requests specific results or designates appropriate outcome measures. As a result, no good data exist or are collected to support or defend necessary child health services. Nor do states collect data on either the dimensions of need, or whether services are actually provided to eligible children or children in need. This lack of data makes it impossible to focus on necessary services and assure that the work done is needed, or that those who need services receive them; it also means that we have no measure of whether services are effective, sufficient, and efficient (Yale Health Policy Project, 1976).

In an impassioned address on behalf of America's neglected children, Vice President, then Senator, Walter F. Mondale elaborated on the doleful details of the consequences of poor health services. His address, "Justice for Children," recounted the effects of our failures on the victims—particularly the impoverished, the migrants, and minority children; but also on those in all income groups, of all races, colors, and geographic residence—whose handicaps and defects are not found early or at all because of the lack of effective treatment programs. Among other things, Mondale stated:

> I wonder why we do not try to find out and report upon how many children are born with or succumb to severe and crippling illness, injuries to their bodies and brains, diseases that affect their growth and development—and then go on to get thoroughly inadequate treatment for such affliction.

> Perhaps if we knew how many children need pediatricians and surgeons, need physical therapists, need child psychiatrists, need one or another kind of medicine, or instrument or mode of therapy—and do not get what they need, then we would be in a position to weigh our priorities, so that when generals and admirals, already in control of enough military hardware to destroy the entire planet, tell us they have needs, they want another kind of plane or ship

or gun, we can say to them: "Yes, we want to protect this country, and protect it not only from outside enemies but from diseases that every single day
unnecessarily kill and maim and stunt and cause pain and suffering to
American children." [He also added harshly]: "What is especially discouraging
is that these remarks of mine are obviously not the first time or the hundredth
or thousandth, that this tragedy has been brought to public attention"
(Mondale, 1970).

The lessons to be drawn from the inadequacies of America's child health
record should be seen in the perspective of what has been accomplished as well
as what has not. That is why we must speak of inadequacies, and not failures. So
little has been attempted, despite our knowledge of what needs to be done; even
where respectable gains have been achieved, they were typically in modest
demonstrations of program effectiveness. Any evaluation of our position must
deal with this framework: we know so much of what is wrong, so much of what
can be accomplished, and we do so little.

At bottom, we all realize that institutional deficiencies are essentially
social decisions, expressions of social values. Creating extensive regulatory
bodies, for instance, to watch over and enforce compliance, has never been
successful. In practically no time at all, the regulatory bodies are captured by
the regulated. Inadequate health services for America's children will not be
remedied by legislating programs that require large-scale regulation.

We have a choice of explanations for the low level of children's health
services: either we don't care much for children, or we have little confidence in
health services, consider them irrelevant, and fail to use or improve those that do
exist. Some argument can be made for lesser concern about children in the
United States than in other countries. An extensive literature connects the
advance of technology with the decline of the extended family and the erosion
of parent-child relationships (Lasch, 1977). Others who see the family under
attack deny that the institution is broken—bent a bit, perhaps—but still a major
national resource, protective of children and available for use in promoting
health, provided that some system worthy of the name is offered (Bane, 1976).

If this latter interpretation is correct, we should be seeking a kind of three-
dimensional attack on health inadequacies—creating first a powerful advocacy
group for children to direct the battle for change; reorganizing the health and
medical care structures; and introducing and sustaining powerful social support
systems. Pursuing this line, it seems useful to examine programs and policies
being followed in those economically advanced countries where the levels of
child health are, statistically at any rate, better than in the United States. A great
deal of information is available on these welfare and social support system
(Kamerman & Kahn, 1978), as well as on the organization and availability of ser
vices for children (Silver, 1978a).

How do other nations view child health and medical care? What is the
social attitude toward children in northern Europe, specifically with regard to

health services? Do these countries do more for their children than the United States? If so, what are the actions taken and how are these reflected in the nature, availability, and effectiveness of child health services? Given the division of medical care into three areas, what is the nature of the social commitment to children? Of the availability of preventive services? Are they easily available and adequate? How are they carried out, and how are they paid for? And finally, what about medical care itself—the treatment of illness—is it easily available?

Throughout European countries, there is social recognition that higher costs for support of larger families could be detrimental to children's health in limiting food or clothing or shelter. Not only children's and family allowances, but in some countries rent subsidies, are provided to help assure that children do not suffer the consequences of high rental costs for housing with adequate space.

Children's allowances may be modest, as in the United Kingdom; or quite substantial, as in France, where fully 25 percent of a family's income can come from this source. Rent subsidies may be substantial, too, as in Denmark, where a low-income family of five may draw its entire rental cost from the government. In the United Kingdom, the children's allowance is taxed, along with other income, meaning that upper-income families benefit very little. In other European countries, the children's allowance is untaxed, and all families benefit, regardless of income. Maternity leaves range from a few weeks, as in the United Kingdom, to six-months paid leave at up to 90 percent of earnings of a working woman—or even seven months of maternity leave as in Sweden.

In European countries, although parents are recognized to be responsible for their children's welfare, the law also views the child as a person who deserves protection, even sometimes against his parents. All European countries have in place a system of official or informal child and youth agencies to hear complaints regarding child abuse and to assess and assign needed legal or social sanctions. The Dutch have a very elaborate system—including "medical referees" who function as ombudsmen for children—that intervenes on demand and spreads protective wings over an abused, or potentially abused, child. And failures to obtain such needed medical services as immunizations for a child is considered actionable. In Sweden, rather than take an abused child out of the home, creating another set of difficult circumstances to which the child must adjust, a social worker may be assigned to live with the child's family.

Finally, all European countries have either a health insurance system or health service in place that provides needed medical services for all, or nearly all, citizens. These services are financed through mechanisms that eliminate any means test; i.e., they are universal systems that provide health care to children without regard to parents' income (Silver, 1978a).

The question that arises, then, is whether universal entitlement to medical services is a sufficient guarantee that children will receive needed preventive services. If the social conditions are met, does a comprehensive medical care system fulfill all of a child's health and medical needs?

In the United States, before Medicaid went into effect, poor people of all ages received fewer physician's services than more prosperous income groups. After Medicaid went into effect, however, poor adults did receive as many physician's services as their more prosperous adult contemporaries. But, poor *children* still continued to receive fewer services. Is it possible, then, that despite universal entitlement to a comprehensive health service, children might not receive all the medical care they need, particularly preventive services? If so, one might be able to discern from among European countries with universal entitlement those that provide a special service for children, as against those who do not, in order to determine whether there are any differences in indices of children's health. As it turns out, if one takes seven northern European countries and ranks them by infant mortality and percentage of children immunized, an interesting grouping is observed when measured against social and preventive services (Silver, 1978b). Nations with specific child health services rank lower in infant mortality and higher in immunization rates.

Obviously, a distinct preventive service for children is quite helpful in raising, or maintaining, a high level of child health. Judging from data on infant mortality and percentage of children immunized, those countries that have positive social policies favoring children and a clearly distinguishable preventive service, plus a strong nursing input into that service, stand at the head of the list. Some of the things we emphasize and consider very important turn out not to be terribly influential—like obstetricians in place of midwives or hospitals as the delivery site for childbirth. Also, whether the service is publicly or privately controlled seems unimportant, provided that there is an advocacy program on behalf of children.

There are interesting anomalies. Holland, for example, encourages home deliveries, yet maintains a fine record in infant mortality. And Holland retains a strong private initiative in its Cross (see below for details) organizations (Verbrugge, 1968; Ministry of Public Health, 1974). In all the countries surveyed, it is the organizational focus that is so impressive. France has a complex, intricately articulated, comprehensive program of preventive services for children, symbolizing the extreme to which planning can be carried. But the principle of focusing on the child's health needs is no different from the approach in Sweden, Finland, or Holland, except that these countries expect more local administrative initiative.

Petersson (1974), a Swedish pediatrician, points out that governmental assumption of maternal and child health responsibilities *must* be met by a highly organized and effectively supervised system. He has developed a "quality index" of infant mortality and prenatal care on this basis. In his tabulation, there is a clear correlation between organized social action on behalf of preventive services for children and the outcome of child health.

In Holland, for example:

—There is a strong central supervision. The National Health Service is responsible for, among other health matters, operation of the preventive health services for children.
—This central supervision is delegated to district directors.
—There is a separate national inspector's office, responsible to the ministry, also delegating authority to district inspectors, for evaluating and supervising all health and medical care services.
—There is a strong private-sector preventive service.
—There is a separate social insurance agency for collecting information on, and paying for, medical care.
—There is a strong link between health and social agencies and the courts (Silver, 1978a).

Scotland, since the reorganization of the national health service, has moved away from a separate preventive service for children in which health visitors were located in the health department or in the school health service. In their new system, the Scots place a special nurse in the local doctor's office, and make every effort to give the family physician responsibility for child care. The health visitor, splendidly trained to be a child health and family preventive service nurse, has been withdrawn from this arena and placed in the doctor's office. This presumably good idea, based as it is on standard public health philosophy fostering the "doctor-nurse team" concept, has had a pernicious effect. The family doctor tends to use the nurse to help relieve him of such onerous duties as services to chronically ill old people. Much as the old people need and deserve attention, the health visitor's time is limited, and so she is less and less occupied with home visiting on behalf of infants and preschool children. Following the extensive governmental reorganization, troubles have also accumulated with the Community Medicine Specialist, a new administrative position that has yet to fulfill its promise. And children's services, particularly the preventive ones, have suffered in consequence. Removing the health visitor from the organized public service and relying on the general practitioner to provide preventive and other health services seem to be largely responsible for the decline in immunization rates and the persistence of a relatively high infant mortality rate—like that of the United States (Silver, 1978a).

Denmark appears to be the only country in which emphasis on the general practitioner's role and maintenance of both prenatal care and well-baby services in his office have not had a deleterious effect. Because midwives and visiting nurses play large and important roles, concurrent with the family doctor, preventive services may account for Denmark's excellent infant health record. In Finland, despite the doctor's primary role, nurses are heavily involved in carrying out preventive activities. And although the physician is unquestionably in charge in Sweden, the nurse and the family doctor share responsibilities for preventive care (Silver, 1978a). This is also true in Holland, where the nurse is very visible in the individual Cross societies and even in the large cities where Cross society services may have been amalgamated, so that while the public health officer is in charge, nurses carry out the bulk of preventive care. This private-sector nursing operation in Holland also helps involve parents and the community in decisions about health services, encourages their participation in health care, and assists outreach efforts in parent education and prevention of child abuse and neglect.

A word about these Cross societies is in order. Families pay dues to belong to these private organizations through which preventive services are provided for mothers and children. Costs beyond the modest family membership dues are met from taxes. Since all services are standardized nationally, and the employees of the organization are paid on national wage scales, budgets are relatively easy to determine and review. There is, then, little danger of wildly incomparable programs or budgets.

The differences between local Cross societies, such as they are, relate not to services, but to the origin of the societies. Cross societies originated in Holland, for example, and reflect the denominational separation which is such a characteristic part of Dutch life; the societies aim to maintain denominational equality. Belgium, with serious problems of bicultural conflict, also attempts this separate but equal approach, though less successfully, in its Oeuvre Nationale de l'Enfance (Querido, 1968).

So far as the legal situation is concerned, Denmark, Sweden, Finland, and Holland have powerful private, as well as public, bodies concerned with child care and children's rights. In Denmark and Sweden the official bodies are the stronger and involve elected and appointed officials who supervise child care, seek out neglect, and legally discipline families when children are being abused or neglected.

These European models, then, serve to instruct us about what steps can be taken to assure the best protection and support for guarding and maintaining children's health. The focus of these models is on families as well as children. Nonetheless, the European experience suggests that a very deliberate emphasis must be placed on services for the individual child. Some specific social measures are absolutely necessary for guaranteeing nutrition, legal protection, and safety for the pregnant woman and the child. Conversely, integrity of the family is maintained better when society protects the individual interests of the child rather than relying solely on parental control.

Universal entitlement for medical care services seems an insufficient base for guaranteeing preventive services to all children. A separate preventive system, along with good liaison to the medical care system, is desirable. A greater involvement of nurses, particularly trained pediatric nurses, in the preventive system is not only an added benefit but may actually be the determinant of quality preventive services for children.

Different countries approach these matters differently, perhaps because of their different histories or because of different professional and social experi ences. Attitudes toward children may be culturally the same, but some countries have a historic basis for government intervention that is lacking in other countries. Attitudes toward work, especially for mothers of young children, and reliance upon private-sector action vary from country to country, which in turn influences the organizational forms of the medical care systems and health services.

In Scandinavia and the Netherlands one finds an explicit social concept called *shared risk,* meaning that *both* society and parents have a stake in what happens to children, owe responsibility to children's health and growth, and share authority. The long history of destructive and savage wars in Europe may have something to do with this feeling of shared risk and the associated sense of mutual dependency. In the United States, on the other hand, only a generation or two removed from the frontier where it was necessary for the individual to be self-reliant, government is viewed as a hindrance, an interloper; and acceptance of government intervention in the family is less palatable.

One tangential aspect of the administration of health services for children bearing further exploration is the matter of centralization versus decentralization. Scotland and France have highly centralized administration in that, although responsibility for administration devolves upon lower echelons, power resides at the center. In Scandinavia, decentralization is the rule, with tax collection and budgeting done at the county level or below. Holland, too, in part because of the Cross organization admixture in the service, is in effect decentralized. The impact of decentralization in these countries is not clear because it is difficult to study separately from other factors that significantly influence operations, such as separate preventive services, heavily nurse-oriented services, and the magnitude of the social (financial) contribution to health care. Nevertheless, it may be that decentralization also has a favorable effect on increasing and improving child health services and it deserves further study.

These European patterns of health care for children are not inflexible, and one can expect further evolution in each of the respective systems. Developments in the European Economic Community and educational activities of the World Health Organization can be expected to have an impact in this regard. One hopes that the better operational and organizational influences will flow into and among the countries modifying services for children. As physicians, nurses, and other health workers begin to cross borders to work, even if only to hold meetings for discussion of their problems and their respective approaches to solutions, the better-organized, more cost-effective, and more satisfactory services and programs are bound to spread.

One can review the experiences and benefits of European child health care programs with a mixture of emotions. Only the naive will expect that spreading the word in this country will result in legislative action to provide similar or identical programs here. We cannot expect this, nor should we. The European experiences, as emphasized, vary from country to country. There is no "European" system of child health care. There is a Dutch, a French, a Swedish, a Finnish system. And there ought to be an American system.

The skeleton outline of what we need in order to devise an American system can be derived from the various European experiences. There are basic elements that must be included. And if we examine the skeleton, surprisingly enough, much of what would be recommended has native roots already, some for quite a long time.

Prevention, of course, is widely preached, and is having a very fashionable renascence. Nurse practitioners, pediatric nurse associates, and midwives have been promoted, educated, and trained in this country for many years. There is even the beginning of a groundswell for delegating childbirth responsibilities to midwives and supporting childbirth centers instead of hospital deliveries (Tew, 1977; Wasserman, 1975; Watkin, 1977). A good many years ago, Montefiore Hospital experimented with nursing programs for well-child services (Ford, Seacat, & Silver, 1966). And Henry Silver had done yeoman work in the development of nurse-guided, well-baby care for many years (Silver, Ford, & Stearly, 1967).

After long years of declamation on my own part as to the inseparability of preventive and curative medicine, I now question the wisdom of this position. Preventive and curative medicine have very ancient *separate* origins. Even in Greek legend, the demigod Aesculapius had among his children Hygeia *and* Panaciea—the goddesses of health and curing. As we look back on the complex of problems we are to deal with in preventive medicine, we might ask: Is a physician really necessary? Certainly in the social component of prevention—parent education, guidance, and support to the family—it is the nurse and not the doctor who does the home visiting. Outreach and family supervision are, after all, the nurse's role. Strengthening the self-healing characteristics of the family, which is the outstanding contribution that prevention can make, will not issue from office visits. Immunization, child-rearing advice, and nutrition consultation are characteristically even now the nurse's role. The person in charge of these services needs to be well informed about things that are rarely included in medical education. Why must they be considered a part of medical practice? Aside from the fashionable shibboleths of our time, is it really what a pediatrician is trained for or wants?

And looking at it from the other side, isn't the nurse actually trained in these areas? Isn't the acquisition of these skills considered a basic objective of nursing education? Prevention requires more and different education, as well as more respectful emphasis, than it is now given in the medical curriculum or medical practice. Too often, because of the excessively clinical training a doctor undergoes, there is a strong tendency to medicalize his role—to seek clinical causes and to test and examine and look for disease entities, to give complaints and difficulties a medical name, a medical diagnosis. You can almost hear it, the inner voice that insists on a battery of tests in case of doubt. What, after all, was I trained for?

Finally, is it economically desirable to have doctors trained for a substantial role in preventive medicine? And even if so trained, would doctors willingly accept the responsibility?

In brief, the idea of a separate preventive system with the nurse as the leading figure, though not completely foreign to the American medical scene, is not yet seen as a critical element of our child health system.

As for the second critical element in the outline of needed services, social support (meaning money and family allowances), we find a growing trend toward this direction right now in the United States. Just below the surface, professionals and legislators are struggling with reform of the welfare system—to reform it out of existence, actually, and replace it with a social support system. Paid maternity leaves are beginning to be part of the fringe benefits in many private pension plans; federal legislation is on the way, and there has been a recent Supreme Court ruling encouraging industrial action in this area.

There are those who consider financial and social support to have priority over a preventive services program. It isn't fair, however, to condition one set of returns on another. Thus, it shouldn't be assumed that, without an appropriate fiscal base for family support, preventive service will fail. It is quite possible, nevertheless, that by creating an organization to promote preventive service, an advocacy group can be organized that will make the social support system operative. The same cannot be said in the other direction. The best social support system will not provide the mixture of health services that can issue from an independently designed and staffed preventive system.

And finally, there is the matter of a comprehensive, universal, easily accessible, medical care treatment system for children. This may be the lowest priority for advocacy at the moment, since considerable congressional attention is being devoted to the design of such a system. After all, people are getting restive about the national health program that has been promised for so long—not just in this administration, but for the past fifty years. Because the high cost of modern technological medical care is frightening to our representatives, they may find a child medical care program increasingly attractive. Children require fewer and fewer expensive treatment services than adults. The overall cost of a child medical care program would therefore be less than national health insurance, and tacking the premiums onto Social Security can take the curse off the idea of an added tax. Thus, a children's medical care program is not entirely out of the question within the next ten years.

But building a medical care system, as evidenced by the European experience, will not guarantee a good preventive service for children. And again, the existence of a good preventive service may very well call into being a comprehensive medical care system for children. Parents will not long tolerate the experience that preventive services are friendly and free, but that one must scour the countryside for medical care and pay heavily for it when found.

Professionals—both general practitioners and pediatricians—will find their busy offices relieved in part because of preventive service in the clinics, the schools, and at home. As a result, they will be able—and willing—to undertake the effective care for children they may not have had time for before.

It could also be that the long hoped-for transformation of the medical care system from fee-for-service to salary would be facilitated by the model of the preventive system. Since nurses and physician consultants would be paid on salary or per session, the preventive system might demonstrate the feasibility of such a payment mechanism for a national health program. Our troubled musings over cost and the legislative struggles to assure cost control and ceilings on expenditures may thus be resolved.

These are the skeletal elements. I would hope that the private sector experience of Holland; i.e., the nonprofit Cross society portion, could be woven into the American pattern of preventive services for children. It seems to me that paying dues and joining a club in which you have a part to play in decision making will make the preventive services work better, will involve parents more, and will build a tighter community structure. I would hope also that the Scandinavian experiences of local funding and local control would be designed into the structure. Size is a great enemy of human functioning, and large bureaucracies create turbulences of their own in which the bureaucracy is generally better served than the clients. I look forward to small district operations and fiscal control.

Perhaps something more ought to be said about the relationship of size to involvement of citizens, especially parents, in both social services and advocacy. We ought not be looking to national organizations for child advocacy, or at least not only to national powerful lobbying forces. Advocacy can be more powerful if it has multiple grass-roots clusters at work. Social intervention, in Charles Schultz's (1977) words, should work both ways—private-sector protection against bureaucracy as well as public-sector protection against antisocial, private-sector actions. And here, the thesis of Berger and Newhaus in their polemical pamphlet *To Empower People* (1977) should be reviewed. They argue that government should take positive steps to strengthen what they call "mediating institutions"—the family, the neighborhood, the church—to defend people against the power and impersonality of the "megastructures." They define *mediating institutions* as those "standing between the individual in his private life and the large institutions of public life." Megastructures, such as the modern state, large economic conglomerates, big labor, and welfare, educational, and professional bureaucracies, can be countered at the very places where people live. That too is advocacy and may well be the most successful kind of advocacy.

Social policy should be seen in the context of social history. Changes may be gestating for a long time before they are expressed in legislation or social action. True, it is difficult, if not impossible, to sail against the current of accepted attitudes and norms of institutional behavior. Nevertheless, it is important to try to detect what incipient currents are flowing below the surface, predict the possibilities of change, and foster or reinforce such possibilities in order to bring about necessary reform and reconstruction.

No matter how stubborn, both social attitudes and institutional forms do get modified over time. Without imaginative and insightful leadership, however, outworn attitudes and behavior patterns will persist longer than necessary. Academic professionals have a responsibility, not only to identify the defects of social institutions and characterize the historic forces working to obstruct change or maintain inadequate, outworn, and defective patterns, but also to recognize the undercurrents that presage better and more appropriate forms.

Because I do believe in man's deep-seated desire for perfectibility, I know there will never be a perfect system or perfect operation of any social institution. Perhaps for this very reason I believe that change is a constant in any society: no situation is immutable. Recognizing what can be done as well as knowing what needs to be done determines progress.

In Kuhn's (1970) elegant formulation of the structure of scientific revolutions, he describes how the accumulation of evidence against the accuracy of a particular scientific belief or theory eventually results in its replacement. There is, however, a period of time during which the evidence has mounted but is not sufficient to dethrone the accepted theory; nor is the successor theory, waiting in the wings, sufficiently well articulated to be recognized. It is in this period that imaginative and interested people can exercise a crucial role in accelerating change. In the natural sciences, investigators recognize this and are constantly aware of the need to test theories and not reject challenging results. Physics, chemistry, and biology are constantly enriched in this way. The cure for cancer, cheap energy sources, multiplication of food resources will come about in this way—by a leap of imagination drawn from barely recognizable current evidence.

Social science and social programs need to use the same approach and challenge received wisdom daily. Only failure of imagination—allowing ourselves to be chained to outworn credos—obstructs the provision of universal health and medical care services for ourselves and our children. We seem now to lack the capability of making the leap of imagination that will take us into new theoretical areas of social policy. Everything that is being done in one or another European country for children has an American analogue. The American counterpart may not be as fully developed, but it is there. We need to seize the opportunity to promote and hasten our uniquely American program into existence.

REFERENCES

Bane, M. J. *Here to stay.* New York: Basic Books, 1976.

Berger, P. L., & Newhaus, R. J. *To empower people: The role of mediating structures in public policy.* Washington, D.C.: American Enterprise Institute, 1977.

Davis, K. A decade of policy developments in providing health care for low income families. In R. Haveman (Ed.), *A decade of federal antipoverty programs.* New York: Academic Press, 1976.

Davis, K. *Health and the War on Poverty.* Washington, D.C.: Brookings, 1978.

Department of Health, Education and Welfare. *Health: United States* 1978 (DHEW Publication No. PHS 78-1232). Washington, D.C.: Author, 1978.

Ford, P. A., Seacat, M., & Silver, G. A. The relative roles of the public health nurse and the physician in prenatal and infant supervision. *American Journal of Public Health,* 1966, *56,* 1097-1103.

Foltz, A-M. The development of ambiguous federal policy: Early and Periodic Screening, Diagnosis and Treatment (EPSDT). *Milbank Memorial Fund Quarterly,* 1975, *53,* 35-64.

Kamerman, S. B., & Kahn, A. J. (Eds.). *Family policy: Government and families in fourteen countries.* New York: Columbia University Press, 1978.

Kuhn, T. *The structure of scientific revolutions* (2d ed.). Chicago: University of Chicago Press, 1970.

Lasch, C. *Haven in a heartless world.* New York: Basic Books, 1977.

Miller, C. A. Health care of children and youth in America. *American Public Health Journal,* 1975, *65,* 353-358.

Ministry of Public Health and the Environment. *Compendium of health statistics of the Netherlands.* The Hague: Author, 1974.

Mondale, W. F. Justice for children. *Congressional Record,* Dec. 9, 1970, 40505-40518.

Office of the Assistant Secretary for Health. *A proposal for new federal leadership in maternal and child health care in the United States.* Washington, D.C.: Author, 1976.

Petersson, P. O. Report of the meeting of the Swedish Pediatric Association. *Acta Paediatrica Scandinavica,* 1974, *63,* 475-481.

Querido, A. *The development of socio-medical care in the Netherlands.* London: Routledge and Kegan Paul, 1968.

Schultz, C. *The public use of private interest.* Washington, D.C.: Brookings, 1977.

Silver, G. A. (a). *Child health: America's future.* Germantown, Md.: Aspen Systems Corporation, 1978.

Silver, G. A. (b). Some observations on preventive health services for children: European and American policies and programs. *Courrier,* 1978, *28,* 1-5.

Silver, H., Ford, L., & Stearly, S. A program to increase health care for children: The pediatric nurse practitioner program. *Pediatrics,* 1967, *39,* 756-760.

Tew, M. Where to be born? *New Society,* 1977, *39,* 120-121.

Verbrugge, H. P. *Kraamzorg bij huisbevallingen.* Groninger: Wolters-Noordhoft NV, 1968.

Wasserman, M. The new nurse-midwives. *The Progressive,* 1975, *39,* 32-35.

Watkin, B. Back to home deliveries? *Nursing Mirror,* 1977, *144,* 42.

Yale Health Policy Project. *The White House Conferences on Children and Youth: Seven decades of evolving national policies.* (Working paper #1). New Haven: Author, 1973.

Yale Health Policy Project. *Politics and social policy: Failures in child health services.* New Haven: Author, 1976.

Comments on Silver's Paper

JONATHAN B. KOTCH is an Assistant Professor of Maternal and Child Health, School of Public Health, University of North Carolina. In addition to being a faculty member of the Bush Institute for Child and Family Policy at UNC, Dr. Kotch is also Public Health Liaison, Maternal and Child Health Branch, North Carolina Division of Health Services.

We are indebted to Dr. Silver for bringing before us, and before a national audience of health workers and policymakers, a controversial notion that has been taboo for the last decade; namely, that prevention and treatment can, and indeed ought to, be separate systems.

Let me agree with Dr. Silver that medical care is but one aspect of the larger concept of health promotion and health maintenance. The contribution of therapeutic medical care to the overall health status of an industrial society may be much smaller than its popular image suggests. What has been even more unnerving to those of us committed to a health model which emphasizes prevention is how this emphasis has been captured and exploited by the medical establishment. Let me propose, for argument's sake, that medical institutions have a kind of "Midas touch." Whatever they touch becomes more expensive and in consequence more inaccessible. Dr. Silver and I agree that preventive services for children are better served by nurses than by physicians, but note what has happened to such nurses in the name of comprehensive medical care. In this country, no less than in Scotland, the professional nurse has been coopted by the medical establishment and her community role undertaken by a new breed of health worker, the community or family health aide. Yet this aide would rather be taking blood pressures, heights, and weights in the clinic, which nurses used to do. Nurses want to be practitioners and do physical exams, diagnose, and treat, which doctors used to do. And doctors, including myself, want to tell everyone what to do.

I think, therefore, that in arguing on behalf of a greater and more responsible role for nurses, Dr. Silver needs to be quite specific. We are not talking about those nurses who have gone beyond the pale, donned white coats and stethoscopes, and found comfortable niches in the clinic and office. Rather, we need to attach new prestige and new money to the public health nurse, our country's counterpart to Scotland's child health visitor, who eschews the clinic in favor of the home and community. Our present value system is revealed by the fact that a hospital-based diploma nurse, in a California county from which I just returned, can make $250 to $300 more per month than a bachelor's level public health nurse (O'Halloran, 1979). No wonder that 10 public health nursing positions in this county remain vacant, and, over a period of years, that monthly immunization clinic sites have had to be reduced from twelve to three (Baiers, 1979). Dr. Silver has referred to *medicalization* of the medical student. Let me add a warning against medicalization of the nurse.

Another example of the way medical institutions suck resources away from children is the case of Medicaid, a fee-for-service reimbursement system designed for the convenience of providers. Dr. Silver has already pointed out how Medicaid has permitted some poor adults to achieve utilization levels similar to those of wealthier patients who can afford medical care. But poor children still have lower utilization levels than wealthier children. They lag behind as well in the amount of public money spent for them—$4.7 billion in fiscal year 1976 for children under nineteen, a group which constitutes 33 percent of the population, compared with $23.6 billion for those over 65, constituting only 10.5 percent of the population (Silver, 1978). Thus, for every dollar spent on children, about $16 is spent on the elderly. I contend that whenever a health program does not specifically address the needs of children, resources are drawn away from children to benefit older people and away from prevention to increase medical treatment.

Even a family-based health plan is not good enough, for families may not include children, and the costs of remediating the problems of adult family members far exceed the cost of protecting children. This concern was expressed by Marsden Wagner, who, in the National Institute of Mental Health study of Denmark's national Family Guidance program, observed the switch from the child-oriented Family Guidance program to a family-oriented Social Assistance program. This transition resulted in the abolition of the Child and Youth Department. Wagner (1978) states: "One result of this change has been that so many families without children have applied that families with children are sometimes unable to receive help. Unless funds are ear-marked for children, it is likely that the more powerful adults will consume the funds" (p. 24).

Similarly, in its report to Parliament in 1976, England's Committee on Child Health Services noted that the decrease in contacts between home visitors and children under five began in Great Britain, not with the attachment of home visitors to office-based practices, but as early as 1946, when the health visitor was officially designated a *family* health visitor and consequently had assignments with adults and the elderly (Committee on Child Health Services, 1976, p. 73).

I must take exception to Dr. Silver's hope that sectarian institutions, such as Holland's Cross societies, would play a major role in child health promotion. For social and cultural purposes, I hope ethnic and religious differences continue to thrive in this country. But once government begins to subsidize institutions based on ethnic and religious allegiance, I have no doubt that poor health outcomes for low-income children would not only be reinforced, but would be even more difficult to remedy. Take, for example, the University of North Carolina's continuing difficulty in equalizing the educational opportunities provided by its previously segregated 16 campuses. I have no doubt that if institutions are encouraged to form along social or cultural lines for health purposes, some will resemble country clubs in their memberships and others would bear a greater resemblance to rural Baptist church groups. Children in groups, such as the latter, would need more resources, yet it would be impossible to convince legislators that such a differential would not constitute reverse discrimination. So, I wish to qualify Dr. Silver's hope that these local child health promotion organizations be encouraged with the proviso that they be constituted on an arbitrary basis, such as geographical criteria, rather than on social or cultural criteria.

We may actually need two different kinds of organizations. In addition to local institutions providing preventive services, we also need child advocacy organizations active in the political arena. These can and perhaps ought to be organized by social and cultural groups. Such a method of organization would encourage the role suggested by Dr. Silver's term *mediating institutions.* Let thousands of such organizations take root and bloom, because there remains a serious political battle to achieve a well-financed, universal health care program for every child in this country, regardless of income, geography, or social background.

But let me urge further that any local organizations which provide preventive services for children need centralized fiscal control. There is no other way in this country to equalize the wide variations in income across social classes, ethnic groups, and geographical areas. There is no reason why local control cannot coexist with centralized financing, as it did in the special projects of Title V of the Social Security Act and in the Office of Economic Opportunity Neighborhood Health Centers, before former President Nixon's New Federalism. There are precedents such as these for bypassing the state bureaucratic machinery altogether. The Family Guidance program of Denmark that I mentioned earlier also was a centrally planned and monitored program with local administration and local service delivery.

Children today face a serious threat—that the gerontocracy ruling this country, fearing for its own myocardial infarctions and malignant neoplasms, will legislate some form of national health insurance, particularly catastrophic insurance, which by its nature favors adults over children and treatment over prevention. The costs will be outrageous, and such costs would fuel the arguments of fiscal conservatives, effectively preventing any further evolution of a genuine national health plan.

I believe we can afford a national health program for children in this country because universal coverage on a prepaid basis, with adequate resources for prevention and with use of less highly specialized staff than physicians, would be much cheaper than the misguided, fee-for-service system we have now.

In North Carolina, for example, a Medicaid child enrolled in the Children and Youth Project of Guilford County costs the state an average of $136 in 1977, whereas another Medicaid child not enrolled in this special project, which provides prepaid medical care along with public health nursing outreach, costs about $247 per year (Division of Health, 1979).

We must not, therefore, let ourselves be coopted by the unmet promises of medical care. Neither must we be bought off by the guaranteed extravagance of catastrophic health insurance. Let us begin any national health program in this country at the beginning, with a program that emphasizes prevention, and with a program specifically designed for children, for all children, and, at least at first, for nothing but children.

REFERENCES

Baiers, T. Contra Costa County Health Department, Martinez, Calif. (Personal communication, March 8, 1979).

Committee on Child Health Services, *Fit for the future* (Vol. 1). London: Her Majesty's Stationery Office, 1976.

Division of Health Services and Social Services, North Carolina Department of Human Resources. (Personal communication, February 1979).

O'Halloran, B., Contra Costa County Health Department, Pittsburgh, Calif. (Personal communication, March 7, 1979).

Silver, G. *Child health: America's future.* Germantown, Md.: Aspen Systems Corporation, 1978.

Wagner, M. *Denmark's national family guidance program* (DHEW Publication No. ADM 77-512). Rockville, Md.: Public Health Service, 1978.

Comments on Silver's Paper

HUGH H. TILSON is the Director of Health Services for the State of North Carolina.

As usual, Dr. Silver has provided us much food for thought. In lucid fashion, he has summarized a complex set of facts from a complicated group of health delivery systems and drawn conclusions which make sense. Indeed, it would be difficult to take issue with Silver's conclusions and suggestions. Thus, it is difficult to disagree that we need, as a nation, a more specific national policy regarding children's health. The cost-benefit ratios seem clear—and have for many years. The need for agreement on federal resource allocation seems likewise clear. Similarly, a national advocacy group to speak out on children's health issues is needed. Nor can we dispute the suggestion that such an advocacy group should address prevention and not simply access to medical care. In addition to the national health care evaluation data speaking so well for such a position, common sense argues it—perhaps even better.

It is paradoxical—if not downright prophetic—that Silver's comments should be addressed to an audience in the state of North Carolina. Within the last year, a very forward-looking governor—Governor Jim Hunt—has articulated an unquestionably forward-looking policy regarding children's health for the state of North Carolina. Although complex in its implementation—because it involves all of the health care delivery system issues known to most of us through years of laboring in the maternal and child health vineyards—Governor Hunt's "New Generation Strategy" is elegantly simple in conceptualization. In November 1978, addressing the Appalachian Regional Commission Conference on Health Care in Appalachia, Governor Hunt said: "The question is not whether we have the knowledge to raise a new generation of healthy, educated children. The question is whether we have the will and the commitment to provide the greatest opportunities that we can and know how to provide." In developing his subsequent legislative agenda, Governor Hunt put together an approach which embodies the principles enumerated by Silver; namely, development of a constituency for children, development of adequate resources focused on the health of children and their mothers, and strengthening of agencies necessary to accomplish both tasks.

The first step in the governor's strategy has been to sponsor legislation to clarify state policy on behalf of children. A 1979 Act of the General Assembly created a statewide New Generation Council of responsible agency heads and contained permissive language encouraging local "New Generation Committees."

Counties were encouraged to create parallel committees to the single Statewide Council. The governor is to chair the Statewide Council; county managers are to chair local committees. At the local level again, concerned, responsible agency heads would be convened, not to advocate for more funds for children or any special interest groups (commissioners pointed out that they had quite enough people advocating for such additional appropriations), but, rather, for better use of existing appropriations through more creative interagency cooperation and collaboration. Important in these days of tax-weary electorates and the bureaucratic multiplication of agencies, the committees envision the use of existing community groups rather than proliferating meetings and bodies. The notion is that communities need to band together to help themselves. And the further notion is that the health of the next generation needs to be of significant concern to the present one.

A related effort was a joint planning process that harnessed the concerns and energies of the state's private pediatricians through the North Carolina Pediatric Society, under the able leadership of Dr. David Williams of Davidson County. Working jointly with officials from the Department of Human Resources, the Assistant Secretary for Children, and the Division of Health Services, a single planning effort—rather than parallel but separate government and private efforts—was launched to devise a single ("the definitive") health plan for North Carolina's children. Issued in a public proclamation by the governor, this health plan articulates child health principles elegantly. The desired product is a "health home" for all children of the state. This *health home* is defined as comprehensive, continuous, compassionate, accessible, available, and acceptable health care. The notion is that there should be a single lead person, or case manager made available to the family as a focus for the child's health care. However, as in all "homes," in the Health Home there needs to be shared responsibility by the agencies and individuals whose efforts must be coordinated to assure the family competent service delivery to every child. In other words, the multiplex of community service agencies needs to be "cut through" to assure that children receive needed services in a timely fashion with follow-through and continuity of responsibility.

In order to bring about this health home, the North Carolina Child Health Plan lays out three prerequisites. First, every community must have its own health plan that establishes priorities and estimates costs. The elements of the plan must be ranked in priority sequence according to urgency, feasibility, and affordability.

Second, planning should be local; i.e., not removed from the community which is the recipient of the activities. Here again, the notion of local involvement in solving problems is critical—and perhaps a bit at odds with the clarion call issued by Silver. For local planning represents an indispensable complement to any national voice for children. But if I could have only a local or a national voice, I would choose the local voice every time because that's where priorities, expenditures, and caring actions are going to occur.

Third, the Child Health Plan institutionalizes cooperative planning between public and private enterprises. This, of course, is the embodiment of the public health vision—that the nation will be blanketed with a set of locally responsible, responsive public agencies—called *public health departments*—whose responsibility it is to promote the health of all people in their jurisdictions. In too many words, the point just made is: every community in the nation needs to be served by a local health department. Dr. Silver does wave a hand at that concept in his paper, but I think his failure to articulate the local public health agency is worrisome. All too often, it is taken for granted. What I am talking about here is not big government, but responsive and local small government. Such agencies will ensure that every community has a local conscience that will help bring about the child health strategy which Dr. Silver so ably outlined.

North Carolina's New Generation strategy is also programmatic, not just organizational and political. Indeed, the professional substance of the program is exciting. It involves a considerable financial and legislative commitment to services for all mothers and children—rich and poor—in the state of North Carolina. These services include family planning assistance, twenty new perinatal clinics for high-risk mother-infant pairs over the next biennium, refunding of intensive maternal and infant perinatal services in the tertiary care centers, and better distribution of high-risk perinatal care outside the four academic teaching centers across the state. In addition, the Crippled Children's Program of North Carolina, which extends far beyond the federally funded "matchable" crippled children's guidelines, has been funded once again. Finally, an exciting new program of high-risk infant tracking and screening has been developed. The planning for this effort involved private and public groups working together to be sure that pediatricians agree to criteria and processes and that public health professionals are able to identify, find, reach, and track those children who are at increased risk of morbidity and mortality. This high-risk infant tracking system is initiated with parental consent and by the signature of the attending pediatrician at the time of birth; it involves people of all income levels, whether the baby's health home is in the public or the private sector. Don't misunderstand. Some significant efficacy questions need to be asked about all such health registries. They are being asked in North Carolina. The point is that the risk registry and tracking system avails itself of all we now know about risk appraisal, follow-through, and continuity of care. In a state in which infant mortality ranks third worst in the country, we must be aggressive if we are to create a new generation healthier than the present one. This risk registry and tracking system seems to be a respectable, efficient way to improve the health of subsequent generations.

Other aspects of the New Generation strategy are many, including intensive efforts at improved infant care, increased use of pediatric nurse practitioners in health departments, improved immunization laws that include compulsory immunization for all students at all levels of school, strengthened efforts at reducing sexually transmitted diseases, contraception services and other services for adolescents, and an intensive effort to reduce the incidence of teenage pregnancy.

In short, it is paradoxical that Dr. Silver should issue a clarion call for a national strategy for child health in a state in which the elements of that strategy are being employed. Indeed, one worries that the national strategy might require additional data requirements beyond those we have already put in place here in North Carolina. The call needs to be for better and more useful data rather than more data.

Finally, one can't help smiling at Silver's comments that state governments still slyly take federal money and use it to offset state general funds. Of course, there probably are states doing just that. In North Carolina, however, if there is any "slyness" in what we do, it is in avoiding yet another federal categorical reporting system, funding restriction, or set of programmatic blinders. We are trying to get on with the business of serving whole people with integrity and dignity in their local communities—and to serve people in a way that does not require them to define their crises and needs in our bureaucratic terms. Let us hope that in proceeding to develop a national strategy for child health, some of the categorical restrictions that require excessive slyness on the part of us state bureaucrats may be reduced. It is my conviction that federal, state, and local health policymakers really see eye to eye on the objectives which Silver lays out. We all want the next generation to benefit from what we know how to do right now. But such benefits can occur only through local advocacy, local planning and organization, and local service delivery.

HENRY M. LEVIN received his M.A. and Ph.D. in economics from Rutgers University. He is currently a Professor of Education and Director of the Institute for Research on Educational Finance and Governance at Stanford University. While publishing a substantial number of books and articles on urban education, education of minority and low-income children, and school finance, Dr. Levin has maintained an active schedule of consultation to domestic and international agencies concerned with educational finance, evaluation, and planning. His recent work has focused on educational vouchers and other mechanisms designed to promote the equitable financing of public education.

5

Educational Vouchers and Social Policy

In periods of growth, social institutions rarely face major challenges to their existence. Issues of control and competition for resources may be ever present within periods of growth, but a peculiar protection is afforded to institutional forms by growth's sheer upward thrust. In the case of the elementary and secondary schools of the United States, the fifties and sixties were decades in which the major problems faced were those of rapid growth. New schools had to be constructed; teachers had to be trained; tax burdens had to be increased to keep up with the dynamic growth of the educational sector. Like the Queen's advice to Alice, educational agencies had to run as fast as they could to maintain pace with demands for enrollment expansion. They had to run at least twice as fast to improve the quality of educational offerings.

Statistics on the growth of elementary and secondary schools over this period are spectacular. Between 1954 and 1970, the number of elementary and secondary enrollments grew from about 34 million to over 51 million youngsters; secondary enrollments alone more than doubled from about 9 million to almost 20 million.[1] Per student expenditures in public elementary and secondary schools in 1976-1977 dollars doubled from $766 to amost $1500, and total elementary and secondary expenditures tripled. But since 1970 the schools have met with significant reverses in terms of enrollments, funding, and even the prospective employment of their graduates. Demographic shifts have resulted in declines in the number of persons of school age; inflation and slow economic growth have created pressures to reduce taxes and to divert resources to other social services. Between 1970 and 1986 it is expected that elementary and secondary enrollments will decline by six million students. At the same time there is activity at both the state and national levels to reduce public spending, including public expenditures on schools (Catterall & Thresher, 1979). Further, there is evidence that young persons at all levels of education are facing inferior job opportunities compared to those faced by similar persons in past decades, and there is also a perception of diminishing academic rigor and increasing disorder in the public schools.[2] Finally, the hopes of the sixties for obtaining greater equality of educational outcomes through compensatory educational

---

[1] All data in this section are taken from Dearman and Plisko (1979).

[2] For trends in the public evaluation of schools between 1969 and 1978, see Elam (1978). Freeman (1976) reviews the job situation.

expenditures and school desegregation have not been matched by progress in either greater equalization or reduced racial segregation.

To a large extent, education has become a declining industry. As such, it is beset with all types of conflicts over resources, policies, and long-term direction. Federal and state governments have increased their demands for minimum educational standards, greater equality of resource use and educational outcomes, and new programs for addressing the needs of handicapped youngsters. But at the same time, the funding for these kinds of activities has become less dependable. Parents have become increasingly dissatisfied with educational offerings and academic rigor; employers have raised serious questions about the preparedness of secondary graduates for work roles. The schools now face a period of decline and retrenchment in which their basic capability for carrying out their traditional roles has been challenged and undermined by a potential loss of public support.

Among the many suggested reforms for addressing this educational malaise, perhaps the most profound challenge has been raised by those who advocate replacing the existing system of publicly operated schools with "schools of choice" in which public funds would be given parents in the form of educational vouchers for the schooling of their children (Coons & Sugarman, 1978; Friedman, 1955, 1962; Institute of Economic Affairs, 1967; Jencks, 1966; Levin, 1975; West, 1965). Parents could use the vouchers for tuition payments at any school that met minimal requirements set by the state. Schools eligible to participate could compete for students and their vouchers and redeem the vouchers for cash from the state. It is argued that a variety of alternatives would arise for each child in comparison with the present system of monopoly which requires attendance at a particular school based upon neighborhood residence.

Advocates of educational vouchers see the approach as one which will resolve many of the present problems faced by the public schools. Parents would be able to choose schools according to their own religious, political, and academic preferences, and schools would have to be responsive to parental and child concerns to maintain their enrollments. It is asserted that such a market approach will improve the efficiency of public spending on education as well as increase parental and student satisfaction. In contrast, it is argued that the present schools must necessarily suffer from a highly centralized and bureaucratic approach that cannot respond to individual needs and preferences or utilize resources as efficiently as a market-oriented approach. As a distinguished organizational analyst has stated:

> . . . . the classic antidote to monopoly is competition. By introducing alternative sources of supply, competition expands the choice available to consumers. Moreover, these alternative sources are likely to use different methods and approaches or even to develop wholly new products. Thus, greater variety makes expanded choice really meaningful. Since consumers can shift their trade from suppliers who do not please them, suppliers have a strong incentive to provide what the consumers want (Downs, 1970, p. 219).

By implication, if parents want to send their children to schools with greater academic rigor, with a particular political or religious orientation, with greater emphasis on the arts or sciences, or with some other specific focus, they need only use the educational voucher provided by the state to select such schools.

HISTORY OF EDUCATIONAL VOUCHERS

Although educational vouchers have become a salient topic of educational reform only in the last decade, they have a rather long history. For example, the father of laissez-faire capitalism, Adam Smith, wrote over 200 years ago in *The Wealth of Nations* that at least part of the costs of schooling should be paid by parents because if the state were to pay all costs, the teacher ". . . would soon learn to neglect his business" (1937, p. 737). A very specific voucher approach was proposed at about the same time by Tom Paine in *The Rights of Man* [see West (1967) for analysis of this plan]. Under this plan, every family would receive a specified amount for each child under the age of fourteen, and children would be required to attend school. Local ministers would certify compliance with the law.

Present discussions of voucher plans derive primarily from the provocative proposal made by Milton Friedman (1955, 1962). Friedman would give each parent of a school-age child a voucher that could be used to pay a specified level of tuition at any "approved" school. Schools would become eligible to receive and redeem these vouchers by meeting certain requirements, such as a minimum curriculum offering and certain safety conditions. Schools would compete for students, and they would have great incentives to meet the needs of potential clients in order to obtain and retain enrollments. Parents would seek that school which best met their own concerns with respect to the education of their children. The role of the state would be that of: (1) providing funds in the form of educational vouchers for all school-age children; (2) establishing criteria for eligibility of schools to receive and redeem vouchers; and (3) assuring that the educational marketplace functions efficiently and effectively by setting out mechanisms for providing information on schools to parents, adjudicating conflicts between parents and schools, and ensuring that all children were enrolled in an approved school.

More recent versions of educational voucher plans build on the foundation laid down by Friedman. For example, Jencks (1966) suggested that vouchers be provided only for children in inner cities in order to enable them to find alternatives to public schools. And in the late sixties and early seventies, the Office of Economic Opportunity (OEO) designed and sought to implement an experiment utilizing an educational voucher approach (Center for the Study of Public Policy, 1970). That experiment was aimed at testing the educational consequences of providing educational vouchers in a large, urban area, with specific foci on the nature of parental choices, the types of schools that would emerge, and the effects of these schools on student achievement and on racial and social stratification of students. The OEO version of educational vouchers was designed to be "pro-poor" in providing higher or compensatory vouchers to persons from low-income backgrounds and in using a lottery for selecting students in those schools where the number of applicants exceeded the number of available places. Because of the various changes in state laws that would have been required to test the voucher plan proposed by OEO, it was not possible to find a state or local school district in which the experiment could be fully implemented. A modified version was attempted in a school district in San Jose, California, but all the alternatives were restricted to the public schools rather than permitting the development of nonpublic alternatives (Cohen & Farrar, 1977; Weiler *et al.*, 1974).

At present (1979), a voucher initiative is circulating in California with the aim of obtaining the required number of signatures to place it on the June 1980 ballot as a constitutional referendum. Essentially, the "Initiative for Family Choice in Education" (see Appendix) would modify the California constitution in establishing three classes of schools. Public schools, independent public schools, and family choice or private schools would be eligible to compete for students. Independent public schools would be those initiated by public educational authorities as nonprofit corporations with their own governance arrangements and would be operated according to the same laws as those affecting family choice schools. Family choice schools would need to meet only the current standards for private schools with no modifications permitted by the legislature. These requirements are rather minimal, so the family choice and independent public schools would have to meet only the most minimal curriculum and personnel requirements. Further, family choice schools would be permitted to teach any social values, philosophy, or religion, with the single qualification that no pupil be compelled to profess political, religious, philosophical, or ideological belief or actively participate in ceremony symbolic of belief.[3]

The Family Choice Initiative has been created and promoted by Professors John Coons and Stephen Sugarman. Many of its basic assumptions can be found in their book, *Education by Choice* (1978). Although some of these assumptions will be discussed in a later section of this paper, it is important to note that this Initiative probably represents the leading edge of a movement to initiate voucher plans among the states. In fact, the strategy is closely modeled after the constitutional initiative to limit property taxation in California which resulted in the

---

[3] It is not clear what this qualification means. If a child is saturated by a particular ideology, religion, or political view, it is reasonable to believe that the child has been socialized or indoctrinated by that point of view. This language seems to be deliberately evasive or misleading with respect to the main issue of whether a school would be permitted to indoctrinate a child politically, ideologically, or religiously. It is clear that the California Initiative would permit such indoctrination.

passage of Proposition 13 in June 1978. Proposition 13, of course, has now been imitated in other states and has provided the inspiration to reduce taxes and expenditures at the federal level (Catterall & Thresher, 1979).

UNDERSTANDING VOUCHERS

One formidable obstacle to understanding educational vouchers is the implicit premise that this terminology refers to a single approach having predictable consequences for education. Perhaps this impression has been created by discussion of the voucher approach as if it were a monolithic device that differs from the present educational system in ways that are well understood. Unfortunately, the world of vouchers is far more complicated. First, there are many voucher plans, and their specific provisions can have profoundly different consequences. Second, most aspects of vouchers are not well understood because an educational voucher plan has not been implemented in the United States. Thus, the actual functioning of the educational marketplace and its economic and educational consequences are subjects for discussion and speculation, but the outcomes of a voucher approach cannot be predicted with certainty.

Because there is not a single voucher plan, it is useful to refer to three major dimensions on which these plans differ in order to assess their likely functioning and results. These three dimensions are finance, regulation, and information (Levin, 1977).

Finance

The *finance* component of a voucher plan refers to such factors as the size of the educational voucher, what it can be used for, whether a school can charge more than the voucher or obtain additional funding through gifts, whether costs of transportation are covered, and the basic sources of funding. Although we shall not review all categories here, it is important to show how arrangements might vary considerably among voucher plans with rather different educational implications.

Under the Friedman approach, a uniform voucher would be given to parents for each child. Parents could, however, provide "add-ons" to the voucher to purchase more expensive education for their children. Obviously, wealthier families and those with fewer children would benefit most from this arrangement, so it would likely have highly inegalitarian consequences relative to present approaches and to recent attempts to provide greater equality of educational expenditures. In contrast, the voucher proposal that was to be the basis of the OEO experiment (Center for the Study of Public Policy, 1970) emphasized compensatory vouchers, giving children from low-income families larger vouchers than those in wealthier families. In addition, "add-ons" by parents, subsidies, and charitable contributions were not permitted, since they would represent ways of circumventing the egalitarian intentions of the plan.

Finally, the present California Initiative states that the legislature may take into account a variety of factors when setting the size of educational vouchers. These factors include grade level, curriculum bilingualism, special needs and handicaps, variations in local cost, need to encourage racial desegregation, and other factors deemed important by the legislature. These variations, however, would be purely optional on the part of the legislature and depend on the politics of the situation. In contrast, by the language of the initiative, schools would be permitted to charge higher fees or "add-ons" to the voucher from wealthier parents without any legislative intervention. Further, the California Initiative has no prohibition against "contributions" to the schools that one's children attend or to subsidies from sponsoring churches or other organizations. · The result is that richer parents could augment vouchers with other resources to obtain far superior education for their children as compared with the education that could be obtained by parents whose resources and institutional affiliations would limit them to the basic voucher provided by the state. Since these privileges of the wealthy would be mandated constitutionally, they could not be altered by legislative action. Rather, a new constitutional initiative would be required in order to repeal them.

Financial provision for transportation is also important, since the number of educational alternatives available to families will surely depend upon their ability to reach different schools. Even without subsidies for transportation, higher-income families will likely have little difficulty in providing access for their offspring to schools over a large geographical area. Since the use of both public and private transportation facilities is heavily contingent on one's income, the poor typically lack such advantages. Thus, without transportation subsidies they would be extremely limited with respect to geographical access. (Note that even a trivial cost of $1 a day for public transportation amounts to almost $200 a year for each child enrolled in school.)

The Friedman plan makes no allowance for transportation; it would permit the voucher to be applied only toward tuition. The OEO plan would make adequate transportation freely available for all students who were included in the experiment. The California Initiative would require arrangements for transportation ". . . in accord with reasonable conditions and limits upon cost to be fixed by law." Since the legislature would decide how to interpret this provision, it is not clear what arrangements would be made for student transport under the initiative. But the relatively high cost of transportation for small groups of students distributed idiosyncratically among schools does not suggest optimism. Even minimal cabfare or minibus fare of $2.50 each way would amount to about $900 a year per child.

Regulation

Although the voucher approach represents a shift from government to market-place production of educational services, that market would be regulated by the eligibility requirements set for schools to redeem vouchers. Just as different financial arrangements of voucher plans will create different educational outcomes, so, too, will differences in regulation. Among the major areas of regulation are curriculum content, personnel, and admissions standards.

The present system of public education provides a highly articulated set of curriculum requirements with respect to the areas in which instruction must be provided. In addition, there are a large number of areas in which teaching is prosocial, the most noteworthy being that of religious instruction. In contrast, the different voucher plans vary with respect to curriculum requirements.

Friedman is not specific about the curriculum requirements under his plan, but it is apparent that they would be minimal, with emphasis on instruction in basic skills and a common set of civic values. The OEO voucher plan is somewhat more detailed, but it also lacks specifics (with the expectation that the plan would have to meet the requirements of the state in which the experiment took place). The OEO plan does, however, require that schools provide standardized test results for evaluation, for parental information, and for the use of prospective clients. The California Initiative would also have minimal curriculum requirements limited to those currently required of private schools.

Further, the Friedman plan and the California Initiative would encourage a large diversity of schools with respect to political, religious, philosophical, and ideological sponsorship and offerings. The state would not intervene nor attempt to regulate instructional content in these areas, except to assure that no laws were being violated. Presumably, Nazi schools could teach white supremacy and hatred of Blacks and Black Nationalist schools could teach conversely racist doctrines, as long as neither school advocated interference with the civil rights of others. That is, the state could subsidize the teaching of divisive social views within the limits of existing laws. The OEO voucher plan would have proscribed many of these options, although the exact regulations on these issues were never clarified because of the failure to implement a voucher experiment.

Personnel requirements of voucher plans also can differ substantially. The Friedman approach would impose no standards, but would let schools and parents determine personnel qualifications. The OEO approach would have been limited primarily to teachers who were qualified on the basis of existing licensing practices of the states in which the voucher experiment was attempted. The California Initiative relies on existing personnel requirements for private schools, and these are considerably more liberal than those for the public schools with respect to training and licensing.[4]

[4] In most cases there are neither educational nor licensing requirements. The school must be staffed by persons capable of teaching, but this is not defined clearly. (See California Education Code Section 48222.)

The regulation of admission practices shows similar diversity among voucher plans. Friedman would allow schools complete freedom in admissions policies. The OEO plan would set fairly detailed requirements, including nondiscriminatory practices, possible quotas for racial composition, and a lottery approach to choosing some portion of the student body for schools with more applications than places. The California Initiative also would prohibit discrimination in admission on the basis of race, religion, or gender, but it would not require any particular composition of enrollments. Thus, if a school of a particular denomination received no applicants from students of other religions, it could remain religiously segregated. Obviously, schools emphasizing a particular political or ideological viewpoint could also be completely segregated—even without discriminating against applicants of other views—by not appealing to parents with other perspectives.

Clearly, depending on permissible curriculum offerings, personnel requirements, and admissions standards, different voucher plans will generate different outcomes with respect to what is learned in school as well as to the degree of segregation of students according to religious, political, ideological, and social class lines. Review of the implications of a particular voucher approach must be based upon examination of the plan's details with respect to regulation. Such an analysis should extend beyond the few basic dimensions that have been discussed here to all dimensions of the curriculum, personnel requirements, admissions requirements, health and safety standards, rights of students to transfer to another school, and procedures of due process and adjudication in cases of conflict between schools and parents.

Information

The final dimension for comparing voucher plans and their implications is the nature of the system for providing information on educational alternatives, to the prospective clients (Bridge, 1978; Klees, 1974). Two points about information are of particular importance. First, education represents a rather complex service that cannot be easily summarized in ways that accurately reflect the educational experience a particular child may face. Second, methods of providing appropriate information on a large number of educational alternatives to a wide variety of audiences are likely to be costly and uncertain—particularly with respect to the least-advantaged persons in society, such as those who are not well educated, who are not English-speaking, and who tend to move frequently because of marginality in job and housing markets.

Regarding the first point, it is possible to provide information on such major distinctions as those of the religious, political, or ideological nature of a particular school. If a school is sponsored by Reverend Moon, the Catholic Church, the Seventh Day Adventists, or the Jewish Community Center, religious orientations will be obvious. Further, if the school is characterized as a military academy, a learning collective, a Ku Klux Klan school, or a Black Panther school, the types of indoctrination will also be straightforward, and voucher advocates would argue that parents could choose according to their preferences. Even schools that emphasized particular curricula, such as the arts, sciences, sports, human potential, and so on, could be so presented that parents could make choices among the distinctions.

However, qualitative aspects of education are much more difficult to characterize. Anyone who reads college catalogs will be impressed with the fact that the majority of institutions in higher education claim to seek academic "excellence" and to have distinguished faculties. Thus, it is much more difficult to ascertain how well institutions carry out their educational mission and to present this information in an understandable format than to present self-serving claims. Further, if schools with various political or religious orientations tend to use clandestine approaches to obtain converts and adherents—as has been reported for certain religious groups—there will be an incentive to distort information in the direction of those descriptions that will secure clients. Of course, advertising and promotional abuses can occur for other types of schools as well (U.S. Federal Trade Commission, 1976).

The second important point about school information is that persons from the most disadvantaged backgrounds are those who need information services the most. Such persons are characterized by low educational attainments, higher probabilities of not speaking English, and higher incidences of neighborhood mobility because of their lack of housing and job stability. In essence, they need to be informed of available alternatives in language they understand and in a form in which the information is comprehensible to them.

Also, one must bear in mind that within any state there will be virtually hundreds of local educational markets, each with its own unique information and changes over time. Therefore the system for providing information must be highly decentralized, with information agencies and counselors available in every community. These services are likely to be very costly. Even with a very extensive bilingual information campaign that saturated the Alum Rock School District in which the OEO modified-voucher demonstration was tried, a surprising proportion of the population was not even familiar with the existence of the plan (Bridge, 1978, pp. 514-516). Despite the use of newspapers, mailings, radio announcements, neighborhood meetings, and information counselors, one quarter of the residents were unfamiliar with even the existence of the voucher demonstration over a four-year period. As might be expected, parents with lower educational attainments and non-English-speaking backgrounds showed the highest levels of ignorance. Most troublesome, any ongoing voucher plan probably could not afford the obviously high costs of the OEO "saturation" approach.

Whereas the Friedman plan made no direct provision for information and the OEO plan provided for extensive information, the California Initiative specifies that reasonable requirements of disclosure be established by law regarding curriculum and teaching methods, qualifications of teachers, resource use, and the possible requirement of standardized test results. This information would be made available through sources independent of the schools, and nonliterate parents and others with special information needs would receive a grant redeemable for the services of independent education counselors. Also, schools would be forbidden to air deliberately false or misleading information. These information requirements appear to be rather extensive and responsive to the needs of disadvantaged families. But the Initiative gives no details for implementing these information services, and the budget provided for them is minuscule (see below). Thus the Initiative is open to a variety of interpretations regarding the form and comprehensiveness of the information plan.

Summary of Voucher Arrangements

In summary, one can try to understand the nature and implications of educational vouchers only by examining and analyzing the specific attributes of particular voucher plans. Different specifics can lead to radically different results. Of special importance are the arrangements for financing, regulating, and providing information for the educational marketplace. Clearly, a voucher plan with "compensatory" vouchers for the poor, no "add-ons," an extensive information system, and regulation of admissions to assure participation of the poor will have vastly different consequences than one which provides a uniform voucher with parental "add-ons," a poor information system, and a laissez-faire approach to admissions. In short, any debate over the desirability of vouchers should be based on a discussion of specific details and their possible consequences.

One additional, but central, conclusion that can be drawn from this discussion is that the claims of advocates for voucher plans may or may not be supported by details of the plans. For example, the California Initiative asserts that one purpose is "To protect freedom of religion, but aid no religion." This statement is obviously designed to give the impression that church-sponsored or church-related schools are not eligible for vouchers. The Initiative would require that such schools incorporate as separate entities for purposes of voucher eligibility, but a careful reading of the Initiative demonstrates that such schools would certainly be eligible for vouchers. Indeed, since church-sponsored schools enroll the vast majority of children in the independent schools of California, they would likely be the primary beneficiaries of the shift to vouchers.[5]

Authors of the Initiative would draw legalistic distinctions in order to show that vouchers aid no religion. First, they would state that children would

[5] For example, in 1976 about four-fifths of the students attending private schools in California were enrolled in church-affiliated schools (California State Department of Education, 1978, p. 14).

receive the benefits of vouchers, not institutions. Second, they would argue that requiring schools to incorporate as separate legal entities will separate the schools from their religious sponsors, despite the obvious content and intentions of the curriculum and instruction. These attempts to create legal distinctions that are likely to mislead the average citizen are unfortunate, for it is very clear that both the intent and impact of the Initiative will be to aid religious schools and to subsidize religious instruction.

The Initiative also calls for decentralized public administration of education through the marketplace, but it does not mention that the shift to vouchers will also shift many functions of schools from the local to the state levels. At present, the state must coordinate and monitor the financing and educational offerings of about 1040 local school districts. Those districts, in turn, address the educational needs of children within their jurisdictions, including the monitoring of attendance and compliance with compulsory attendance laws.

Under the voucher system, the state will need to monitor the attendance patterns and enrollments of almost five million youngsters as well as to ascertain their eligibility for vouchers and the appropriate amount of the voucher. That is, the state will have to ensure that each of the five million students is enrolled in an approved school as well as to diagnose the educational characteristics of each child in order to ascertain how large the voucher should be. Recall that the California Initiative would award different vouchers, according to grade level, curriculum, bilingualism, special needs and handicaps, variations in local costs, need to encourage racial desegregation, and other factors. Presumably, each child would have to be located by the state and screened for voucher eligibility. Further, the state would have to establish relations with individual schools rather than school districts in order to determine whether a school is eligible to redeem vouchers. The state would have to provide information services in every community as well as a means of adjudicating complaints and conflicts between parents and schools. In short, many school functions presently carried out at the local level would become functions of the state and would be administered centrally at that level.

Moreover, the Initiative would limit the expenditures of the state on such functions to no more than one-half of one percent of the total public cost of education. Using the present level of expenditure in California, the Initiative would limit annual state expenditures on all of these functions to less than $10 per child. Precisely how the state will carry out the extensive functions implied by the Initiative and create an extensive information system, screen children for voucher eligibility, certify schools, handle complaints, and so on, for less than $10 a year per child is not addressed. Clearly, either the state will perform these services in only the most perfunctory manner, or the cost will be considerably higher. Of course, one could question whether the state has the administrative and technical capacity to handle these functions for five million students at any cost. Experiences with government regulatory agencies hardly suggest cause for optimism.

Finally, the Initiative argues that it will limit costs by mandating that expenditures cannot rise beyond those costs associated with school population and the consumer price index. But by absorbing an additional half million students presently in private schools who would be eligible for vouchers, the state would become responsible for another $1 billion a year in additional costs under the Initiative. Thus, over the next decade, the costs of public schooling would be at least $10 billion higher—even without increases in the consumer price index—by underwriting the 10 percent of California's elementary and secondary students who are now in private schools.[6]

Clearly, if voucher initiatives are put before the voters, the nature and intentions of the details ought to be clear rather than obfuscatory. The California Initiative has been constructed in such a way that citizen debate is likely to be highly misinformed on each of the issues previously detailed. Some of these points will be obvious to persons familiar with the educational system; others will be obscure to all but the most careful and best informed analysts of the subject. Unfortunately, few of the "true" provisions will be apparent to the average citizen who is being asked to vote on the Initiative.

[6]This interpretation is based upon the ambiguities and contradictions among a number of passages in the Initiative. For example, paragraph 4 states that: "For school years 1980-81 through 1986-87 the total public costs of elementary and secondary education in all common schools shall not exceed the total public costs of elementary and secondary education in 1979-80 adjusted and compounded for changes in the consumer price index and total school age population." I have interpreted this as meaning that adjustments will be made for the number of students who become eligible for common school support. Since this number would increase under the Initiative, the total school age population would rise. Others have interpreted this as a demographic phenomenon. If this were the case, however, then the age categories would have to be specified in order to obtain a precise classification. For example, if the compulsory attendance laws were used to define "school age population," students below the age of 5.75 years and above the age of 16 years would not be calculated in the measure. Accordingly, I have interpreted this as the number of children who will actually be attending the newly-defined common schools, since any age criterion that does not specify the particular age range is ambiguous.

There is a further point of ambiguity in interpretation. If the Initiative intends that the budget will not rise to accommodate additional students who become eligible for public support by shifting from existing private schools to "independent public and family choice schools," then how will the additional financial obligations be covered? Paragraph 15 provides for educational expenditures in support of students enrolling in independent public and family choice schools at ninety percent of that cost in public schools. But only if all students enrolled in independent public and family choice schools would total costs be contained while absorbing almost half a million additional students. As long as students choose to stay in public schools, then real educational expenditures *for each public school would decline* within the total expenditure limit in order to accommodate the new students who become eligible for public support in the independent schools.

Perhaps the greatest social dilemma raised by vouchers is the potential divergence between private choices and the social benefits of education. Presumably, so many of our social resources are devoted to education because the reproduction of our social, economic, and political systems depends heavily on preparing the young to understand and participate in these systems. Even Friedman argues that the state ought to pay the cost of basic education because of its important role in providing the common values and knowledge necessary for an effectively functioning democracy (Friedman, 1962, p. 86).

This concern has at least two major dimensions: First, the schools are expected to provide students with an understanding of the role and functioning of our democratic system of government as well as to prepare them for participating in such a system. Second, the schools are expected to create and sustain a system of social mobility in which a child's eventual income and occupational status are not linked inextricably to those of his parents. The schools are expected to more nearly equalize adult opportunities among youngsters born into different racial, social, and economic circumstances. In this section, we shall explore the probable impact of the voucher mechanism on these two social goals of the schools.

Vouchers and Preparation for Democracy

A major function of the public schools is the transmission of a common language, heritage, set of values, and knowledge necessary for appropriate political functioning in our democratic society. To a large degree, the schools attempt to reproduce these traits through a common curriculum and heterogeneous enrollments. That is, we presume that exposure to a variety of students from different backgrounds and to a common curriculum of social studies and civic content will prepare students adequately to participate in democratic institutions.[7]

In almost every respect, the voucher approach would violate these premises by encouraging separation and stratification of students according to parental commitments and orientations and by tailoring curricula to appeal to and reinforce these parental concerns. Neighborhood residential patterns in the United States prevent complete heterogeneity in student attendance patterns; even within most neighborhoods different religions, political viewpoints, ethnic backgrounds, and ideologies are represented. Further, there is some degree of racial heterogeneity in a large number of public schools, even

---

[7]The major treatise on this subject is John Dewey's *Democracy and Education* (1916). It is important to emphasize that these arguments are not germane to the postsecondary educational sector, where the emphasis must be on other goals. Rather, the arguments pertain to the compulsory portion of education.

though the overall picture on racial integration is not a happy one. The voucher approach would systematize the allocation of youngsters to schools according to family background and identity to an incomparably greater extent than even the more segregated of our current neighborhood-based schools.

Indeed, the great appeal of vouchers is that parents can choose the type of education they desire for their children by simply selecting a school that addresses those needs. True, parents might wish to choose schools that emphasize to a greater degree the arts or sciences or sports or basic skills or humanistic objectives than the present schools, but these differences can be sought and attained through a variety of arrangements in the current public school system. (We return to this matter in a later section.) What makes the voucher approach unique is that parents will be able to send their children to schools that will reinforce in the most restrictive fashion the political, ideological, and religious views of the family. School will be treated as a strict extension of the home, with little opportunity for students to experience the diversity of backgrounds and viewpoints that contributes to the democratic process.

The importance of being exposed to conflicting positions in forming democratic values cannot be overstated. This fact is illustrated by a recent study of attitudes toward dissent among West German youth (Weiler, 1971; Stiefbold & Weiler, 1970). The central finding of this study was that young people who showed high tolerance for viewpoints different from the majority ones on specific subjects had been more exposed to controversy or conflict than those who had little tolerance for dissenting views. Even more to the point, the greater the reported frequency with which controversial topics had been entertained in classrooms, the higher the tolerance of students toward dissenting viewpoints.

But if we consider that under a voucher approach, parents will tend to select schools that reinforce their own views, the opportunities for exposure to constructive conflict and controversy will be significantly narrowed for their children. It is highly dubious that Catholic schools will or even should promote discussions about the pros and cons of birth control and abortion; that Ku Klux Klan schools will provide anything but the most negative stereotypes of Blacks, while Black Panther schools will treat whites similarly. John Birch schools are not likely to expose students to a debate on the virtues of Medicare and public assistance under monopoly capitalism; Maoist schools are not likely to find any virtues in the political institutions of America. This situation is hardly likely to have salubrious consequences for a democracy in which disputed issues must be addressed and resolved continually.

Vouchers and Equality

As I indicated previously, how a voucher approach is financed and regulated, and how information about the voucher is provided will have an important impact on how egalitarian will be its consequences. Even though there will be differences from plan to plan, vouchers will tend to create greater transmission of inequalities from generation to generation than the present public schools. This problem tends to assert itself because parents seem to pursue child-rearing patterns that are consistent and reinforce their own values and class position in the society (Bowles & Gintis, 1976; Kohn, 1969). This can best be understood by considering what these values are and how they might affect the choice of school.

Let us assume parents wish to select that school which they believe will have the most chance of making their child a success in life. Clearly, the rules for success differ according to where parents are situated in the productive and occupational hierarchy. Kohn (1969) has shown that working-class families seem to emphasize conformity in their children (obedience to rules), whereas parents in relatively higher occupational positions stress independence and ability to choose among available alternatives. The research of Hess and Shipman (1965) on maternal-child interactions also tends to substantiate these differences, with lower-class mothers stressing a "do as I tell you" approach in teaching their children and middle-class mothers seemingly using a more heuristic approach. Obviously, conformity and "do as I tell you" are ingredients for success in working-class occupations. Such occupations require workers to report to work on time, follow orders of superiors, carry out repetitive tasks, and obey all the rules and regulations of the firm in order to succeed (Edwards, 1979). Individuals in these occupations who do not conform are not rewarded with steady work and job promotions. Thus, the research on behavior of working-class parents suggests that they will select for their children highly structured schools that emphasize a high degree of discipline, concentration on basic skills, and following orders.

In contrast, the occupational experience of the upper middle-class parent suggests that independence and mastery of principles or concepts breed success. Managerial and professional roles require the ability to consider alternative production techniques, products, marketing strategies, and personnel, to create the rules and regulations which define the work organization, to maintain relatively great flexibility in personal work schedules depending on individual needs, and to have the ability to give orders even more than to take orders. Parents with a background in such occupational positions are more likely to stress a great deal of freedom in the school environments of their children with a heavy emphasis on student choice, flexible scheduling, few significant rules, and light enforcement of rules that exist. These parents will expect the school to place a great deal of responsibility on the student in choosing and undertaking his educational experiences. The attainment of basic skills will be taken for granted, and the curriculum will pay much greater attention to written and verbal communication skills.

If parents choose those school environments they believe will maximize the probability of success as defined within the context of their experience, the working-class child will get schooling that reinforces working-class orientations, and upper-class children will attend schools that orient them toward the upper echelons of the occupational hierarchy. As Kohn has concluded from his study of the effect of parental occupation on the values of children:

> The family then functions as a mechanism for perpetuating inequality. At lower levels of the stratification order, parents are likely to be ill-equipped and often will be ill-disposed to train their children in the skills needed at higher class levels ... No matter how dramatic the exceptions, it is usual that families prepare their offspring for the world as they know it and that the conditions of life eventually faced by the offspring are not very different from those for which they have been prepared (1969, pp. 200-201).

Vouchers would make this class stratification and socialization even more "efficient" by making it possible for parents to choose particular primary and secondary schooling environments based upon these values. Thus, the differences in child socialization among classes in our highly stratified society would be augmented by a more perfect correspondence between the social class orientations of the parents and the schools they choose. In contrast with the present system where at least some children find themselves in schools that do not necessarily reflect their parents' social origins, the voucher approach would streamline the transmission of status from one generation to the next.

Further, to the degree that social class stratification increased, it would become easier to identify individuals for particular positions in the social class hierarchy by the schools they attend. Each school would connote a different breeding or charter that would have a certification value in preparing individuals for further educational opportunities or positions in the labor market.[8] Even without identifying the actual proficiencies of students as individuals, the information connoted by the class orientation of schooling would tend to serve a stratification role.

The voucher approach to education represents a paradox. It seems reasonable to believe that greater choice among consumers and increased institutional responsiveness will enhance the welfare of society. At a rhetorical level, we would be improving the ability of families to obtain the education they want for their children. But as I have demonstrated, the expansion of choices and market responsiveness will be much greater for upper-income groups than for lower-income and minority citizens, and the element of choice will lead insidiously to an even greater degree of class stratification and socialization than exists now. That these latter effects will be based upon individual "choices" and "preferences" means that the exacerbation of social-class differences in the fortunes of children will be considered the responsibility of parents who chose

---

[8] Meyer (1970) develops a theory of "charter" effects of education. Thurow (1975) explains how a job queue of educationally certified workers can explain the behavior of United States labor markets and the distribution of earned income.

the schools rather than the responsibility of the class-oriented society that predetermined the parents' values leading to the choices.

In summary, in two important respects the voucher approach would violate the underlying premises of schooling in a democratic society. By segregating students in school environments that tend to reinforce the values, prejudices, attitudes, and behaviors of their parents, the diversity of experience and exposure to other viewpoints, which are at the base of the democratic process, will be largely eliminated from the schools. Further, to the degree that parents tend to choose schools that emphasize the ingredients for success consistent with their niche in the occupational hierarchy, the schools will tend to reproduce in children the work values and orientations associated with the occupations of their parents. To a large degree, public support of education will be utilized to support educational outcomes that are in conflict with the social purpose of schooling.

ARE THERE OTHER OPTIONS?

One of the most unfortunate aspects of the current voucher debate is its tacit constriction of options that are posited for improving American education. The advocates of both vouchers and the existing public schools tend to place the choice at two poles—a voucher system versus the present system of public education. Since it is the voucher advocates who must provide a persuasive case for change, they pose the question in a way that is conducive to the answer supporting their case: "Who should make the decisions about how each child will be educated?" They then limit the answers in this multiple choice quiz to two possibilities—the family or the state.

The family is characterized as being deeply concerned with the educational needs of its children and anxious to make good decisions on their behalf. The state is characterized as an insensitive bureaucracy of functionaries whose concerns for children are relatively low on their schedule of priorities. We are then asked to choose one of these sources to make decisions for our children. Needless to say, most people would choose the family over this faceless bureaucratic state for making sensitive decisions on behalf of children.

But the comparison is so largely contrived that it is not helpful. First, the state is hardly a monolith, but is composed of different levels and degrees of personal concern and citizen access. For the average parent, it is the personnel in a single school or a single classroom that have relevance, rather than an abstract notion of bureaucracy. Many teachers are deeply committed to the educational needs of children in their classes, and many are very amenable to suggestions from parents. Other teachers are indifferent or worse. Of course, the same can be said for parents. Many parents are deeply committed to the educational needs of their children and will work with teachers, administrators, and other school personnel to fulfill those needs. In other cases, parents are hard pressed by the demands of work, marital difficulties, poverty, or illness, and are therefore unable to devote much time or attention to the educational needs of their children. In still other cases, parents do not have the appropriate rapport with their children or understanding of their children's needs.

Given the relatively high rates of divorce and separation, alcoholism, and other stresses on family life in America, it is somewhat difficult to argue that families *are always* preoccupied with what is best for their children. One finds examples of sensitivity and dereliction among both families and schools. The real question is what overall arrangement can best contribute to the development of children in meeting both their individual needs and those of society. The answer to this question may suggest options that are ignored when the debate is limited to the existing public schools or vouchers.

A second artificial aspect of the voucher debate is the tendency of voucher advocates to ignore or denigrate any social purposes of schooling beyond those reflected in family choice. In general, these conclusions are reached by arguing: (1) there is no unanimity on the social purposes of schooling; (2) schooling should not be concerned with social purposes, but only individual needs; or (3) almost any voucher arrangement will meet the social purposes of schooling, whatever they are. Coons and Sugarman (1978) argue the first point; West (1965) asserts the second; and Friedman (1962) seems to support the third.

Indeed, much of the explanation of why family choice should replace the existing system is predicated on arguing away the relevance of schooling's social benefits. Yet, if voucher advocates truly believe that schooling confers benefits on only those who choose and receive schooling, one must surely raise the question of why education should be funded from the public trough. That is, one must justify government's levying taxes to provide families with vouchers that will be used to serve only their own personal desires with no important social benefits. If schooling is designed to meet only the narrowest private desires of citizens, the basis for public funding is undermined. Without social purpose, the demand for public revenues from the state is indefensible.

In summary, voucher advocates tend to frame the debate on schools as one which can be resolved only by choosing between the existing public schools and a voucher approach. Thus, they intimate that if we are dissatisfied with the public schools as they are constituted, vouchers represent the only alternative that will be responsive to our needs. Moreover, this conclusion is reinforced by the tendency to ignore or dismiss the social purposes of schooling, thereby strengthening the family choice arguments. Unfortunately, they fail to point out that if schooling provides no social benefits beyond those received by the families and children receiving the schooling, there is no justification for public funding. Yet the dilemma remains. Given the legitimacy of many of the complaints about the existing schools, are there other options besides vouchers? More specifically, is it possible to maintain the social purposes of the public schools with improvements in their responsiveness and diversity?

Public Choice Approaches

The purpose of a public choice approach to improving education is to capitalize on the social benefits conferred by the public production of education, while encouraging a greater degree of choice and diversity within that framework. These approaches are premised on the view that the virtues of utilizing public schools for preparing youth for democracy and social mobility do not obviate the need for greater educational diversity. Fortunately, there are public choice approaches that represent alternatives to both the existing public schools and vouchers. Paradoxically, at least two systems of public choice in education have developed as by-products of the quest for vouchers.

The OEO attempt to provide an experiment with educational vouchers was not successful in finding a state that would relax its educational code to accommodate the experiment, particularly with respect to the use of public funds for private schools. After an extensive search for an appropriate site and a concerted effort to persuade state legislators to pass enabling legislation for the experiment, OEO finally decided to initiate a "modified voucher" experiment. The modified approach was not a voucher approach at all, but a system of public choice (Cohen & Farrar, 1977). Participating schools in the Alum Rock (San Jose, California) School District were required to provide a minimum of three distinctive educational alternatives or minischools at each school site. Teachers at each school site joined forces with other teachers to create the types of minischools in which they wanted to teach. The personnel in each minischool had considerable discretion over the educational approach and curriculum, although they still had to meet certain curriculum requirements. They were also given a budget for the acquisition of materials and other instructional needs (Weiler *et al.*, 1974).

Each neighborhood school was converted into a complex of from three to five minischools, at least tripling the number of options that families had at their disposal. In addition, transportation was provided to minischools in other neighborhoods, so that the actual number of options was considerably larger—over fifty in the latter years of the demonstration. The particular orientations of the various minischools were quite diverse. The major categories included minischools emphasizing basic skills, fine and creative arts, multicultural activities, individualized learning, and innovative open classrooms (Haggart, Rapp, & Wuchitech, 1974). Parents were also provided with considerable information on the fifty or so alternatives, including the availability of counselors with whom they could discuss their child's educational needs. The early evaluations of this approach suggest fairly high levels of satisfaction among parents and participating teachers, and summary evaluations of the five-year demonstration (which ended in 1977) will be available shortly (Weiler *et al.*, 1974).

From the perspective of a public choice model for education, the Alum Rock demonstration has a number of important virtues. First, it represents an approach that can be implemented in the existing public schools with no alterations in the state constitution or the state educational code. Second, it enables the school system to preserve basic social objectives that can be expressed in curriculum policies and the composition of student enrollments. Third, the approach would minimize the costs of monitoring the attendance of students and transportation in comparison with a statewide voucher program. Finally, the considerable evaluative data on Alum Rock now available should be helpful in refining and improving the approach.

An alternative public choice approach is embodied in the California Initiative which sets out a category of public independent schools. These schools would be established as independent entities within school districts and would serve as alternative schools within the public sector. Without commenting on the specific provisions in the Initiative for this class of schools, the overall idea has provocative consequences for establishing greater choice within the public schools. Moreover, the approach would not require modifying the state constitution, but would only require an action of the legislature to establish the conditions under which this new class of schools would operate.

A third option for greater public choice would be the establishment of somewhat more decentralization in the governance of local schools. In many school districts, the emphasis on uniform policies tends to homogenize educational offerings without taking account of the specific needs of student populations in particular school settings. A movement toward a more meaningful system of community involvement in the governance of local schools could improve the responsiveness of schools to the special concerns of their students and parents. This emphasis on "community control" would also enhance the democratic functioning of schools in that parents, students, and teachers would work together to define and implement the educational process in a democratic fashion (Levin, 1970). Control over much of the curriculum, budget allocation, personnel selection, and managerial practices would be relegated to the persons who are most closely affected by them.

In summary, there are a number of intriguing options for improving the responsiveness of public schools while ensuring that they address their social purposes. If the voucher proposals stimulate the development of these public choice approaches as well as citizen awareness and political efforts to implement them, the debate on vouchers will have performed an important public service. Up to now, the discourse on vouchers has tended to ignore these other options. Surely consideration of such a major change in America's educational structure as represented by the voucher approach ought to be accompanied by an informed debate on all the feasible options. I hope this paper has contributed to that goal.

REFERENCES

Bowles, S., & Gintis, H. *Schooling in capitalist America: Educational reform and the contradictions of economic life.* New York: Basic Books, 1976.

Bridge, G. Information imperfections: The Achilles' heel of entitlement plans. *School Review,* 1978, *86,* 504-529.

California State Department of Education. *1976-77 California public schools selected statistics.* Sacramento, Calif.: Author, 1978.

Catterall, J., & Thresher, T. *Proposition 13: The campaign, the vote, and the immediate aftereffects for California schools.* (Program Report 79-B5). Stanford, Calif.: Stanford University Institute for Research on Educational Finance and Governance, 1979.

Center for the Study of Public Policy. *Education vouchers: A report on financing elementary education by grants to parents.* Cambridge, Mass.: Author, 1970.

Cohen, K., & Farrar, E. Power to the parents?—The story of educational vouchers. *Public Interest,* 1977, *48,* 72-97.

Coons, J. E., & Sugarman, S. D. *Education by choice: The case for family control.* Berkeley, Calif.: University of California Press, 1978.

Dearman, N. B., & Plisko, V. W. *The condition of education.* Washington, D.C.: National Center for Educational Statistics, U.S. Department of Health, Education and Welfare, 1979.

Dewey, J. *Democracy and education.* New York: Macmillan, 1916.

Downs, A. Competition and community schools. In H. M. Levin (Ed.), *Community control of schools.* Washington, D.C.: Brookings, 1970.

Edwards, R. C. *Contested terrain: The transportation of the workplace in the twentieth century.* New York: Basic Books, 1979.

Elam, S. M. (Ed.). *A decade of Gallup Polls of attitudes toward education, 1969-1978.* Bloomington, Ind.: Phi Delta Kappa, 1978.

Freeman, R. B. *The overeducated American.* New York: Academic Press, 1976.

Friedman, M. The role of government in education. In R. A. Solo (Ed.), *Economics and the public interest.* New Brunswick, N.J.: Rutgers University Press, 1955.

Friedman, M. *Capitalism and freedom.* Chicago: University of Chicago Press, 1962.

Haggart, S., Rapp, M., & Wuchitech, J. M. *Instructional aspects of the 1972-73 minischool programs in the Alum Rock Voucher Demonstration.* Santa Monica, Calif.: Rand Corporation, 1974.

Hess, R. D., & Shipman, V. C. Early experience and the socialization of cognitive modes in children. *Child Development,* 1965, *36,* 869-886.

Institute of Economic Affairs. *Education: A framework for choice.* London: Author, 1967.

Jencks, C. Is the public school obsolete? *Public Interest,* 1966, *2,* 18-27.

Klees, S. The role of information in the market for educational services. *Occasional papers on economics and politics of education* (74-1). Stanford, Calif.: Stanford University School of Education, 1974.

Kohn, M. L. *Class and conformity: A study of values.* Homewood, Ill.: Dorsey Press, 1969.

Levin, H. M. (Ed.). *Community control of schools.* Washington, D.C.: Brookings, 1970.

Levin, H. M. Educational vouchers and educational equality. In M. Carnoy (Ed.), *Schooling in a corporate society* (2d ed.). New York:David McKay Company, 1975.

Levin, H. M. Postsecondary entitlements—An exploration. In N. Kurland (Ed.), *Entitlement studies* (NIE *Papers in Education and Work,* No. 4). Washington, D.C.: National Institute of Education, 1977.

Meyer, J. W. The charter: Conditions of diffuse socialization in schools. In W. R. Scott (Ed.), *Social processes and social structures: An introduction to sociology.* New York: Holt, Rinehart and Winston, 1970.

Smith, A. *The wealth of nations.* New York: Random House, 1937.

Stiefbold, R. P., & Weiler, H. N. *Political socialization in West Germany: Tolerance of conflict and dissent.* Paper presened at the annual meeting of the American Political Science Association, Los Angeles, September 1970.

Thurow, L. *Generating inequality: Mechanisms of distribution in the U.S. economy.* New York: Basic Books, 1975.

U.S. Federal Trade Commission, Bureau of Consumer Protection. *Proprietary vocational and home study schools.* Washington, D.C.: U.S. Government Printing Office, 1976.

Weiler, D. *et al. A public school voucher demonstration: The first year at Alum Rock.* Santa Monica, Calif.: Rand Corporation, 1974.

Weiler, H. N. *Schools and the learning of dissent norms: A study of West German youths.* Paper presented at the annual meeting of the American Political Science Association, Chicago, September 1971.

West, E. G. *Education and the state.* London: The Institute of Economic Affairs, 1965.

West, E. G. Tom Paine's voucher scheme for public education. *Southern Economic Journal,* 1967, *33,* 378-382.

An Initiative for Family Choice in Education

THE FOLLOWING SECTION SHALL BE ADDED TO ARTICLE IX OF THE CALIFORNIA CONSTITUTION

1. Purpose

The People of California have adopted this section to improve public education and to increase the authority of parents and teachers. It is their further purpose:

- a. To empower every family to choose among different kinds of schools;
- b. To eliminate the use of property taxes for schools;
- c. To place a constitutional limit on school expenditures;
- d. To eliminate the administrative costs of excessive regulation;
- e. To decentralize the public administration of education;
- f. To protect freedom of religion but aid no religion;
- g. To protect children against discrimination on the basis of race, creed, gender, or family income.

2. Family Rights

Every family shall have the right:

- a. To enroll its children in public schools, independent public schools, or schools not administered by government but which meet the standards specified in this section;
- b. To choose among such schools in a manner unaffected by family income;
- c. To petition its school district of residence to establish independent public schools governed by combinations of parents, teachers, trustees, and others.

3. Elimination of Property Tax for Schools

Except to the extent that *ad valorem* taxes or special assessments are necessary to pay the interest and redemption charges upon debts of any school district existing on July 3, 1980, including reserve or sinking funds required in connection with such indebtedness, no taxes or assessments upon property shall be used for the support of elementary or secondary education after school year 1981-82.

4. Limits upon Public Expenditure

For school years 1980-81 through 1986-87 the total public cost of elementary and secondary education in all common schools shall not exceed the total public cost of elementary and secondary education in 1979-80 adjusted and com-

126

pounded for changes in the consumer price index and total school age population. The Controller shall authorize no payment in violation of this subsection and where necessary shall prorate uniformly the value of subvention and of educational certificates. Public cost here and in subsection 14 shall mean every cost to state and local government of conducting elementary and secondary education in the relevant year as determined by the Department of Finance according to law; it shall not include the costs of funding employee retirement benefits which are unfunded on June 3, 1980.

5. Limit Upon Central Administration

Appropriations for administration of the State Department of Education shall not exceed one half of one percent of the total public cost of education as defined in subsection 4.

6. Classification of Common Schools

Parents and guardians are entitled to choose among three classes of common schools for education in grades kindergarten through twelve. These shall be known as public schools, independent public schools, and family choice schools; together they shall constitute the common schools of California. Public schools are those publicly owned, funded, and administered and not certified to redeem education certificates issued by the state. Independent public schools are those organized by school districts, community colleges, or public universities and which are certified to redeem educational certificates. Family choice schools are those privately organized and certified to redeem educational certificates.

7. Admission to Independent Public and Family Choice Schools

Parents or guardians of school age children may enroll them in any independent public school or any family choice school. This right is subject to the authority of every such school to set its enrollment limit at each grade level and to limit applications to children of either gender. The school may exceed its enrollment limit at each grade level by five percent; it may be directed by law to do so where the total number of places in the common schools of an area is insufficient to serve the pupil population. Where applications to any school exceed its enrollment limit, a public agency designated by the Legislature shall select by lot among all its timely applicants. However, pupils attending a school at the time it becomes certified shall have priority as shall their siblings. Children and siblings of former students and children of full-time employees of such schools shall enjoy similar priority. With reasonable notice a child may transfer during the school year from any school to any independent public or family choice school with available places. Subsequent enrollment rights of pupils validly dimissed from a school shall be regulated by statute. Appropriate free education is guaranteed every child who is subject to compulsory education. Common schools shall transport their pupils in accord with reasonable conditions and limits upon cost to be fixed by law.

8. Admission to Public Schools

In assigning pupils to public schools, and in considering requests for transfer to any public school located within or outside the applicant's district of residence, boards of education, both district and county, shall give substantial weight to family choice. The Legislature shall with appropriate legislation facilitate transfers to public schools chosen by the parent or guardian.

9. Pupil Rights and Discipline

A pupil subject to compulsory education who attends an independent public or family choice school may continue in that school unless she or he derives no substantial educational benefit or is responsible for grave or habitual misconduct related to school which seriously impairs the education of others. No pupil enrolled in a common school shall suffer discrimination on the basis of race, religion, or gender. The Legislature shall enact uniform standards of procedural due process for common schools and provide for independent review of dismissals.

10. Independent Public Schools

All school districts, community colleges and public universities are authorized to establish independent public schools. Each school shall be organized as a separate public nonprofit corporation. It shall employ personnel with such qualifications as its responsible officers deem appropriate. Governing boards of such schools may include, but are not limited to, faculty, principal, pupils, parents and guardians of pupils, independent trustees, and any combination of such individuals. The form of governance for each school shall be determined by the organizing authority. Except as stated in this section, independent public schools shall be operated according to the laws affecting family choice schools.

11. Parental Petition for Independent Public Schools

Parents may petition their school district for the establishment of an independent public school or schools. The Legislature shall facilitate this right, and petitioning parents shall have standing to challenge unfavorable decisions. Parental petitions shall propose the grades to be included, the form of the governing body of the corporation and the educational goals of the school. School districts shall grant such petitions and lease available facilities to the corporation at cost whenever:

a. The signatories affirm their intention to apply to the proposed school and waive alternate choices for the initial year;
b. The signatories represent pupils sufficient in number to make adequate enrollment probable, the number 100 per school or 30 per grade being deemed sufficient unless otherwise provided by law; and
c. Such school can operate without additional cost to the public or substantial hardship to other pupils.

12. Family Choice Schools

Each family choice school shall organize under California law as either a public benefit or mutual benefit corporation and may be neither a religious corporation or a corporation sole.

13. Certification of Schools

Independent public schools and family choice schools shall be certified upon proper application to an agency designated by law. A school whose application satisfies the curriculum requirements and standards for teaching personnel fixed by law for private schools on July 1, 1979, shall be entitled to immediate certification; the Legislature may not augment such requirements and standards. Certification shall continue so long as such school complies with this section. A certified school may neither advocate unlawful behavior nor engage in unlawful hiring practices. The deliberate provision of false or misleading information to public agencies or to individuals shall be forbidden. Every certified school shall be subject to reasonable requirements of law including disclosure regarding its curriculum and teaching methods, the qualifications of its teachers, and its use of resources. The Legislature may require standardized testing and publication of results where it deems such results to indicate quality of instruction; it may establish a minimum standard of competency in language and mathematics for the high school diploma for all common schools.

No school shall be ineligible to redeem certificates because it teaches moral or social values, philosophy, or religion, but religion may not be taught in public schools or independent public schools; a curriculum may be required by any school, but no pupil shall be compelled to profess political, religious, philosophical or ideological belief or actively participate in ceremony symbolic of belief. The Legislature shall encourage diversity among schools. Health and safety standards applicable to independent public and family choice schools shall not be more restrictive than the standards imposed upon facilities of private schools on July 1, 1979.

No school shall suffer decertification or other penalty except upon proof of substantial violation of law after notice and opportunity to defend. Agencies responsibile to initiate and conduct decertification proceedings shall be designated by the Legislature.

14. Educational Certificates

Every child of school age is entitled to a certificate redeemable only for educational purposes in independent public and family choice schools. Any provision in this Constitution notwithstanding, the Legislature may facilitate redemption of such certificates through establishment of individual school drawing accounts or otherwise. Certificates shall be adequate for a thorough education as defined by the Legislature. They shall be equal for every child of similar grade level and circumstance and shall reflect the reasonable cost of the transportation guaranteed by subsection 7. The redeemable amount may also differ by such factors as grade level, curriculum, bilingualism, special needs and handicaps, variations in local cost, need to encourage racial desegregation, and any other factor deemed appropriate by the Legislature so long as the right of every child to enroll in any school remains unaffected by his or her family's capacity to purchase education. Schools shall accept no fees or consideration other than state certificates nor impose any other financial public burden except in a manner accommodating family capacity to discharge the burden. When during a school year a pupil transfers or ceases to attend a common school the Legislature shall provide for an appropriate division of the certificate.

15. Average Cost Per Pupil

The average public cost per pupil enrolled in independent public and family choice schools shall approximate ninety percent of the cost in public schools.

16. Information to Parents

The Legislature shall assure provision of adequate information through sources independent of any school or school authority. Nonliterate parents and others with special information needs shall receive a grant redeemable for the services of independent education counselors.

17. Employee Rights

The Legislature shall provide on reasonable conditions, for continuation and funding of retirement and other benefits for employees who transfer from public schools to independent public schools and may do so for employees of public schools who transfer to family choice schools. Employees of independent public and family choice schools have the same right to bargain collectively as those employed by public schools, but the bargaining unit shall not be larger than the employing school corporation.

18. Educational Facilities

The Legislature is authorized to establish programs of loans, guaranteed loans, or similar aids for common schools designed to promote the acquisitions, creation, expansion or maintenance of educational facilities serving public educational objectives; family choice schools may participate to the extent they serve such objectives. No capital aid may be extended where facilities are available which are adequate for the educational use intended. Express space in common schools shall be available to other common schools at actual cost.

19. Federal Aid

The Legislature shall ensure that federal aid, within the limits of federal law, advances the objectives of this article.

20. Transitional Provisions

The Legislature shall promptly implement this section, ensuring eligibility for educational certificates of one-fourth of all pupils in school year 1982-83, and a similar additional number yearly thereafter.

21. Termination by the Legislature

Ten years after all children have become eligible for educational certificates and thereafter the provision of this amendment may be repealed or modified by statute receiving the affirmative vote of two-thirds of the elected members of both houses of the Legislature.

22. Severability of Invalid Provisions and Applications

Should any provision of this amendment be held invalid under the federal Constitution, the balance of its provisions shall continue as the law of California. If particular applications to specific schools be held invalid, it shall remain the law for all valid applications to such schools. In the event of partial invalidity the Legislature shall adopt a system of family choice which conforms to the purposes of this amendment to the maximum degree consistent with the Constitution of the United States.

II. ARTICLE IX, SECTION 5, IS HEREBY REPEALED.

III. ARTICLE IX, SECTION 6, IS AMENDED AS FOLLOWS:

The provisions of the fourth paragraph of Section 6 of Article IX beginning "Except that there shall be" and ending "($2,400)" are hereby repealed.

IV. ARTICLE IX, SECTION 8, IS AMENDED AS FOLLOWS:

The words "common schools" in this section shall be replaced by the words "public schools or independent public schools."

Comments on Levin's Paper

ROBERT P. STRAUSS is an Associate Professor of Economics at the University of North Carolina at Chapel Hill and a faculty member of the Bush Institute for Child and Family Policy at UNC (Dr. Strauss is now an Associate Professor of Economics at Carnegie-Mellon University).

In this and earlier papers, Henry Levin (1973, 1975) has constructed a series of arguments against educational vouchers and in favor of other organizational forms of educational service delivery. He has clarified the debate over vouchers by providing a framework for evaluating alternative voucher schemes, reviewing our experience with vouchers, and pointing out that the operational details of a voucher scheme are crucial to understanding its likely impact. I think that Levin has not conclusively argued that vouchers are inferior to either current arrangements around the country or the arrangements proposed by Levin to supplant them. Indeed, I would argue that the case against educational vouchers remains yet to be soundly made.

At the outset, it is important to understand what educational vouchers, in the generic sense, are designed to do; namely, provide the family not only an annual choice about where to obtain educational services, but also an effective fiscal control mechanism which rewards productive educational services and fails to reward unproductive services. Essential to any voucher plan is the ability of a family to send Johnny to school B if, in its judgment, school A is not doing its job. Contrast this paradigm of choice with current options available to families who are unhappy about school A. First, they may complain to the teacher or school directly or through the PTA. Second, they can enroll their child in a private school and thus pay twice for educational services (first via property taxes for the public school services which are not used and second via tuition fees to the private school). Third, the family can change residence to another school district and begin anew.

Levin correctly perceives that parents are increasingly unhappy about the education their children receive; however, parental concern goes beyond ". . . a perception of diminishing academic rigor and increasing disorder in the public schools." The simple facts are that per pupil expenditures have at least equaled the inflation rate at the same time that SAT scores have been declining. Concomitant with these trends of the past ten years is the increased unionization of teachers and administrators and their increased isolation from calls for accountability. Parents sense that they are paying more and getting less—and the less involves a deterioration in the ability of many school systems to ensure that basic skills are obtained by the time of high school graduation. As a result, more than 30 legislatures—over the objection of educators—have required that students pass some sort of competency examination as a condition of high school graduation. Educational vouchers, then, attempt to increase accountability within a framework that permits the family to make choices without extraordinary expense or inconvenience. And I would stress that such voucher schemes are being discussed within a context that amounts to a crisis of confidence in public education. Levin, by contrast, views educational vouchers within the context of education as a declining industry which is now having difficulty raising further public monies.

The core of Levin's objection to educational vouchers is based on the following line of argument: in a world of educational vouchers, families will choose schools on the basis of their religious, political, or academic preferences. As a result of such choices, he expects poor families to make less well-informed choices than nonpoor families, since poor families will know less to begin with. Further, when such choices are made by poor families, they will be based on a particular school's ability to teach certain values held by the poor; namely, conformity and discipline. Such values doom poor children to lower-class occupations later on. Since the two social justifications for public education are the maintenance of historical continuity in teaching democratic values and the equalization of opportunity by giving all children similar starting positions, vouchers are found deficient. The very fact of family choice, in Levin's view, militates against democratic values being transmitted, and the proclivities of the poor ensure that they will send their children to schools which emphasize lower-class values. These values, in turn, ensure that poor children will remain at the bottom of the social strata as adults.

I would raise four objections to this series of arguments against educational vouchers. First, Levin's definition of the social benefits of education seems to ignore basic literacy as a public good. Simple compliance with laws (e.g., tax laws)—as pointed out some time ago by Burton A. Weisbrod (1964)—requires literacy on the part of the population. In this respect, creating a literate population actually saves significant amounts of public resources. Moreover, I would argue that basic literacy, rather than religious or political education, is of utmost concern to almost all families. Nationwide declining church attendance and declining rates of voter turnout would suggest that religion and politics are of decreasing importance to American families (Jacquet, 1978, table 1-J; U.S. Bureau of the Census, 1978, table 836). Thus, I would argue that basic literacy is the most sought-after private component of education.

Second, it seems likely that educational authorities could design regulatory or accreditation requirements which would ensure that our history and democratic values would be transmitted from generation to generation. This could be easily achieved without materially altering the choice of schools inherent in voucher plans.

Third, I find the argument that the poor will be worse off because they are least informed to be patronizing and elitist, a view which is contrary to that held by both liberals and conservatives in other areas of social policy. For example, it is now widely agreed that some form of negative income tax would be a productive replacement for our existing hodgepodge of welfare programs. An important aspect of this reform of the welfare system is the widely held and substantiated belief that the poor can better manage their use of money in the purchase of housing, food, and so on, than a social worker or a set of government regulations (Michael, 1978). Indeed, many observers regard the provision of in-kind services as demeaning to the poor. It would seem that reluctance to permit poor parents to choose education services for their children is equally demeaning.

Associated with the question of whether one can trust the poor to choose wisely when vouchers come into place are the correlative questions of whether external market pressures will force the poor to make better decisions over time and whether poor children have expectations and desires that differ from those of the nonpoor. Too frequently, educators ignore the linkage between educational services and the skills demanded by private industry and the public sector. Information about job opportunities, starting salaries, and salary paths over time are constantly being generated by the marketplace, and are of interest to students of all backgrounds. If poor parents choose unwisely, then there will be subsequent adverse economic consequences for their children in the job market. At the extreme, for example, no one will hire a graduate of a revolutionary Black Panther school. Unemployment will result, and information about the utility of that particular type of education will inevitably be generated. It is very difficult for me to believe that, even in this extreme case, parents and children would not adjust their educational demands over time. In other words, irrespective of initial parental misinformation, powerful market forces will force them to adapt their educational choices.

The only circumstance in which job market pressures will not force parents to adapt their educational choices over time is one in which they (and their children) do not care about job market outcomes and pecuniary success. Only if the poor have substantially different expectations can they continue to ignore job market failures and successes. At issue ultimately is whether the poor (and their children) have a different definition of the American Dream. Psychologists tell us that in most important respects people want the same thing—especially a good education for their children (National Academy, 1976). One need only look at the intraurban migration patterns of middle-class Black families to realize that they object to "problem schools," a synonym for schools that fail to improve the basic literacy of children. Again, if indeed the American Dream is shared by the poor, I would argue that market pressures will force parents to make informed educational choices for their children.

My fourth objection to Levin's criticisms of educational vouchers involves the absence of a reference point in his analysis. Throughout, vouchers are viewed as inferior, but inferior to what? Educational vouchers, in the generic sense, have yet to be demonstrated as inferior to existing arrangements. Certain kinds of vouchers have been experimentally tested in a very limited manner with mixed success. Moreover, I would argue that for the poor, who cannot afford to pay twice for educational services and cannot afford to move into an expensive suburb with better schools, it is difficult to envision how vouchers could make them worse off.

In sum, I think the debate on educational vouchers is far from over. As long as public education fails to provide basic literacy to the population, the public demand for greater accountability in the schools will continue, and the logic of permitting parental choice through educational vouchers will remain compelling. Whether Levin's worst fears about the adverse effects of vouchers on the poor are realized remains an empirical question. I think that the risks are far smaller and the benefits to parents and children far greater than he envisions. Therefore, it is my hope that we get on with trying various voucher schemes to see whether indeed they are workable.

REFERENCES

Jacquet, C. H. (Ed.). *Yearbook of American and Canadian churches.* Nashville, Tenn.: Abington, 1978.

Levin, H. M. Vouchers and society equity. *Change,* 1973, *10,* 29-33.

Levin, H. M. Educational vouchers and educational equality. In M. Carnoy (Ed.), *Schooling in a corporate society* (2d ed.). New York: David McKay, 1975.

Michael, R. T. The consumption studies. In J. L. Palmer & J. A. Pechman (Eds.), *Welfare in rural areas: The North Carolina-Iowa Income Maintenance Experiment.* Washington, D.C.: Brookings, 1978.

National Academy of Sciences. *Toward a national policy for children and families.* Washington, D.C.: Author, 1976.

U.S. Bureau of the Census. *Statistical abstract of the United States* (99th ed.). Washington, D.C.: Author, 1978.

Weisbrod, B. A. *External benefits of public education: An economic analysis.* Princeton, N.J.: Princeton University Press, 1964.

Comments on Levin's Paper

JAMES J. GALLAGHER is Kenan Professor of Education, University of North Carolina at Chapel Hill. In addition, Dr. Gallagher is Director of the Frank Porter Graham Child Development Center and Director of the Bush Institute for Child and Family Policy at UNC.

When the concept of educational vouchers first hit the educational scene, I was working in the vineyards of the United States Office of Education near the end of the Johnson era and the beginning of the Nixon era. It was not a happy time for American education. It was a time filled with disillusionment about the problems of educating disadvantaged children and about the rising costs of education at a time when many powerful politicians wanted to find additional funds to support the Vietnam War. In this atmosphere, the concept of educational vouchers had that degree of simplicity and clarity that has strong appeal to people who like simple solutions to complex problems.

I suspected then, and my suspicions are even stronger now, that vouchers were popular, not so much because of their educational validity, but because they could hide the real purposes of some of their supporters. First, by changing the major system of educational financing, vouchers could make it relatively easy to reduce the total sum of money spent on education. Second, vouchers could disguise the controversial issue of public support for parochial schools. Proponents of such support had been—and continue to be—frustrated by court decisions based on the principle of separation of church and state. They reasoned, however, that if all families were choosing their own schools, parochial schools might successfully withstand a court challenge because they would then be one among many schools that parents could choose. Finally, there were those who wanted to use vouchers as a device to resegregate the schools by permitting white families to choose white schools for their children.

Levin correctly identifies a number of the ironies associated with voucher proposals. One of the strongest ironies is that although vouchers are theoretically designed to equalize educational opportunity, they actually encourage the conditions for remarkably unequal education. It is a rare occurrence when a state legislature appropriates enough money to provide for even a basic level of education through local schools. This does not pose a serious problem for wealthy communities that can supplement state appropriations with enough money to provide a reasonable education for their children, but it is a severe blow to poor communities in which the financial base is inadequate to supplement state appropriations. Vouchers would do nothing to alleviate this basic source of inequity in our nation's schools and may well enhance the gap between poor and wealthy districts.

A second irony that Levin identifies is that vouchers are touted as a means of providing some degree of power and authority to those who are powerless—the poor and minority groups—but they actually do nothing of the sort. It is no surprise that many proponents of vouchers can be found at the University of Chicago or Harvard or Stanford, the fortresses of wealthy and upper-class citizens. The notion that parents will shop around to find the best school for their child easily draws forth the image of wealthy families taking their sons and daughters on tours of elegant prep schools that will prepare them for higher education. But try to muster a picture of a poor family with six or seven youngsters on a similar tour, even if the "tour" covers only their own limited community. Thus, the control that vouchers give parents would be used mainly by middle- and upper-class families to ensure that their children get a quality education while low-income youngsters might well have a decreased opportunity for a similar quality education.

That these predictions would be confirmed by practice can be inferred from one situation in which vouchers have actually been tried. A number of states now have introduced the voucher concept in providing specialized or supplementary education for handicapped children. In the State of New York, for example, local communities have had the option of providing either services for handicapped children or a voucher allowing parents to seek appropriate educational programs for their handicapped youngster wherever such programs can be found. Before the introduction of this system, New York State had shown a year-by-year increment in the number of public school programs for handicapped children. When the voucher concept was introduced, allowing school systems the option of providing a voucher instead of increased services, the expansion of local programs stopped abruptly. School systems found it much easier merely to hand parents a check than to design and operate an effective special education program. The check, incidentally, often did not cover the real cost of special education.

The potential for success of the voucher system really depends on whether the condition it is designed to remedy is, in fact, the true problem. Basically, the voucher system suggests that the fundamental problem of education is that educators lack the motivation to perform their job correctly. Only the threat of a free marketplace hanging over them will force educators to straighten out and fly right. But is lack of motivation really the problem? Can one picture in this era of modern education a series of self-contained school systems dotting the land, each competing busily against the others? And what of the inefficiency caused by each system providing its own speech therapist, psychologist, and a whole range of special services for its youngsters, while three miles down the road another school or school system is doing the same?

Most states, for efficiency and economy, have organized support services on a regional basis including regional dissemination and training programs. Vouchers would place such across-system cooperation at a definite risk. Educational programs have become increasingly interdependent in their use of resources. Vouchers would encourage the opposite trend.

In my opinion, the sole value of vouchers has been to loosen people's assumption about educational financing. In a field where discussion tends to be remarkably rigid and sterile, such a result is not without its desirable effects. We need to think creatively about our educational problems and what can be done about them. Vouchers, however, are in my judgment, the wrong solution to these problems, based both on the wrong diagnosis and a completely mistaken conceptualization of educational systems.

JAMES P. COMER is Associate Dean for Student Affairs and the Maurice Falk Professor of Child Psychiatry at Yale University's School of Medicine. He also directs the school unit of the Child Study Center at Yale where he has headed an inner-city school program since 1968. In addition to serving as a consultant to numerous government agencies, public school systems, and universities, Dr. Comer has lectured on topics related to child development and social welfare programs throughout the United States and in eight foreign nations. Among his numerous publications, many of which have been reprinted in scholarly and popular books, Dr. Comer received widespread acclaim for his book, *Black Child Care* (Pocket Books, 1976), coauthored with Dr. Alvin F. Poussaint.

6

Relationships between School and Family— Policy Implications of an Inner-City School Program

Every society must make adequate provision for the development and socialization of its children. The family, the smallest unit of society, is universally charged with this responsibility. In our society, and in most of the world, the school has been developed to aid in this task. Thus, the family and the school are the backbones of society, the foundation and center beam upon and around which it grows and thrives or sags and collapses.

For the young, family and school are the templates of society, miniatures and models of the world they must function in as adults. Parents, teachers, and other school personnel are important carriers of the culture. Through interaction with children, they stimulate their psychological, social, moral, and intellectual development consistent with the expectations of a given society.

In order to do so adequately, those responsible for caretaking or child rearing must have a reasonable level of psychological, social, and intellectual competence and morality themselves. They must be motivated to carry out the child-rearing task in a fashion deemed desirable by the society. Economic, political, educational, and other societal conditions and arrangements, as well as individual endowment, determine whether these conditions exist.

Driven largely by scientific and technological developments, societal conditions have changed over time, particularly in the last 75 years. So too has the relationship between home and school, though this change has not always been recognized and responded to appropriately. For this reason, it will be helpful here to outline the timeless developmental needs of children and the child-rearing tasks of parents and school staff before addressing the relationship between home and school. I then explore the manner in which scientific and technological developments have altered the needs of children and the task of adults responsible for rearing children. In addition, I shall discuss the impact of relevant economic, educational, and other social arrangements on the ability of parents and the school to carry out the child-rearing and educational tasks.

Finally, based on an example of the kind of family-school relationships needed for these two institutions to collaborate successfully, I shall draw some conclusions about policy.

CHILD DEVELOPMENT AND CHILD REARING

Children are born totally dependent for survival on parents and other caretakers. They possess only a biological potential for growth and a biopsychological force often called *aggressive, libidinal,* or *survival energy.* They have a capacity to form a psychosocial attachment to caretakers or other frequently interacting individuals. These people are in a position to influence the growth and development of the dependent child in every area. Thus, the caretaker's task is to help the child move from total dependency through a level of maturation necessary to function optimally as an adult in a given society.

Children are born with numerous potential capacities which can be developed. I shall outline rearing and resultant development in the six most critical areas—biological, intellectual, speech and language, psychological, social, and moral.

The diffuse, unchanneled life energy of infants and toddlers is first expressed in aggressive, selfish, and self-centered behavior. They want what they want now, instantly, immediately, even yesterday. When frustrated, they bite, fight, and have temper tantrums. The desired toy of another child is taken, not requested or shared. A brother or sister receiving too much of a parent's attention is pushed aside or abused.

Every parent can provide participant-observer evidence of the young child's potential for exploitative and abusive attitudes and behavior in relationships with others. Where there are failures of psychosocial and moral development, these traits persist with only slight modification into later childhood and adulthood. Parents begin the civilizing and socializing process at birth.

Providing body care, food, and other pleasure stimulates curiosity in the child. This promotes grasping, sitting, standing, and actual physical growth. As the child achieves one new skill after another and the important caretaker displays approval, the infant becomes "addicted" to a pattern of performance and approval and actively seeks it.

Initially, the caretaker is the only available model and is imitated by the child. Eventually the child takes over, with personal modifications, the behavior of the caretaker as his or her own. In time this occurs with other members of the family or close social network. Thus, the child learns and assumes much of the behavior pattern of the caretaker and social network and through them, of the larger society. From this base, individual thought and expression emerge.

Talking to, and otherwise interacting with, the child encourages efforts at vocalization. In the process the child learns to say "Bye Bye" and wave, one of the first social skills. The accumulation of social skills continues.

The caretaker can encourage the toddler to ask for a desired toy, share it with others, or do something else rather than take it by force. He points out that other children will be angry or will not want to play with him if he pushes or shoves them. In this way, the child develops control of impulses, restraint, and negotiation skills. The caretaker anticipates the child's movement toward the hot stove and either stops him or urges caution, explaining the danger without the child having to experience the painful consequences.

The caretaker promotes and enlarges the child's investigative play and interests through attention and questions which support the development of language, thinking, logic, and reality testing. The child is motivated to give up harmful and unacceptable behavior, partially because of negative experience, such as injury or unpleasant sensations, but primarily because of disapproval of the parent whose relationship is important.

In this process, the child learns to use speech for communication. He learns to think about the consequences of behavior before acting on every impulse. He learns to relate yesterday's experience to today's and tomorrow's. He begins to learn to organize and plan. Diffuse energy is channeled and made available to be used in sustained and creative activites and learning. Children who have those experiences are on their way to becoming the masters of their life energy. They can use this energy to achieve rather than be embarrassed by its uncontrolled expression in undesirable behavior.

Through the relationship with the caretaker, the child also obtains several critical moral values. The pursuit of pleasure characteristic of childhood makes manipulation, exploitation, lying, and stealing "legal" or normal. Parents, in a number of encounters, establish the notion that these traits are undesirable. They establish, or should establish, the notion that honesty, fair play, justice, respect for the rights of others, and contributing to the common good are desirable values. The competent caretaker encourages the child to accept attitudes, values, and styles which enable him (or her) to meet her (or his) needs without compromising the rights and needs of others.

These traits represent a high level of human functioning and are not easily acquired. They must be established and reinforced over the entire period between infancy and mature young adulthood.

The relationships established with the parent or early caretakers should be transferred to the school or teacher and the child's development should continue. Teachers should set new and appropriate models of social behavior. They should help children develop skills and capacities necessary to cope in the world beyond the home. They should help children learn the rules, laws, and values of the larger society. Successful performance in the world beyond the home brings the child the respect and approval of peers, parents, teachers, and important others. This, in turn, enhances the child's self-esteem and competence and makes successful performance a greater possibility as well as a worthwhile goal in the future.

The achievement habit first established in infancy is strengthened in the school-age child who is developing well. Eventually the encouragement of caretakers and important others becomes less necessary to reinforce and motivate achievement and desirable behavior because the child sets and lives up to his or her own developing prosocial inner standards.

Finally, parents help youngsters through the difficult period of adolescence in which moving from a dependent to a more independent state in a complex and challenging society is often a traumatic experience. Parents do this best by allowing and encouraging reasonable independence and by establishing fair and consistent rules. They must be compassionate and tolerant of adolescent struggles, yet they must not abdicate their responsibility for guiding and facilitating the youngster's development. The same is true of school personnel.

Development along all of these important lines can be impaired when parents and teachers cannot or do not interact with children in appropriate ways. Chaotic conditions in the home and at school can interfere with development. The existence of troublesome and strongly antisocial peer groups can undermine the teaching and modeling of parents and school personnel. Difficulties among parents, teachers, and children, chaotic home conditions, and antisocial peer groups all complicate the task of child rearing. And each of these complicating factors is related to, and exacerbated by, the technological changes that have changed the face of American society during this century. It is to those technological changes that we now turn our attention.

SCIENCE AND TECHNOLOGY

At the turn of the century, this nation had only entered the world of electrical technology. Most people lived on farms and in small towns. Mobility was limited; cultural life was provincial. The economy was less complicated. Social relationships and expectations between powerful and less powerful people, between adults and children, and within families were explicit. Social life was centered around personal institutions—family, church, and social clubs.

Parents, teachers, ministers, policemen and others came in contact with each other in nonofficial ways. The teacher sometimes assisted the head of a farm family with business matters. The policeman was a deacon in the local church. He and other community leaders held the same jobs for many years. With limited travel, communication, and information, rural people generally spoke with a "common tongue" about right and wrong attitudes, values and ways, or desirable social customs and practices. As the holders of vital and unchallenged information, protectors and providers for the young, they had a great deal of authority.

Obviously abuse of authority was possible under such conditions. The rights and opportunities of minorities, women and children were often abused. But these conditions also gave individuals few options for correct behavior and made life quite predictable. It was possible to earn a living or produce basic survival needs—food, clothing, and shelter—with a low level of education and training. Belief systems—from religion to nationalism—reduced uncertainty and anxiety about life conditions.

Despite injustice and poverty, these conditions created a natural climate of community. Belonging was possible, even though in a prescribed place and way for many. Sharing and communal activities needed for survival contributed to a climate of community. In such an environment, the school was often a trusted and integral part of local society. Parents, teachers, neighbors, fellow church members, and others were expected to aid parents in helping their children to grow physically, intellectually, psychologically, socially, and morally.

Failure to master school subjects created no real problem. The level of education, training, and social skills needed to obtain and hold a job remained low to moderate until the 1940s. When economic conditions in the society were reasonably good, most heads of households could earn a "living wage" or provide goods needed to care for their families. Because change was slow, many rural, native, white American parents reared their children as they had been reared, for an adulthood like their own and like their parents' and grandparents' before them. But this slow pace of change was disrupted.

Transportation technology moved from the horse-and-buggy level of sophistication through the automobile, airplane, jet, and superjet level to a rocket-age level in the short span of 70 years. One can now have breakfast in New York City and late lunch in California. Television brings us information and visual images of attitudes, values, and ways of life from around the world. One can hear differing opinions about desirable morals, social arrangements, and life-styles on newscasts every hour, if not half-hour.

Cars and roads have changed us from rural to urban and suburban dwellers. Movement for employment, pleasure, and status has altered the make-up of our neighborhoods. Mechanization of farming and related changes have vastly complicated our economy. Mobility, urbanization, and technology have facilitated commercial recreation. Sports are often presented or performed by professionals, decreasing healthy, active personal expression.

These and other scientific and technological developments served to increase information but to reduce neighborhood and community intimacy. We are now literally a nation of strangers. There is no "common tongue" about what attitudes, values, and lifeways are right or wrong. Reduced acceptance of religion and other guiding principles and belief systems has increased uncertainty and anxiety about life's problems and possibilities. Parents and schools are trying to prepare children to function in a future nobody can accurately predict. Earning a living wage requires a higher general level of education, training, and social skills than ever needed in the history of the world.

Few parents are in a position to promote such levels of development. The task falls heavily on the school. But the school is no longer a trusted and integral part of the neighborhood. School officials often live outside the community. They often differ in race, religion, income, or social style from the families served by the school. They are no longer, with parents and others, the unchallenged holders of vital truths. The climate of community needed to make it possible for the school staff to facilitate psychological and social development, and in turn academic and intellectual development, no longer naturally exists in many areas. It has to be created.

Probably influenced by the training needed for scientific and technological work, teacher education began to focus almost exclusively on techniques for promoting intellectual development. Although school teachers and administrators today are professionally highly credentialed, few are systematically trained to create the kind of experience in schools which aids psychological, social, and in turn, academic and intellectual development, of children.

Many educators argue that providing a social and psychological growth experience for children is the responsibility of the home exclusively. They view teaching academic skills as their only mission. This denies the inextricable relationships between psychological, social, and intellectual development and academic learning previously outlined. It ignores the fact that the kind of skills needed by children to function well as adults today and in the future are as much social and psychological as academic or intellectual.

From time to time, grave concern is expressed because academic achievement scores of modern students have declined slightly. Unfortunately, no attention has been given to the threshold level of academic achievement needed to perform well at even the most technical and highest-level jobs in our society. Even less attention has been given to the necessary motivational and character traits. There is no real shortage of persons adequately qualified to hold high-skill positions. Indeed, many students are performing at an achievement level high above what is needed. Because of the reduction in unskilled and blue collar jobs, the real shortage is of people with the social and psychological development necessary to hold jobs created by a scientific, technology-based economy. The vast majority of people have the intellectual endowment to do so.

In the past, persons with poor interpersonal skills, low impulse control, and other personal limitations could hold jobs in fishing, farming, and industrial labor. A technology-based economy with an increase in service jobs requires good interpersonal skills, social skills and sophistication, education, and technical training. A child who cannot function well at home and in school— the mold for the adult world—is less likely to fare well in the job market, care for self and family, and contribute positively to the society.

Finally, urbanization facilitated the emergence of a powerful labor movement. Science and technology improved information, communication, and mobility, and eroded the rationale for the denial of rights to anyone. The civil rights movement gained momentum. These developments significantly changed power relationships and increased economic and social expectations of the vast majority of Americans. Now the school is expected to play a key role in making greater opportunity available to greater numbers of people.

Because of the reduced control and direction possible from parents, teachers, and others, children need social and psychological development which facilitates inner control, motivation, direction, and responsibility. Highly authoritarian child-rearing techniques in this age produce dependency or increased parent-child conflict and rebellion. Highly permissive techniques produce selfish assertiveness, inadequate life guidelines, and rebellion. Many families and schools are structured to function in either excessively authoritarian or permissive ways.

The reality of the scientific and technological age is constant change, interaction with differing people and ideas, and increased options for young people in attitudes, values and lifeways. Thus, they must be reared to develop an initial prosocial set of attitudes, values, and lifeways; flexible enough to vary with the demands of a changing society; and tolerant of the attitudes, values, and ways of others. Young people must be prepared to be good problem analysts and solvers, decision makers, and planners. In addition, they must be capable of the organization necessary to implement their plans. They must be competent and motivated to participate in a political and economic system in which negotiation for, rather than imposition of, rights, opportunities, and limits is becoming more and more a reality and perhaps the only viable alternative.

FAMILY SECURITY

Relatively secure parents are best able to carry out the child-rearing task necessary to prepare children to function well in this complex age. The simpler economic system of the past made the provision of basic needs—food, clothing, shelter—reasonably possible for most people. Being able to provide for one's family gave most parents a sense of security. In addition, security came from a sense of belonging in churches, close-knit communities, and other social networks. Religious and other belief systems contributed to this climate of security.

Science and technology continue to decrease unskilled and blue collar job opportunities and to weaken sustaining belief systems. As discussed in the foregoing section, these developments have eliminated the natural sense of community which once existed in neighborhoods. Moreover, economic relief continues to be provided in a demeaning way. No systematic effort has been made to help people receiving public assistance obtain a sense of value, worth, and resultant security and so strengthen their motivation to provide for their families and contribute to society.

The ethos of work and upward mobility is still widely held by individuals in this society. Radio and television comments, newspaper articles, and daily contact with social workers, school officials, grocery store clerks, policemen, and others abuse persons unable to care for themselves and their families. This experience intensifies whatever psychological or social problems interfere with their ability to work in the first place. When no work is available, the outrage is even greater. All these factors combine to make child rearing and emphasis on school achievement much more difficult for these families.

Frustration in the effort to participate in society in a prosocial way often leads to participation in antisocial or illegal economic and social systems. A set of attitudes, values, and lifeways that compete with those of the larger society exist in such systems—selling stolen goods, illegal gambling, prostitution, drug use and sales, beating the system (perceived as the enemy), and so on. Those attitudes, values, and lifeways are transmitted to children just as mainstream prosocial messages and lifeways are transmitted. As large numbers of affected persons are created, schools often find themselves in areas where the attitudes, values, and lifeways are incompatible with academic learning beyond a minimum level.

Many families function well but transmit a culture different than that of the school. This can be a source of conflict and insecurity. Differences in attitudes, values, and lifeways can lead to erroneous or distorted assumptions about the abilities, interests, and motives of children and parents on one side and about the school personnel on the other. Conflict between home and school is more likely in this situation. Because the school represents the mainstream culture, fear of inability to relate well to the school contributes to insecurity among culturally different communities and families. This is true whenever families and school personnel differ in any significant way, such as income, education, or belief systems.

Until very recently, little attention was given to helping parents and teachers develop child-rearing techniques appropriate for this time in our history. Because technological changes have outrun child-rearing changes, serious intergenerational problems often exist. As a result, an increased number of children from middle-income families are challenging the attitudes, values, and lifeways of the mainstream society. Thus, even families with adequate income and members of the mainstream culture are often overwhelmed by the child-rearing task.

THE SCHOOL AND THE FAMILY:
A RATIONALE AND RELATIONSHIP MODEL

Child rearing is a universal function of the family. In spite of rapid past and future scientific and technological developments, this task is not likely to change significantly. Because of the high level and sustained period of development needed to function in present and future society, the school must be intimately involved with parents in the child-rearing and educational task. The latter, education, cannot proceed adequately without the former, appropriate child rearing.

The child-rearing task has been complicated by the loss of a natural sense of community. Trust and reinforcement of attitudes, values, and lifeways between home and school authority figures no longer naturally exist, i.e., there is less of the natural transfer of the authority and affection from home to school necessary to manage and motivate child behavior and learning. Today the sense of community and trust needed for school personnel to serve as parent surrogates must be carefully created.

Even in the past, the conditions necessary to promote high levels of academic and social development were not widespread. The potential of many students was not realized. But they could easily be absorbed into an unskilled work force. Today young people without reasonably high levels of social and educational development cannot be easily absorbed. Their frustration, anger, and alienation give rise to many social problems, all of which can grow worse in future decades without more efficient child development.

To fully address these problems, community economic development with resultant employment is necessary. When this is not possible, unemployment with dignity will be required. More attention must be given to the way cities and neighborhoods can create a climate of community, value, and worth among its families. But it is possible for most schools to address this need now, even without the major social changes needed. I turn now to an example which illustrates the process of developing positive family and school relations that create a climate of community and promote improved social and academic performance without change in society at large.

THE YALE CHILD STUDY CENTER SCHOOLS PROGRAM

Since 1968, the Yale Child Study Center has collaborated in a school development program in an almost all Black, low-income section of New Haven. The program started in two elementary schools and continued for five years until 1973, when the Child Study Center withdrew from one school because of internal conflicts. Minimal services were provided to the remaining school, a 350-student, K-4 institution, until 1975 when a social skills curriculum project was developed and implemented. Since 1977, a field test of the intervention process has been conducted in a third elementary school and a middle school serving grades 5-9.

The Child Study Center uses a preventive approach focusing on the complex network of relationships among *all* participants in the school program—administrators, teachers, support staff, children, and parents. The intervention team—two social workers, a psychologist, a psychiatrist, and a teacher—is particularly concerned with developing a mutuality of purpose among school people, parents, and university staff. Recognizing that there is no "quick fix" to the complicated problems of schools, our choice was to develop long-term strategies for institutional change through working closely with one or two schools, eventually moving the process throughout the New Haven school system and beyond.

In the ten years we have worked at one of the original elementary schools—the Martin Luther King School—there has been gradual neighborhood change from a population with a small core of middle-income Black families to a predominantly Black, low-income group with a disproportionately high number of transient and very troubled families. In 1969, King ranked thirty-second of the 33 New Haven elementary schools in Metropolitan Achievement Test reading and math scores. There was a high student and teacher absentee rate, as well as frequent conflict between children, between children and staff, and between parents and the school.

In 1976 and 1977, despite the increased percentage of children from poor families, King students who had been in the program two years or more scored at grade level on both reading and math achievement tests. As a group, King students had the highest scores of any of the 22 Title I schools in New Haven. King also had the third best citywide attendance in 1976 and second best in 1977. Many factors were responsible for these changes, but involvement of parents and subsequent improvement of the relationships among school, community, and family have perhaps been the most significant.

Like many 1960s school intervention programs involving collaboration between mainstream institutions and poor Black communities, this one had a troublesome first year. Conflicts over the value of open education, race-related problems, and decision-making authority were but a few of the many problems. Parents were angry with the establishment—the New Haven public schools, Yale, New Haven city officials, and so on. They were concerned that these people enjoyed prestige, power, and privilege, but did not meet their responsibility to improve the quality of education or the opportunities and conditions of life for people in poor and minority neighborhoods.

The initial engagement with parents was heated, potentially all-consuming, and destructive to the program. But it was also the energy source which eventually made the program work. The very parents most involved in the initial fighting about whether Yale should be involved in their school became the first parents to participate in child-development and parenting programs, to work on decision-making committees, and to initiate and develop special projects.

The struggle between parents and professionals, whether expressed actively or by the passive hostility of noninvolvement, is not a necessary ingredient for successful parent participation in school programs, but it is common. A longer, closer period of pre-program collaboration and planning, better organization, and other situational factors might have prevented this struggle. The point here, however, is that program leaders engaged the parents in a dialogue about problems, needs, and goals and established the mechanisms to address and achieve them. The mechanisms and processes devised to achieve program goals were based on principles of social science and behavior. Parent-school engagement based on such knowledge is needed widely.

That the school was not a natural part of the community was a major cause of mistrust and alienation between home and school. The intervention team also noted that because teachers and administrators were not trained to deal with behavior problems or to create a climate of community, relationships between administrators and teachers or between teachers and support staff were troublesome. The resultant conflicts and difficulties made good relationships between children and teachers impossible in all but the most exceptional situations. Thus, the intervention team created a Steering Committee designed to deal with these problems.

The Steering Committee was representative of all participants in the program—administrators, parents, teachers, and support staff. Subcommittees were responsible for personnel selection, and extracurricular and curricular program development. The Steering Committee served a number of functions: problem identification, resource identification, program development, implementation, and evaluation. It also established priorities and overall school program direction. Because this body was representative, each group in the school could feel that it had a part in the decision-making process.

Because such an arrangement can create a paralysis of analysis and bog down in power struggles, the body was advisory to the principal who had legal responsibility for the educational program. On the other hand, the principal understood that he would lose parent interest if he were not responsive to group input.

The make-up of the Steering Committee facilitated the growth of trust and cooperation between all participants in the educational process. Had the program been conducted in middle and secondary schools, students would have been involved in the governance process so far as they could make responsible contributions.

The participation of parents in program planning and decision making gave them an investment in the outcome of the school program. Such participation took place at three levels. A core of 25 to 30 parents in each school was responsible for planning extracurricular activities for each school along with school staff. Parents who were comfortable and successful at this level were usually selected by their peers to represent them on the Steering Committee, the most influential and demanding level of participation. Parents who, for one reason or another, could not be involved at the other two levels turned out for school functions because they were encouraged to do so by participating parents who had a high investment in the outcome of programs they helped develop. Also, participating and nonparticipating parents came to trust the school staff.

Summer workshops in which parents and teachers learned together and associated socially reduced most of the stereotypes they held about each other. The workshops permitted parents and teachers to get to know each other as individuals rather than as professionals or nonprofessionals, Blacks or whites, middle-income or low-income people. The workshops also permitted parents and teachers to explore old and new concepts in education.

The involvement of parents encouraged healthy elements of the culture and community life to be brought into the school. Without this, the culture of the school is often a foreign body in many communities. Bake sales, fashion shows, gospel choir presentations, and the like—activities familiar to parents from their church participation—helped to raise money in support of academic programs, permitted lively extracurricular school activities, and fostered a positive relationship between home and school.

The Intervention Team focused on health, not illness or weakness. The team helped administrators understand and appreciate the value of shared decision making. The social worker who had major responsibility for the day-to-day work of the program helped parents develop the skills necessary to participate in decision making—privately helping the parent organizing president learn to run an effective meeting, helping the secretary keep notes, and the treasurer learn to keep a financial record. In return, parents shared insights about their children and contributed to a friendly climate of accountability often missing when professionals have sole responsibility for what goes on in schools. For example, parents working with staff were particularly good in selecting new school personnel with traits that would contribute to a positive climate of living and learning in the schools.

The Intervention Team also helped teachers develop child-rearing techniques that should have been, but were not, taught in school. Using lecture techniques to teach child-rearing skills was not successful. The problem was less a lack of knowledge than ability to apply it under stress in the classroom. Thus, in case conferences and in classroom observations, the team and individual teachers observed and discussed behavior and learning problems and worked out ways of coping based on social science, educational, and behavioral principles. In most cases, such approaches were sufficient. In rare cases, children received individual therapy.

The case conferences proved so successful at King school that teachers began to come to the presentations of other teachers voluntarily. Eventually these conferences turned into seminars in which teachers shared suggestions about dealing with social and educational problems. Teacher inquiries and perceptions gradually changed from what was right and wrong with a child's behavior or performance to a concern with the child's psychosocial situation; from the notion that a child was bright or stupid to a search for the learning problem and a focus on strengths. The search for problems focused as much on school procedures and operations as on the "acting-up" or withdrawn child and the poor learner.

As problem after problem was reduced, teachers were able to give more energy to teaching, to academic curriculum development, and to identifying problems and strengths of children in their particular school. As conditions improved, parents found themselves called to school less and less for problems and more and more to contribute to the positive social and learning processes of the school. This situation was largely responsible for the fact that parent attendance at various performances and programs at King school increased from about 20 to between 200 and 250. Indeed, nearly 400 parents came to one Christmas program in this school with a population of only 350 students.

At this stage, innovative programs worked. A special program for apathetic and "turned-off" youngsters was successful. A program to increase continuity of relationships by keeping teachers with the same class for two years was successful. Nonsuccessful programs and programs proposed by outsiders could be evaluated and accepted or rejected on the basis of school needs rather than because they were supposed to be "progressive."

With growing success, future planning took place in a climate of hope. Parents themselves initiated child-rearing seminars. This made it possible for the Intervention Team to introduce child-rearing approaches appropriate for modern conditions. Parents planned and participated in programs with staff designed to familiarize them with the academic subject areas. Some eventually became involved in a paid classroom assistant program. Parents and teachers also developed a curriculum which integrated the teaching of the arts with social and academic skills.

One social skills unit on politics involved inviting the mayoralty candidates into the schools. In preparation for this visit, parents financed a bus tour to introduce children to problems and opportunities in the city and explained the responsibility of public officials to address these issues. Teachers and parents prepared the children to ask the candidates responsible questions and to engage in give-and-take discussions with them. The children were prepared to serve as hosts and hostesses for the affair. They received a practical language arts lesson through related invitation, thank you note, letter, and report writing. In this way, low-income children were being introduced to and receiving the social skills necessary to participate in the mainstream adult society.

The participation of parents and the inclusion of community-based activities assured that the program was culturally relevant. Indeed, when parents and teachers work together, cultural differences are not as marked as they first appear; differences are appreciated and respected.

This approach was useful in a low-income, predominantly Black community in New Haven. It is not being proposed as an ideal model for parent-school relations everywhere. What is suggested is that a problem identification, resource identification, program development, and evaluation group is needed in all schools. A systematic effort to identify and reduce the source of distrust and conflict is universally needed. Parental involvement in the school program is perhaps not needed in the intimate manner of the King-Child Study Center Program, but parent involvement can restore the climate of trust and bring about better home-school and intergenerational understanding and relations.

Schools cannot continue trying to teach academic skills in a social climate which works against such skills and which interferes with healthy psychological and social skill development. Schools cannot continue to ignore the inextricable relation between academic learning and social and psychological development. The high level of such development now required for good adult functioning necessitates a school climate in which such development can take place.

A word of caution is important here. Other schools and individuals have looked at one or more components of the King-Child Study Center Program and attempted to transplant them in their own setting. This will not work. The process is more important than program content in establishing a good home-school climate and a good in-school climate. Comprehensive change in programs involving every aspect of school life and all the people concerned is necessary.

I have overly simplified a very complex process. I have not discussed the many mistakes, frustrations, disappointments, and traumatic incidents which occurred in this particular program. My purpose is to promote discussion and to show that improved school operation and home-school relations can take place even in socioeconomically stressed communities.

POLICY IMPLICATIONS

A number of policy implications may be drawn from this program. Some are related to schools and education; others, to the functioning of families. Those related to families—income opportunities, social network membership and participation, and so on—are too complex to discuss here. Thus, I will confine my comments in this discussion to policies relevant to parent participation in schools where there is alienation between home and school.

Parental support of school efforts—whether it is direct and within the school setting or the general support of school staff and goals from outside the school—requires school staffs to appreciate relationship issues and to improve their ability to promote students' social and psychological development. Despite some increased attention to theories of child development and human relations, most teacher and administrator training programs provide too little supervised field work in which these issues are stressed. Most teacher and administrator field experiences focus more on the transmission of academic knowledge and on system operations than on the techniques needed to establish and maintain a high quality of relationship between home and school, among school staff, between teachers and students, and among students.

Although adequate attention must continue to be given to history of education, theory of education, teaching methods, and academic subjects, educators need to develop policies and programs which will enable future teachers and administrators to work with parents to create a school climate that enhances psychological and social development.

A related problem is that most teachers are exposed to the expectations and realities of a classroom and school too late in their training. Some could and would leave the field if they were exposed to the classroom earlier; others would be counseled out. Early exposure would also put pressure on college educators to develop policies and programs geared to the "front-line" needs of teachers, and particularly working with families. The trend toward providing future teachers with supervised school experience during the first year and throughout their undergraduate period is a useful policy which one hopes will become standard practice.

In addition, if teachers and administrators are to support the psychological, social, and intellectual development of students—a stated goal of education—then they must be prepared to use the services of behavioral and social science specialists—social workers, psychologists, psychiatrists, special education teachers—and vice versa. Currently, each of these professions is trained separately with a distinct value system and treatment techniques. As a result, there is little understanding, and sometimes even disdain, for the capabilities and limits of others' disciplines. This situation contributes to a much less than optimal working relationship among professionals in education, and to a poor working relationship between home and school. Policies and programs which would bring all school professionals together in a core curriculum early in their training could improve their later working relationships and their ability to work with families and students.

The pace of technological and social change has not slowed in recent years, but the growth in student population has. School program and policy changes in response to rapid social change over the past two decades were never the rule, and are now even less so. These trends mean that fewer new teachers and administrators will be added to existing school staffs. School personnel in many places are retreating from even relatively minor and limited curriculum innovations adopted in the 1960s and 70s. The back-to-basics movement, elimination of arts and athletic programs, elimination of parent participation programs, and others are evidence of this trend. At the same time, evidence mounts that a return to "old ways" is not a realistic approach to providing good education today.

The program discussed in this paper is not the answer to educational problems everywhere. But a search process like the one used at the King school is a reasonable approach everywhere. Policies and programs can be developed allowing a school or schools within each school system to function as research and development units in which every aspect of the educational process—including the value of parent participation—is explored. Findings from work in a particular unit can be used by other similar schools. Such an approach should not be imposed on a system nor carried out by an outside group in isolation. Rather, the initiative should come from each school system—perhaps supported by, or done in collaboration with, an outside group—in order to change or improve its own functioning.

Where school systems do encourage parent participation in school governance and management, attention should be given to preparing administrators, teachers, parents, and human relations specialists to work together. School systems should attempt to finance such training as well as research and development efforts. Support for these programs from state and federal government would be a wise investment, for the benefits of much financial support for education are limited by poor working relationships among educators, human relations staff, and parents.

Finally, either locally or nationally, some program effort to integrate the teaching of social skills, the arts, athletics, and subject area academics is indicated. Academic material in many subjects has little meaning to many students in the abstract. Yet presented in the context of adult experience, simulated or real, mathematics, reading, history, and other subjects can interest the same students. In addition, we found that arts and athletics provided an excellent milieu in which to support the social, psychological, and moral development of students who had not had enough supportive experience. The inclusion of parents in this process gave it legitimacy and direction. Given the complexity of today's society, students from all income groups could benefit from such an emphasis. In short, we need policies which broaden the objectives of our current curriculum and provide students with skills enabling them to deal with the complex adult world of today and tomorrow.

Comments on Comer's Paper

DALE C. FARRAN is Assistant Professor of Special Education at the University of North Carolina at Chapel Hill and an Investigator at the Frank Porter Graham Child Development Center. Dr. Farran is also on the faculty of the Bush Institute for Child and Family Policy at UNC.

This paper begins with a short quiz. No one needs to see your paper and there are no right or wrong answers. Simply, the test asks, do you know these names: Ivan Illich, John Holt, Jonathan Kozol, Herb Kohl, George Dennison, James Hearndon, Mario Fantini? If you do, chances are you are:

—Over 30.
—Concerned about education; and
—A past participant in the great radical reform education movement of the late 1960s.

Many of the factors Dr. Comer mentioned in his talk were responsible for the radical reform education movement of the '60s—such factors as a sense of loss of community; a great separation, daily growing wider, between minority cultures and the schools attended by minority children; the failure of schools to educate children who came to them most in need; and the steadily diminishing job possibilities for those who were not educated.

For a while, North Carolina was a participant in the great reform movement. In 1964, Terry Sanford, then governor, established the North Carolina Advancement School to help *underachievers*—those who were not doing as well as they should in school. In keeping with the *zeitgeist* of the times, a *zeitgeist* enhanced in large part by the availability of a large number of idealists who did not want to fight in Vietnam and who could avoid it by teaching, the Advancement School quickly decided that the problem lay not with the individual student but with the schools. It was not that children were not learning; it was that they were not being taught.

My first job after graduating from college was in the North Carolina Advancement School. I mention the school not to tell you about my background particularly nor even to tell you about the school's efforts here in North Carolina. I mention it as a way of commenting on urban education; for in 1967, one year before Yale began in the Baldwin and King schools, the legislature of North Carolina decided it no longer wanted the Advancement School as it was then constituted. The legislature invited us, in effect, to leave, and 17 staff members packed up their families and moved to Philadelphia at the behest of the new superintendent in the Philadelphia School District. We were convinced, with complete optimism, that we could solve the ills of urban education. After all, we had a three-year Title I grant. The difference between us and the Yale Child Study Center is that Yale is still involved in the King School and all of us, along with some 30 other staff members, have long since departed from Philadelphia for calmer, more rewarding pursuits.

Why were we there? One is familiar with the statistics: big cities had (and still have) poor achievement, low attendance rates, great violence among students, and poor morale and high turnover among teaching staffs. One can trade anecdotes about the horrors of the urban educational system. Dr. Comer has refrained from giving you his, but I want to mention a couple from my own experience so that you can appreciate the extent of his accomplishments at the King School:

- —As of April 1971, there were four junior high schools in Philadelphia in which more than 50 percent of the faculty had less than two years' experience.
- —As many other urban systems had done, Philadelphia had emphasized large plants in its school building construction. In one city block in Philadelphia, a school complex enrolled nearly 4000 children—2500 in a junior high and about 1500 in an elementary school.

  The problem here was that large numbers of children in one building with inexperienced staff created an explosive situation. In Philadelphia, street gangs added another element. In one new magnet school in Philadelphia, it was estimated that there were 22 street gangs represented in the student body. In neighborhoods around the buildings, school administrators created "safety corridors"—patrolled by principals, vice-principals, and nonteaching-assistants—consisting of streets which were safe for children to use while walking to school.

- —In one junior high school, by February 1972, there had been five gang-related deaths among the student body in that school year alone, including one on the front steps of the school building.
- —Many schools sawed the handles off all except the front door to allow only supervised entrance to the school.

Teachers are frightened in such schools, students are frightened—and so are their parents. Is a solution possible? If it is, it must be of the type Dr. Comer described—slow, persistent, and determined, aimed at changing the relationship between the schools and their communities, moving that relationship from one of mutual distrust and antagonism to one of mutual concern and willingness to work on joint problems.

The Advancement School in Philadelphia was peopled by too many of what Jonathan Kozol termed the "eloquent failures" (Kozol, 1972, p. 75)—white, affluent, young people with advanced degrees, who briefly devoted some time to revitalizing urban education much as they once tried brown rice and health foods or joined the political process by working for George McGovern. None of it worked. They moved on, but the problems persisted. For as Kozol also claimed, it is ". . . an irrefutable, if agonizing, fact that poor kids in this nation have been technically retarded in a thousand measurable ways by public education. They know it. Their folks know it. Their white racist school boards know it. Only their liberal friends are scared to say it" (1972, pp. 149-150).

Of course, this was not the way education was supposed to work. The common school was brought into being as a means of educating the "common" people. But as early as 1833, Silberman noted that "the very success of the public school tended to remove it further from the very class of children for whose benefit it was originally established" (1970, p. 60). Silberman's *Crisis in the Classroom* also reported that public education had helped very few immigrant ethnic minorities to achieve middle-class status. Status tended to be achieved through business, politics, and crime. Once such status had been achieved, education was valued. Poor Blacks, however, have been denied access to middle-class status through avenues other than public education and denied public education as an avenue as well. They have not been helped by well-meaning, liberal, highly educated whites who told them in the late '60s that they did not need to be educated—only to be "happy" and "doing their own thing." Kenneth Clark commented at the time that it was easy to deny the importance of a Ph.D. once you had one.

Dr. Comer's approach seems quite understandably to have had more success. His intervention efforts have affected both parents and children, a major feat. He has raised the skill levels of children, the involvement of parents, and the ability of teachers to focus on individual children and solutions to problems. Universities which sit in the midst of urban decay—Temple and the University of Pennsylvania in Philadelphia, Johns Hopkins in Baltimore, the University of Chicago, Columbia in New York, UCLA in Los Angeles—often wonder what they can do to be relevant to their surroundings and to show commitment to the communities around them. The efforts of the Yale Child Study Center at the King school offer an excellent model. Universities are stable while government grants come and go; federal money given to school districts often fails to make any difference to the schools which need it most. But universities could do more of what Dr. Comer has done. Instead of running lab schools of their own, they could work in inner-city schools. Only, however, with the stamina which Yale has shown at King; only if those in charge believe change is possible and are determined to work until it is achieved; only if there is respect for the people with whom the university works; and only if universities become involved and then stay indefinitely to guarantee results.

REFERENCES

Kozol, J. *Free schools.* Boston: Houghton Mifflin, 1972.
Silberman, C. E. *Crisis in the classroom: The remaking of American education.* New York: Random House, 1970.

Comments on Comer's Paper

WILLIS D. HAWLEY is Director of the Center for Educational Policy and Associate Professor of Policy Sciences and Political Science at Duke University.

Jim Comer's talk is significant for at least three reasons. First, we have all too few successes to which we can point when we talk about efforts to enhance the effectiveness of schools, especially those in central cities. Second, at a time when we are focused on so-called basic skills, it is useful to be reminded of the central importance of values and interpersonal skills and the relationship between cognitive and other aspects of learning. Third, Comer emphasizes that we need to reduce the discontinuity between home and school experiences.

An important cause of Jim Comer's success in the New Haven schools is the involvement of parents in decision-making. Indeed, one is tempted to argue that Comer's program is set apart from so many other "innovative" education programs by the direct participation of parents at all stages of the intervention process. Because of my own belief that parents are a necessary part of any program designed to reverse the steady decline in student performance and public confidence in education, I would like to summarize the arguments supporting the importance of parent involvement and to propose a series of policy recommendations for fostering effective parent involvement in the public schools.

There are at least four powerful arguments for increasing the level and type of parent involvement in public education. First, recent educational research suggests that when parents participate in educational programs, their children's performance improves. The connection seems to lie in parent and student attitudes. When children observe their parents having an impact on the school situation, the children's self-image becomes more positive. When parents are involved, they probably communicate more positive attitudes to their children. Many parents need to learn how to be better teachers and what behavioral patterns are most likely to result in higher achievement. Schools that understand this and seek to address the need are likely to be more effective. From these findings, it appears that increasing public and parent involvement in education has a beneficial effect on learning—an effect that would not be costly to achieve.

Second, substantive interaction among parents and school personnel can reduce the discontinuity between school and home environments. In school, children often confront different priorities and expectations than they do at home and in their neighborhoods. This discontinuity probably increases as the child grows older and is exacerbated by policies like desegregation and mainstreaming which increase the social heterogeneity of schools. Discontinuity of these sorts can be a source of discipline problems, student confusion and alienation, and other behavioral difficulties. Parents who are treated with respect and made to feel that they are expected to shape the learning environment are likely to assist teachers in understanding their children and seeking accommodations—which may involve changes in both school and home—that reduce the disparity between school and nonschool contexts.

A third reason for increasing parent participation in education is that such involvement is likely to increase parental and community support for, and commitment to, school improvement. One may think of schools as organizations and parents as members. It is a well-established principle of behavior in organizations that people who share in setting goals and designing ways goals can be achieved are more committed to the organization and to assuring its effectiveness through their own efforts. In other words, opportunities for participation are likely to create a greater commitment to the school's success. One might go a bit further, with the risk of appearing overly optimistic, to suggest that a positive disposition by schools toward parent involvement in decisions and activities affecting their children might serve to redirect antisocial participation into prosocial activity. Involvement is a recognition of worth.

Finally, parental involvement may facilitate adaptiveness in schools. The needs of learners and the things to be learned are many and varied. To be effective, schools and teachers must be *adaptive*. They must avoid routinization, stereotyping, and other sources of rigidity while seeing themselves as problem solvers. To solve problems one must have good information, resist the tendency to assume that past answers will be appropriate to present and future challenges, and develop new resources. When parents feel they can and should identify problems and can make suggestions that will be listened to, they are likely to provide useful information and ideas. This, in turn, can cause school personnel to rethink or question behavior and programs that will benefit from reexamination.

Despite these reasons for increasing the role of parents in public education, parents are not often provided opportunities to directly shape the learning opportunities available to their children. And even when such opportunities exist, parents may fail to bring about the outcomes I suggested are possible. The ways to best address these matters will vary by community. The bottom line, however, is that parent involvement needs to be structured and institutionalized. It is not "natural" at this stage of public school history for most parents and most educators to feel comfortable with parent involvement in policymaking and implementation. Yet, it is extensive rather than peripheral involvement which holds the greatest promise of fostering higher-quality education.

Let me suggest, then, some types of structural arrangements that seem to hold promise for fostering effective parent involvement in the schools. First teacher-parent councils should be set up at the school level. Some mechanisms for information sharing across a school district may be appropriate, but parents are most likely to have the needed motivation and information with respect to the schools their children attend. Districtwide citizen or parent committees are too removed from the action and too easily manipulated by professional educators.

Second, teachers and parents should have equal representation on the school council. Teachers and parents should be partners in the change process. Teachers need to be empowered to the point that they are not defensive and do not lose their identity as a group. This, in turn, may reduce the tendency of administrators to dominate PTA's or school councils.

Third, persons serving on the council should be elected, and the processes for nominating candidates should be open. Procedures such as these are often thought to be more trouble than they are worth. But elections provide motivation and a sense of responsibility to a constituency. Moreover, they legitimize the actions of those who serve and reinforce the decentralizing consequences of parent-teacher councils.

Fourth, basic responsibilities of the councils should be well defined. For example, roles for councils in personnel matters (especially recruitment and selection), curriculum development, and budget making should be specified. These roles need not be determinative to be effective, but they should be formal, and opportunities to present issues to the school board directly should be provided.

Fifth, some funds should be made available to local boards for discretionary expenditures, perhaps allowing for principals to veto decisions they feel are unwise. Such vetoes seem unlikely to be used often, and this power over some expenditures will tend to provide councils with a way to act directly and with some resources that can be used to bargain and to motivate.

Sixth, a small, districtwide office providing assistance to school councils for training, information sharing, and logistical support could improve their effectiveness.

These suggestions will not guarantee success, of course. It does not seem likely that most school districts will take the steps necessary to maximize the payoffs from teacher-parent councils. But until they do, parent involvement will be relatively ineffective and perfunctory. As Jim Comer has shown with his work in New Haven, teacher-parent organizations that have actual power and support can help turn a school around. Most school administrations, however, are reluctant to release such power to teachers and parents. And so it goes, despite the potential benefits of parent involvement, it seems probable that schools will continue to be the most isolated and insulated of America's institutions providing public services.

ELLEN HOFFMAN, a well-known speaker on child-care policy, received her Master's degree in history from Georgetown University. She is currently the Director of Governmental Affairs for the Children's Defense Fund. Before working with CDF, she was staff director and a professional staff member of the U.S. Senate Subcommittee on Children and Youth. In her role as staff director, she was responsible for a wide variety of domestic policy issues in the areas of children and youth, women's rights, and education. Ms. Hoffman also spent five years as a reporter for the *Washington Post* covering education and urban affairs. This diverse background provides her with a unique and broad perspective on child and family policy.

7

A National Policy for Children— How Do We Get There?

What should be our national goals for children? Here are some possibilities from an agenda worth considering:

> For every child a home and the love and security which a home provides; and for that child who must receive foster care, the nearest substitute for his own home . . .
>
> For every child from birth to adolescence promotion of health.
>
> For every child a dwelling place safe, sanitary, and wholesome . . .
>
> And for every child an education which, through the discovery and development of his individual abilities, prepares him for life and through training and vocational guidance prepares him for a living which will yield him the maximum of satisfaction.

Few social scientists, politicians, or citizens would disagree with these goals. They are part of the agenda established by Herbert Hoover's White House Conference on Children in 1930.

Forty-nine years later it is estimated that nearly half a million children live out of their homes, many of them in inappropriate or even dangerous settings far away from their families. Our national government encourages such arrangements by providing open-ended funding for children who are outside their homes in foster care. But the government provides almost nothing to help children in foster care return home or to prevent them from having to leave home in the first place.

In 1978, some ten million children received no health care, and five million children received no dental care. This situation exists even though we have a federal program designed to provide early health care to all the nation's poor children—the ones who most need it.

Some ten million children live in poverty. The Head Start program can provide the comprehensive services and parent and community involvement which could give many of these children the extra push they need to succeed as adults. But funds are available to serve less than one-quarter of the eligible children.

History has demonstrated that these are not problems which can be remedied easily or cheaply. It has also demonstrated that our existing process of setting national policy for meeting the basic needs of children and families is miserably inadequate. Who is responsible? Who are the policymakers? Why should it be so difficult to create and implement policies that encourage the healthy development of America's next generation?

FORCES IN POLICY DEVELOPMENT

Several types of forces and several types of policymakers interact to produce national policies affecting children and families. The three main forces are the executive branch of government, the legislative branch of government, and interest groups. Although the judiciary also plays an important role, it is not a visible force in day-to-day policymaking at the national level and thus will not be discussed here.

Without attempting to draw a comprehensive picture, I'd like first to sketch the dimensions of the large, amorphous apparatus that makes policy in the executive branch. It consists, first of all, of several Cabinet-level departments. In addition to the Department of Health, Education and Welfare, a number of other departments operate programs which directly affect the lives of millions of American children and their families. Among the most important are the Agriculture Department, which operates food programs, such as school breakfasts and Food Stamps, and the Labor Department, which supports employment training programs, including child care and other services authorized by the Comprehensive Employment and Training Act (CETA).

There are also a number of other executive agencies which we don't hear about as often and which we often do not consider when analyzing the policy-making process. These include the White House, with its domestic policy staff; the Office of Management and Budget which must approve all testimony presented by the administration to Congress; and other, more specialized agencies such as the Civil Rights Commission or the Community Services Administration (which operates what used to be the Community Action Program of the Offfice for Economic Opportunity).

In HEW alone, policy development occurs in several different bureaucratic arenas. In education, for example, all the following players become involved: special assistants to the HEW Secretary; departmental legislative staff; the Assistant Secretary for Planning and Evaluation; the Assistant Secretary for Education; the Commissioner of Education; and budget officials. Once a decision has been made within HEW, it may then be filtered through a number of other executive branch channels including the Office of Management and Budget, the domestic policy staff, and other White House offices. Many subunits of the Cabinet-level departments also have their own administrative, policy, and legislative staffs.

Turning now to policymaking by the legislative branch, we find that three types of congressional committees play crucial roles; namely, authorizing, appropriations, and budget committees. Authorizing committees (e.g., the House Education and Labor and the Senate Agriculture committees) create programs, renew them, and make substantive changes. Appropriations committees make item-by-item decisions each year on funding levels for each federal program. And since 1974, the budget committees in the House and Senate have responsibility for developing general spending targets for the federal government each fiscal year.

These committees are assisted in their tasks by several agencies not well known to the public, but which produce information that is often the basis for important policy decisions. They include the General Accounting Office, a technical analysis arm of Congress; the nonpartisan Congressional Budget Office (counterpart to the Office of Management and Budget); and the Congressional Research Service of the Library of Congress. Each of these agencies has the capability for developing—on its own initiative or at the request of a member of Congress—a wide variety of information used, and generally taken very seriously, by members of Congress and the committees.

A number of other groupings of members can also be important in shaping congressional decisions. Perhaps the most important is the leadership of the House and Senate. These are senior, highly respected members—the Speaker, the Majority and Minority leaders, and so on—who make key decisions about management of congressional business on a day-to-day basis, and who thus control the congressional agenda. In recent years, a series of other groups representing members' specialized interests have been formed. These include the Democratic Study Group; the Black Caucus; the Women's Caucus; the (Republican) Wednesday Group; and a number of regional caucuses. Most such groups are supported and staffed through contributions from the office accounts of the congressional representatives whose interests they represent. Typical activities of these groups include providing research support on pending legislation and organizing their members for joint action on particular legislation.

Then there is the third force—the interest group sector. In the field of child care and family policy the groups involved are diverse. Some represent units of government or public administrators. These include the National Conference of Mayors and the National Governors' Association as well as a host of more specialized groups, such as public welfare administrators. Professional groups (such as the National Association for Education of Young Children or the National Association of Social Workers) and unions are also involved in shaping child and family policy. The interest group category also includes organizations of providers, groups such as the Child Welfare League, and a range of public interest and consumer groups including the Children's Defense Fund, the Children's Foundation, civil rights and parent organizations, and such groups as the League of Women Voters.

This very brief description of the many players in the children's policy game is not intended to be comprehensive but only to suggest the complexity of the process and the difficulties of mastering it. The interaction—or lack of it— among all these forces produces our national policies affecting children and families.

INTERNAL CONSTRAINTS TO CHILD
AND FAMILY POLICY

Many factors—some internal, some external to the federal government—militate against accomplishing the goals many of us would like to see achieved for children and families. The internal constraints grow out of the nature of the government. First and foremost is the federal budget. Especially this year, the budget is crucial in determining what policies can be initiated or undertaken within the government. The President's proposed budget emerges from a long, complicated, decision-making process. Once general decisions about budget size and priorities have been made, they produce rigid internal constraints on policy-making within the executive branch.

A second constraint is the lack of a systematic process for developing federal policy for children and families. It is simply not possible to identify the point where policy originates and the points through which decisions flow in a definitive way. The general principles do not apply in many particular cases. For example, leadership for developing national health insurance and welfare reform legislation in the Carter administration has originated in the White House rather than in HEW. Similarly, many policy decisions are ultimately the product of informal negotiations between Congress and the executive branch.

A third internal constraint is what could be called a *crisis management* attitude. Anyone who has been in Washington for any length of time is familiar with this attitude. Whatever is judged the crisis of the day stimulates all of us to drop what we're doing and rush to meet the crisis. This type of behavior, of course, is the enemy of planning and methodical progress toward clearly specified objectives.

Bureaucratic inertia constitutes a fourth internal constraint on child and family policy. Often very good policymakers and very good thinkers push creative programs through the Congress only to see the programs flounder during the implementation phase because of disinterest or resistance from the bureaucracy. Somehow, even excellent policy decisions just never seem to make their way through the red tape to reality.

All these internal constraints—tight budgets, lack of a policy development process, the crisis management attitude, and bureaucratic inertia—make the development of a coherent children's policy difficult.

EXTERNAL CONSTRAINTS TO CHILD
AND FAMILY POLICY

In addition to these internal constraints on children's policy, there are also what I would call *external constraints.* Foremost among these is the lack of a long-range planning system. Those of us outside the government do not have a means of cooperating in long-range planning or of developing a strategy for accomplishing shared goals. In addition, the lack of a well-defined policymaking process within the government often makes it difficult even to figure out whom we should try to influence: The domestic policy staff in the White House? The secretary of HEW? Someone in the agency with direct administrative responsibility for a particular program? And having selected a target, we may be on the verge of successfully lobbying for our policy only to find that none of the other actors in the process is interested because they did not originate the policy. There is simply no clear process or series of steps for outsiders to follow in attempting to influence the federal system.

A second external constraint concerns the fragmentation of federal programs and particularly the constituencies of those programs. During the Great Society years, for example, many new child and family programs were created. The constituents of these programs began to concentrate their energies on maintenance and funding of their categorical programs. During the Nixon and Ford years, however, federal efforts became fragmented when a frustrated Congress acted on the assumption that "something is better than nothing" and created even more small, categorical programs aimed at assisting children and families. Each of these new programs also created its own constituencies working to maintain and, if possible, expand its own piece of the pie. We now must face the problem of bringing together these many constituencies and persuading them to subordinate their own narrow interests and work together toward broader goals that would benefit all of them. It will, however, take tremendous political and possibly financial resources and energy to do this.

Another external obstacle to a coherent child and family policy is the need to use many different advocacy tools to accomplish what needs to be done. It is not sufficient just to litigate. It is not sufficient just to do research and hope somebody will notice. Nor is it sufficient only to lobby. Rather, all these activities must be orchestrated in a systematic way if we are successfully to influence the different levels of policymaking structures previously outlined. We must recognize that policy development has only begun when a law is enacted; implementation also requires our serious attention and resources.

Finally, there is the external constraint of political trends. At the moment, these trends are very negative for those concerned with child and family policy. The most important of these trends is fiscal austerity—the Proposition 13 mindset that prevents Congress from spending additional funds on any new programs. Another facet of this negative political trend is an increasing antifederal attitude—a feeling that the federal government creates more problems than it solves when interacting with state governments, local governments, or individual families.

A third facet of political constraint on policy initiatives for children and families can be seen in the controversies raised by current efforts to rewrite the Federal Interagency Day Care Requirements (FIDCR). Many feel that the federal government has no business regulating anything, even when it has millions or billions of dollars invested. Thus, for those concerned about using federal standards to improve the quality of programs receiving federal funds, there is a strong trend that will have to be overcome in Washington.

Nor shall it escape our notice that we are in an intensely political time. As far as I can tell an election year begins one or two years prior to its calendar date. Candidates start their campaigns and are concerned about the mood of the voters well in advance of election day. Politicians may sense that the national mood is changing, but not be clear exactly how they must adapt to assure re-election.

In sum, many complicated and interacting factors now militate against development of a sensible, coherent, effective set of national policies for children and families.

CONGRESSIONAL BUDGET PROCESS

A number of the problems just discussed have taken on larger-than-life proportions in this year's concern about the size of the federal budget. For this reason, I want to focus attention on the budget process, and particularly the role of Congress in this process. Although the current process of creating the federal budget has been in existence for five years, this year budget deliberations in Congress have become the vehicle for key policy debates and decisions.

To understand the central role of budget deliberations in the policy process, one must recall that Congress created the current budget process because it had no way of developing its own version of the federal budget. The President had his Office of Management and Budget, his computers, and his economists, and could use these resources to produce each year a huge and complex budget document that reflected his own priorities. All the Congress could do with its few appropriations committee staff was react to particular items in the President's proposal.

As a result, Congress decided it needed a more independent force to respond to the budget proposal of the executive branch. Thus, the Congressional Budget Office and budget committees in both the House and the Senate were created in 1974. At the same time, Congress enacted a series of detailed requirements and deadlines for approval of a budget each year. One requirement of the law was that no later than March 15 of each year, the authorizing committees (those that create and amend education or social programs) must make recommendations to the budget committees about funding priorities for programs in their jurisdiction.

That this deadline has created serious problems for policymaking can be illustrated by one example. The Senate Finance Committee probably has more programs under its jurisdiction than any other committee in Congress—including social services, social security, welfare policy, trade and tax legislation, and much more. Despite this diversity of complex programs, the Finance Committee must decide by March 15 of each year how much money should be set aside for each program for the fiscal year that begins October 1. Included in the estimates this past year were figures representing how much money would be saved by hospital cost containment legislation. But this legislation had not been written or even studied by Congress!

Consider further the problems these deadlines create for the committees, and especially for new senators or staff persons. Suppose you were not familiar with the intricacies of the welfare program or social security; or that you didn't know whether hospital cost containment legislation would save $1 or $2 billion a year. It would be almost impossible for you to make budget decisions about these programs in a short period of time and on the basis of very limited information. But this is what has been happening. As a result, legislative policy options are foreclosed very early in the year, long before the economists can make reliable predictions about unemployment, inflation, and other key trends that will affect the budget. And this year, for the first time, Congress is trying to limit its budget choices as far ahead as five years.

One outcome of the new budget process has been to increase the power of traditionally influential members of Congress—those who have been there the longest, those who understand programs best, those who can manipulate the system. Congresspersons who are new and therefore unfamiliar with either specific programs or the budget process are often reluctant to raise a question or to challenge their most senior colleagues.

These problems are exacerbated because very few individuals and organizations are working on children's issues in Congress at any given time. The demands created by the budget process—for monitoring, attending committee hearings and action sessions, and educating members on the budget—compete with demands the advocates already face in trying to keep up with authorizing and appropriations activities.

I have stressed the congressional budget process because it is relatively new and unknown, yet is having an important impact on child and family policy by demanding a level of political and economic sophistication and effectiveness often lacking among advocates for human services.

MEETING THE CHALLENGE:
PROPOSALS FOR A NATIONAL CHILD
AND FAMILY POLICY

Thus, if we are to accomplish our goals for children and families—including those articulated by the 1930 White House Conference—we must create a systematic and pragmatic strategy. Different individuals and organizations react to this challenge in different ways. To illustrate how one particular organization is responding to the challenge, I turn now to a description of current activities of the Children's Defense Fund (CDF) on behalf of children and families.

This year for the second time CDF has formulated and published a "National Legislative Agenda for Children" (see Appendix). This agenda is not a comprehensive statement of what we hope to achieve in the area of children's policy. As in the past, we shall continue to carry on research, litigation, community education, administrative monitoring, and other activities designed to improve public policies affecting children and families. But in the last two years we have begun to realize that these activities alone will not provide health care to a child in rural Mississippi, or a permanent home to a youngster who has lingered for years in an inappropriate foster care placement. It is time for us to use what we have learned about children and the programs designed to serve them in order to achieve tangible goals that will make a difference in the lives of some of our neediest, most forgotten children—before they grow up and it is too late.

CDF's legislative agenda contains two types of goals: (1) specific proposals that have a realistic chance of passage in the current session of Congress, (2) broader goals that must be accomplished over a longer period of time by working, step-by-step, from the more immediate goals.

Immediate Goals

Last year Congress almost passed laws that would have made a dramatic difference in the lives of half a million children who live outside their own homes, and of several million children who are eligible for but do not receive even the most basic health services. The two pieces of legislation that would move us toward these goals are top priorities on CDF's agenda again this year.

The first is a bill that would address the needs of those children who live away from their families in facilities ranging from individual foster families and group homes to large institutions. It would shift our existing, antifamily federal policies from their emphasis on out-of-home care to a policy that would prevent inappropriate placements outside the home and encourage either the return of children to their families or adoption. Among the tools this bill would provide

173

are preventive services and subsidies for the adoption of children with special needs (see background study by Children's Defense Fund, 1978).

Although the bill had strong bipartisan support in Congress, the administration, and a wide variety of outside organizations, last year it became bogged down in the Senate Finance Committee as part of a larger package of public assistance amendments and died in the last hours of the session.

The second bill, the Child Health Assessment Program (CHAP), also died in the last few hours of the 1978 congressional session. CHAP is a package of amendments designed to improve the existing Early and Periodic Screening, Diagnosis and Treatment (EPSDT) program under Medicaid. The EPSDT program now reaches less than one-fourth of 13 million eligible children, and many children in need are not even eligible under current rules. CHAP would address a number of specific problems identified in a CDF study of EPSDT, including lack of effective outreach, inadequacy of coverage, need to improve incentives for provider participation, and the need for better service delivery systems (Children's Defense Fund, 1977).

A third item on CDF's legislative agenda is child-care services. CDF remains committed—despite Senator Alan Cranston's recent announcement that he would not push ahead with new child-care legislation this year—to increase the quantity and quality of child-care services for all children and families who need and want them. In pursuit of this goal, we are working in the 96th Congress on a number of legislative concerns: increased funding of the Title XX social services program; assured funding of the specially earmarked Title XX day-care funds; expansion of training for child care, child welfare, and other personnel; renewal of the Appalachian Regional Child Development Program; and expansion of Head Start to serve more of the many unserved, but eligible children.

In a fourth area of concern—family support—CDF will continue to work toward a policy that guarantees access to steady, long-term employment opportunities for all families with a member able to work, and a guaranteed annual income with a uniform minimum benefit level high enough to eliminate poverty in the next generation for families without a member able to work. We intend to continue calling attention to the fact that any change in the welfare system will have its greatest impact on children, who account for over two-thirds of the recipients in the Aid to Families with Dependent Children Program.

I have drawn a very sketchy list here that does not include every item on CDF's legislative agenda, but the items mentioned illustrate the types of issues that concern us and the priority we place on them.

Longer-Range Goals

CDF believes it is also crucial to identify goals that both can be achieved in the foreseeable future and can serve as stepping-stones to broader changes in our system that may be necessary to prevent—rather than simply react to—the problems of children and families. We believe it is important to be aware of, and capitalize on, the political atmosphere in trying to accomplish legislative goals. For example, both CHAP and child welfare are proposals that offer substantial hope of reducing future budgets by replacing costly "after-the-fact" services with less expensive preventive measures. This may be the most effective argument we can make for such legislation at a time when the federal budget is widely perceived as too large and still growing.

But our experience in recent years demonstrates that even such seemingly uncontroversial issues as permanent homes and health care for children cannot be achieved without systematic mobilization of outside interests to bring such issues to the attention of policymakers. As a result, we are trying to identify and work with many groups around the country that share these concerns. In many communities, the most active and interested groups are not those generally seen as "children's groups." Rather, they are the Junior League, the churches, the American Association of University Women, and many similar organizations.

As part of our effort to build an active national force on behalf of children, CDF is looking to people who work with children and have personal knowledge of their needs; to organizations and individuals who have traditionally been active in the areas of social welfare, human rights, and civil rights; and to groups of professionals—including teachers, social workers, lawyers, and others—who can apply their knowledge, understanding, and commitment to problems faced by children and families. And we look to the academic community for intellectual leadership, for critical analysis of children's needs, for assessment of the effects of existing policies, and for creative new approaches to solving some of the problems discussed in this paper.

CONCLUSIONS

We are living in a period that offers many symbolic opportunities, such as the International Year of the Child and the proposed White House Conferences on Families and on Children and Youth. But the real question faced by those committed to helping children and families is whether we are going to put some substance behind these symbolic and rhetorical opportunities.

Are we going to take the next steps toward providing basic health and child-care services, increased educational opportunities, and an adequate income and decent home for children?

Whether we succeed will not be determined by an abstract and anonymous institution called *government.* Whether that institution responds depends on what we offer it to respond to. The task will not be easy, but no significant human achievement ever is.

Grace Abbot, Chief of the Children's Bureau in the 1930s, described as well as anyone the forces that confront those who would take on the challenge of forging policies that provide a chance for all of America's children:

... Sometimes when I get home at night in Washington I feel as though I had been in a great traffic jam. The jam is moving toward the Hill where Congress sits in judgment on all the administrative agencies of the Government. In that traffic jam there are all kinds of vehicles . . . . There are all kinds of conveyances that the Army can put into the street—tanks, gun carriers, trucks . . . There are the hayricks and the binders and the ploughs and all the other things that the Department of Agriculture manages to put into the streets . . . the handsome limousines in which the Department of Commerce rides . . . barouches in which the Department of State rides in such dignity. It seems so to me as I stand on the sidewalk watching it become more congested and more difficult, and then because the responsibility is mine and I must, I take a very firm hold on the handles of the baby carriage and I wheel it into the traffic (U.S. Department of Health, 1976, p. 70).

REFERENCES

Children's Defense Fund. *EPSDT: Does it spell health care for poor children?* Washington, D.C.: Author, June 1977.

Children's Defense Fund. *Children without homes: An examination of public responsibility to children in out-of-home care.* Washington, D.C.: Author, 1978.

U.S. Department of Health, Education, and Welfare. *Child health in America* [DHEW Publication No. (HSA) 76-5015]. Washington, D.C.: Author, 1976.

Appendix—Children's Defense Fund
Second National Legislative Agenda for Children

CHILDREN WITHOUT HOMES

The Problem

Over 500,000 children live away from their families in facilities ranging from individual foster family and group homes to large institutions. Some are the responsibility of the child welfare system; others of the juvenile justice system; and still others of the mental health and mental retardation systems. Some are infants. Many more are pre-adolescents and adolescents. Some have special needs stemming from physical or emotional handicaps; some have been involved with the juvenile court; others have no disabilities but are removed from families where pressures to cope are too great or where there is abuse or neglect.

Far too many of these children are unnecessarily or prematurely removed from their homes before attempts have been made to work with or to provide preventive services to their families. Tens of thousands are placed in inappropriate facilities for long periods of time, often away from their communities and even out of their states. They languish in a twilight area, neither returned home nor provided a permanent new family through adoption.

Their treatment makes a mockery of our national rhetoric about the importance of the American family and current emphasis on cost-effective use of the taxpayers' dollars. Current federal child welfare dollars encourage family breakup, and discourage children from being returned home or placed with adoptive families—both less costly and more humane options.

Early in the 95th Congress, child welfare reforms were introduced which would have shifted federal fiscal incentives away from costly maintenance of children in unmonitored foster care. Passed by the House of Representatives, they would also have supported preventive and reunification services and adoption subsidies. However, the reform bogged down in the Senate Finance Committee as part of a larger package of public assistance amendments. Separate action on the child welfare provisions was not taken by the full Senate until the closing days of the session—too late to help homeless children. This must not happen again.

Immediate Goals

1. Passage of comprehensive child welfare legislation which would:

—erase current federal fiscal incentives to remove and maintain children out of their own homes;

—provide targeted funds for preventive and reunification services, adoption subsidies, and a periodic review mechanism to prevent unnecessary removal and lengthy placements outside a permanent family setting;

—ensure placement of children in the least restrictive settings appropriate to their needs and within reasonable proximity to their families; and

—provide children and their families with due process protections prior to removal and termination of parental rights, and ensure needed services throughout the placement process.

2. Enactment of legislation that would enable the Department of Justice to bring suit to protect children and others against institutional abuse.

Longer-Range Goals

1. Legislation that provides financial incentives for family support services and programs in communities as an alternative to inappropriate institutionalization; and ensures appropriate services for children when they return to their communities to prevent unnecessary future institutionalization.

2. Legislative and administrative efforts to encourage development of a differentiated juvenile justice system which protects the community from and meets the needs of the minority of juvenile offenders who threaten its safety, and serves all others with a full range of services in the least restrictive settings appropriate to their needs.

3. Legislation that increases the range of medical, psychological and social services available to meet the special needs of children involved in the child welfare and juvenile justice systems.

CHILD HEALTH

The Problem

One in every 65 American infants and one in every 43 nonwhite infants dies each year. Our nation's capital, where one in 33 nonwhite infants dies annually, has the highest infant mortality rate in the nation. One in seven American children—or an estimated 10 million—has no regular source of primary health care. Two of five American children are not even fully immunized against the major childhood diseases we know how to prevent. One out of every two children under fifteen—or 15 million children—has not seen a dentist in over a year. Yet the largest federal health program providing funds for the detection and care of children's health problems, the Early and Periodic Screening, Diagnosis and Treatment (EPSDT) program, reaches fewer than one-fourth of the 13 million eligible Medicaid children. And it often serves inadequately even those it reaches.

The Maternal and Child Health and Crippled Children's program (Title V of the Social Security Act) provides care to only a fraction of the mothers and children who need its help.

In April 1977, President Carter proposed the Child Health Assessment Program (CHAP) to "expand and improve" EPSDT, and during the past session of Congress, both the House Interstate and Foreign Commerce Committee and Senate Finance Committee developed CHAP proposals. CHAP is, in effect, a cost-containment program which, through timely preventive care, can help keep our neediest children out of hospitals, both now and when they become adults. Because it was not a high priority, however, action on CHAP was delayed until it was too late to pass a bill before Congress adjourned. CHAP's fate in the 96th Congress could be similarly endangered if its consideration is postponed or if its funding is dependent on the enactment of broader health cost containment measures.

EPSDT and Title V, which must be improved in the short-run, provide only partial and temporary answers to the health care needs of millions of our neediest young. American children and families will not get adequate health care without: (1) the expansion of federal support to develop, organize and, where necessary, subsidize the creation of needed health services; and (2) the enactment of a universal comprehensive health insurance program. It should be noted, however, that any national health insurance program is worthy of the name only if it provides for changes in health delivery and equitable access to quality services at a reasonable and predictable cost.

Immediate Goal

Enactment of a strengthened Child Health Assessment Program (CHAP) which will improve the EPSDT program by:

—assuring effective outreach;
—increasing coverage of health services;
—expanding Medicaid eligibility;
—developing mechanisms to assure that services get to needy children;
—encouraging participation by qualified providers; and
—strengthening states' capacities to deliver services to needy children.

Longer-Range Goals

1. Improvement of existing federal programs which finance or provide child health services, including the Maternal and Child Health and Crippled Children's program (Title V of the Social Security Act) and Medicaid (Title XIX of the Social Security Act).

2. Legislation that will fund programs to promote the more effective delivery of health services, including expanded and improved support of neighborhood and community health and mental health centers, children and youth projects, primary care centers and HMOs.

3. Enactment of a sound comprehensive national health program.

CHILD-CARE SERVICES

The Problem

Today an overwhelming majority of American families are likely to need child-care services at some point to aid in raising their children. One preschool child in five and one Black preschool child in two live in a single-parent household. They are among the 9.7 million children growing up in single-parent families.

One white child in three and one Black child in two, under age six, has a working mother. They are among the 28.2 million children whose mothers work. Five million families have at least one child with a physical, mental, or emotional handicap. The ability of these children to function in society now and as adults is enhanced by access to child-care services. Hundreds of thousands of children are without homes altogether. Removing many of these children from their families might have been prevented by flexible child-care services. An additional 10 million children live in abject poverty, and an unknown number are abused and neglected because their parents have few supports.

For all these children, there is no national policy guiding the development of child-care services. A patchwork of programs serves a fraction of the very poor and tax credits benefit the affluent. The vast numbers of families in the middle have no system of dependable, quality child-care arrangements. Project Head Start, a model of comprehensive, family-centered, community-based child development, reaches only 20 percent of the eligible children. Over one-and-a-half million children and one thousand counties lack this essential and successful program.

Immediate Goals

1. Retention of the child-care targeting within the Title XX social program on the current basis of 100 percent federal funding.

2. Enactment of legislation that will lead to a comprehensive program of child care and family support services for children and families who need and want them.

3. Enactment of revised Federal Interagency Day Care Requirements (FIDCR) that will ensure a high quality of care provided to children in the Title XX program.

4. Incremental Head Start budget increases to serve greater numbers of eligible children and communities.

Longer-Range Goals

1. Expansion and funding of a comprehensive program of child-care services for all children and families who need and want them.

2. Ensuring that income maintenance and job creation proposals provide working parents access to quality child care that they can afford.

FAMILY SUPPORT

The Problem

Poverty is one of the most persistent problems affecting great numbers of children in this country. Children are the most disproportionately poor of any age group in America. In 1976, while 11.8 percent of the general population lived in poverty, 15.8 percent of all children did. These 10.1 million children—and millions of others living barely above the government's arbitrary "poverty line"—often lack the basic physical necessities of life.

One in every four American children lives in poverty at some time during his or her childhood. In 1977, children 18 years old and younger accounted for well over two-thirds—7.7 out of 10.9 million—of Aid to Families with Dependent Children (AFDC) recipients. Reform of the AFDC system to provide a guaranteed minimum income has long been recognized as a priority step to encourage family stability and healthy development for poor children. But "welfare reform" continues to elude us, remaining one of the most emotional and least understood issues on the national agenda.

Adequate jobs and income support programs alone, however important, are not the entire answer to breaking the cycle of poverty for millions of children. Their families—indeed all families, whether rich, middle-class, or poor—at some time need the helping hands of others. The main difference is in families' ability to locate and pay for services, and the quality of services they can find and buy. Title XX of the Social Security Act is designed to begin to eliminate this difference by funding supportive social services for eligible families who want them. But the quality and availability of Title XX services have never been properly monitored and enforced.

Immediate Goals

1. Incremental action to ensure more adequate income support for children through establishment of a national AFDC benefit floor at least at 75 percent of the poverty level.

2. Elimination of discrimination against poor children in two-parent families in 24 states through mandating the now optional AFDC-Unemployed Parent program.

3. Increase in the funding ceiling of Title XX to protect against inflation and ensure continuation of necessary child and family services at least at their current levels.

Longer-Range Goals

1. Guaranteeing all families with a member able to work access to steady, long-term employment opportunities, and all those without a member able to work, a uniform minimum benefit level high enough to eliminate poverty for the next generation of children.

2. Strengthening Title XX and other existing and proposed social service programs in an attempt to establish an effective family support system based on principles of equity, universality, diversity, accessibility, prevention and accountability.

Comments on Hoffman's Paper

FLORENCE C. GLASSER is the Human Development
Coordinator and Policy Advisor in the Division of Policy Development,
Department of Administration, State of North Carolina.

I want to begin by congratulating Children's Defense Fund (CDF) on its fine
advocacy efforts on behalf of children and families. CDF has focused attention
on the important children's issues of our time and has spoken on behalf of children whose needs would not otherwise have been articulated or addressed. CDF
has also been willing to address tough problems and complicated issues—issues
that could be addressed only by advocates who are persistent, courageous, sensitive, insightful, and strong. And most important, CDF has now translated these
issues into the legislative agenda outlined by Ellen Hoffman.

The CDF agenda calls for a comprehensive child and family policy. I shall
focus my remarks on identifying some forces that can support the development
of child and family policy. In addition, I shall offer some specific proposals concerning what child and family policy should include.

Ellen Hoffman has carefully outlined the external and internal constraints
on the development of a national children's policy. I want to suggest that we
first look at the possibility of developing good comprehensive state policies for
children and families. There are a number of reasons for adopting this approach.

States have an important role in planning and implementing programs for
children and youth. Primary government responsibility for education, mental
health, juvenile justice, and youth vocational programs resides with state and
local governments. In addition, health, child care, and family support programs
require increasingly large state and substate investments. For each of these
services, states set priorities, plan, develop, and operate their own systems.

In North Carolina, for example, we have been working on a comprehensive
child and family policy called "Raising a New Generation." This policy is built
around the recognition that the best way to support children is to strengthen
families. Families are the primary providers of services to meet children's basic
needs for clothing, food, and shelter. But the cost to the family of providing for
these needs is higher than it has ever been. In order to support the family by
improving family income, the governor and the Advisory Budget Commission
recommended a tax-relief program that would give a cost-of-living raise to
families. More specifically, they recommended a $40 million a year permanent
tax-relief package that would increase the family's state income tax exemption
for children. In addition to such indirect savings that result in more disposable

income for all families, state general revenues are heavily invested in children's programs. Almost half of the total North Carolina budget serves children—$1.9 billion in the current year. Over two-thirds of this amount—$1.3 billion—are state general funds. Federal funds represent the remaining third. State general funds invested in children are increasing three times more rapidly than federal funds. Spending for North Carolina children increased by $16.2 million in fiscal year 1978-79, and nearly $14 million of these increases are state general funds. Spending for North Carolina children will increase by $89 million in 1979-80 and $119 million in 1980-81. Clearly, this state—and many others—are responding to the needs of children and families.

In addition to planning and funding state programs for children, the states are involved in implementing federal initiatives. Foster care, adoption, day care, Early and Periodic Screening, Diagnosis, and Treatment, and programs for exceptional children are—to quote CDF's Marion Wright Edelman—"about as good or bad as state performances." The implementers and the administrators are state and local policymakers.

Children's Defense Fund understands the key role that states play in developing and implementing children's policy, and I think that is the reason CDF has begun to set up a network of state-level child advocacy groups. I applaud this CDF effort and hope this network will provide some assistance in helping CDF pass at least part of its legislation agenda.

In addition to state-level organizations, regional organizations of states can also contribute to the development of a national children's policy. In November 1978, the 13 states that are members of the Appalachian Regional Commission met in Asheville, N.C. to discuss the needs of the region's children. Vice-President Mondale, White House staff, governors, and 300 invited guests proposed some new ideas for guiding the investment of Appalachian dollars in programs of benefit to children. Subsequently, the governors approved conference recommendations that would commit resources to reduce infant mortality, continue comprehensive child development programs, and support basic skills education. The commission will also continue to attract high-wage industry to the region so that parents can find jobs that will provide family income adequate to meet the basic needs of children.

A similar effort is now under way under the auspices of the Southern Growth Policies Board. Governor Hunt of North Carolina, as chairman of this 14-state regional organization, called on his fellow governors to designate a representative to serve on a regional committee that would examine the needs and strengths of Southern children and their families. Are Southern families and children unique? Do they have special needs? The data to answer these and similar questions are now being collected and will serve as the first step in a careful assessment of needed policy initiatives for the region's children and families.

Finally, the most important organization of state policymakers that can provide the political force necessary to legislate and implement family policy is the National Governors' Association (NGA). At the last meeting of the NGA, the spouses of the governors discussed the International Year of the Child. Perhaps at the next NGA meeting, the subject of children and families can be an agenda item for the governors themselves.

Having briefly outlined the forces that can support the development of state, regional, and federal family policy, let me briefly suggest what this policy should include. First, family policy must be comprehensive. If the goals of policy are to be comprehensive, then we must move away from the categorical approach to the sixties and seventies and toward the goal of offering comprehensive support to families. Above all else, policy at the state, regional, and federal level should seize every opportunity to improve the economic status of families. That is not just rhetoric. In order to improve the economic status of families, we must identify family support programs and argue and advocate strongly for those programs. We must all lobby as vigorously for Social Security and Supplemental Security Income and Veterans' benefits as CDF has for CHAP and 7200. Child advocates must closely examine the under-utilization of income transfer programs and promote greater education and outreach efforts so that eligible children can benefit from these programs.

Tax spending is another way of improving the economic status of families. Tax reform that would correct the present inequities suffered by families with two wage earners is important to a comprehensive family policy. Other possibilities include child health bill credits, income disregards for families with handicapped children, and income tax credits for corporations that provide subsidized child care for their employees.

Legislating, implementing, and coordinating these elements of family policy can be achieved only through advocacy and planning efforts at the federal and state levels. CDF must continue to argue for child and family policy positions at HEW and the White House. But those of us at the state level must continue to press the view that comprehensive family policy can be best developed if federal planners work closely and cooperatively with policymakers at the state level.

Editor's Note: CHAP—the Child Health Assessment Program—was a bill that nearly passed the Congress in 1978. It would have strengthened the Early and Periodic Screening, Diagnosis, and Treatment program under Medicaid. The term "7200" refers to House Bill 200 which was introduced in 1978. The thrust of this legislation would have been to provide funds for improving the foster care and adoption systems in the various states.

Comments on Hoffman's Paper

DONALD J. STEDMAN is Acting Vice President for Research and Public Service Programs and Professor of Education at the University of North Carolina at Chapel Hill. Dr. Stedman is also a faculty member of the Bush Institute for Child and Family Policy at UNC.

I detect a certain weariness in Ellen Hoffman's presentation. I can hardly blame her. She is slugging it out in the bureaucratic quagmires of government along the Potomac. For her work and energy we are grateful. For the vigilance and diligence of the Children's Defense Fund we are thankful. For the insights provided by her paper we are indebted.

Her paper has stimulated some random thoughts about child and family policy which I will share.

First, a growing problem is the complex of barriers and restrictions of freedom placed upon local agencies that seek to improve the quality of life for children, and with increasingly high turnover rates, these local organizations spend more time backpedaling in response to federal mandates, the pressures of professional organizations, and the delegated standards setting of private organizations than on improving the curriculum of the schools, addressing the inadequacies of teacher education, or improving the learning environments provided for the community's children.

Second, we still have not resolved who the "we" are that ought to "shape the policy" and "take the steps." Self-appointed advocates too often misperceive the situation and even innocently compound the problems already present for children. Consumer activities and consumer legislation are not always well grounded in fact and do not necessarily work in the best interest of children and families.

Third, I think that no new laws or legislation are necessary. We must first learn to implement what we now have, especially on the state/local axis. We have ground out enough legislation in the past twenty years to keep us busily occupied for the next decade or more. Perhaps the task for the '80s is to consolidate our gains, to review our concepts and principles, to reassess the results of our research, and to refuel those mental engines that developed some of the great ideas of the '60s.

Fourth, we continue to play out and attempt to solve adult problems in the context of children's systems. Busing, for example, is an attempt to solve the problem that adults have in determining access to property.

Fifth, we must become increasingly cautious with the use of child development research data. We are dangerously close in some existing and some pr posed federal legislation to outrunning our technology and severely straining the credibility of our approach to improving life for children and families.

Sixth, we continue to have a preoccupation with government. We need less—not more—of it. The political star system in Washington and in many state capitals has created an unhealthy disregard for pragmatic and realistic approaches to children's programs. National goals for children cannot be developed when individuals or small groups focus primarily on their own ambitions and are dedicated principally to reelection rather than reform.

Seventh, it is clear that the complexity of obtaining federal and state resources (the legitimate hustle) is an effective deterrent to improved services at the local level. For example, the relationship between federal standards for residential care and drawing down federal funds under Title XIX had led to *diminished* state budgets in some states rather than increased state budgets and improved quality of service. Federal funds are being drawn down by institutionalized hostages whose Social Security benefits are being passed along to the general treasuries of states for the improvement of highway systems and other non-child- or non-family-related enterprises. This procedure is not illegal, but it approaches immorality.

Eighth, it may be that we have emerged from a period of "entitlement" into an era of "disentanglement." *Back to the basics* means back to the agencies and local organizational building blocks that have always been the backbone of services to families in this country. There may well be taking place at this moment a relocation of the original intent for local agencies. The problem then will be to resist a competitive Balkanization of the country and consequent regional struggles for diminishing national dollars. Somewhere we must find the opportunity and a set of pathways to strengthen traditional local agencies as an alternative to the development of new and unique local organizational formats that attempt to develop and to institutionalize change. The concept of the community action program was useful and effective in the '60s. It would not stand a chance today. Instead, young leadership at the local level wants to work within the existing framework to provide improved opportunity, more effective services, and greater access to material well-being than has heretofore been available. The activities on behalf of children and families over the past two decades have been sobering. We still know too little about what really works. We do not have a firm understanding of why successful programs work. We still have an inclination to legislate change before we are capable of following through on national initiatives at the local level.

All this adds up to an even heavier responsibility for consumer advocacy organizations, such as the Children's Defense Fund, and for supreme advocates such as Ellen Hoffman. I would not seek to alienate her affection or to cause her to flag in her efforts. I would, however, ask that she constantly check her sources, choose her battles wisely, and listen carefully to alternatives lest the credibility of all our organizations and efforts be so severely undermined as to negate our potential for effecting change in an increasingly conservative and cynical world.

MARTHA H. PHILLIPS is the Assistant Minority Counsel of the Ways and Means Committee of the U.S. House of Representatives. In her role as Minority Counsel, she specializes in assessing the impact on families of various programs under the committee's jurisdiction including welfare, income tax, and social security. Before serving on the Ways and Means Committee, she directed the House Republican Policy Committee, a 26-member leadership group charged with identifying and articulating positions for House Republicans on pending legislation and political issues. Ms. Phillips is also a member of the legislative core group of the National Women's Political Caucus, the American Educational Research Association, the American Political Science Association, and the Family Impact Seminar.

The Needs
of American Families—
The Current Federal Agenda

In this paper, I want to focus on the setting against which some of the broad decisions regarding child care and families are being made and to suggest some of the implications of this setting for future policy goals and strategies. Frankly, my view is not very optimistic. Perhaps that is because I have just finished going through the mark-up process for the First Concurrent Resolution on the Fiscal 1980 Budget, which followed on the heels of a hotly debated effort to use the public debt limit to force Congress to balance the federal budget beginning in fiscal 1981.

Not very many years ago, federal public policies for children and families were approached with optimism and enthusiasm. We asked what were the problems, what solutions were possible; and finally, almost as an afterthought, how much would they cost. A number of ambitious undertakings were launched with federal seed money in the expectation that more substantial sums would soon be forthcoming—Head Start, health screening, remedial and preventive education, social services to low-income families.

Today, we appear to be entering a different, and far more austere, era—one of fiscal constraint, balanced budgets, and tax revolt. This federal tightfistedness has been building throughout the seventies. Ending the war in Vietnam did not produce the expected fiscal dividend that would finance all the "butter" required by many recipes for social progress. The sharp recession in the middle of the decade was a further setback, one which erased much of the progress that had been made in reducing poverty and dependency. That recession is still with us in the form of incredible annual rates of inflation which eat into every family's sense of well-being and of a disappointing lack of the real economic growth which must occur if we are to generate the public revenues required to finance new initiatives. To top it off, we are being told to expect another recession—which government will induce in order to stave off an even worse dislocation later on. We have been expecting that recession and because it has not yet occurred, despite government's best efforts to bring it about, we are becoming concerned as to how precipitous it will be when and if it finally gets here.

These economic dislocations have taken their toll on public policies affecting families and children. Now, instead of contemplating new programs, we find ourselves defending the existing ones. We ask how much it is likely to cost to continue current policies, whether that much is available or whether current policies must be trimmed in order to squeeze into the already tight federal

190

budget. We eye hungrily the surpluses at state and local levels of government and try to figure out ways to leverage that money in directions we think are desirable —toward day care and not dump trucks, for example.

CURRENT TRENDS IN THE FEDERAL BUDGET

Examining overall priorities, we find that more of the federal budget already goes into the functional category called *income security* than anywhere else— next year some $179 billion out of a total budget of $532 billion. National defense gets only $126 billion, or $146 billion if you include payments to veterans. What's third? Not health ($53 billion). Not education, training, employment and social services which altogether come to $30 billion. Third is interest on the public debt which in 1980 will total $65.7 billion, the legacy of years of deficit budgets. In fact, 40 percent of the federal deficit has accumulated in the 1970s.

All these figures add up to one conclusion—money is tight. Few now doubt that tight money is one of the most significant factors in the policy process controlling child and family programs. This preoccupation with the immediate and long-term cost of government initiatives dominates any discussion of options and alternatives. Although healthy in the long run because of the realism and sense of proportion it forces on planners and politicians, this preoccupation is bitter medicine to those who had pinned their hopes on a much larger share of the public purse than they now enjoy.

Nor is fiscal austerity the only trend currently blocking new initiatives on behalf of children and families. A second trend is what columnist Ellen Goodman has called the "grasshopper phenomenon." What she had in mind was the betrayal people feel when they carefully plan ahead for upcoming needs—education, health care, housing, retirement, and the like—only to find that others who have not made similar sacrifices have their responsibilities taken care of by the government. She pointed out, for example, that a college education these days costs about as much as a new Mercedes. The parents who spend their money on the Mercedes and therefore have no cash in the bank can expect that Junior will get some federal assistance to pay for his education. The parents who are still driving the beat-up old VW in order to save for Junior's college, on the other hand, will find that they are expected to pay for his education, even though their earnings over the years may have been less than that of the folks driving the Mercedes. The poor mother who saves a few thousand dollars in hopes of getting off welfare loses in the long run because the welfare department penalizes her for this savings if it is discovered. The parents who both work in order to afford the middle-class life they want for their children are frustrated at the huge bite taken by taxes, the benefits of which are not clearly apparent.

Both of these trends—tight budgets and the grasshopper phenomenon—are leading policymakers to pare back existing programs and focus them as exclusively as possible on people who are truly in need.

In the recent House Budget Committee consideration of spending targets for the fiscal 1980 budget, several examples of this trend were debated:

- —School lunch program subsidies for nonneedy children would be reduced by a nickel apiece in order to achieve an annual savings of $146 million. Similarly, free lunch eligibility would be cut back to children at the poverty level plus annual food stamp allotment ($7270 for a family of four);
- —Stepparents' income would be counted in computing AFDC benefits, even though stepparents may not be legally responsible for the dependent child (saves $100 million a year);
- —Three administrations in a row have proposed ending student benefits under the Social Security program and relying on the Basic Educational Opportunity Grants program to pick up the slack for those in need (would save over $1 billion by fiscal 1984);
- —The "runaway fathers" program would be vigorously enforced for both welfare and nonwelfare recipients alike, generating over a billion dollars in child support in the last fiscal year and possibly contributing to a reduction in welfare dependency.

A GUARANTEED INCOME FOR FAMILIES?

Initiatives of this sort respond to budget constraints, but they also reflect an answer of sorts as to what the relative responsibilities are of individuals and the government. This trend toward more reliance on individual initiative and less on government intervention is clearly contrary to what many analysts of public policies for children and families have advocated. Thus, for example, two major publications—the volumes of the National Academy of Sciences (1976) and the Carnegie Council on Children (Keniston, 1977)—have drawn similar conclusions about the status and problems of children growing up in America today. To oversimplify, both studies suggest that a certain amount of income is critical to a family's ability to meet the needs of its children. They suggest further that a large percentage of our nation's children and youth are being raised in impoverished surroundings which harm them and their chances of success in life and which put them "at risk" for a number of negative physical, emotional, and intellectual outcomes.

Based on this analysis of the problem, both reports conclude that the best solution is to redistribute income or wealth. In particular, families in the bottom fifth of the income ladder, who currently receive only 5.4 percent of money income, should be the beneficiaries of redistribution so that "no child [would] be deprived of access to a family living standard lower than half of the median family income level (after tax) for a substantial period of his or her childhood" (National Academy of Sciences, 1976, p. 5). This redistribution would take the form of a negative income tax system in which everyone is taxed at a higher rate than they presently are so that a portion of these new revenues could then be returned to those at the lower end of the economic spectrum.

There is virtually no chance of such a scheme being enacted in the foreseeable future. Whatever case can be made in favor of the outcomes that might be expected from income redistribution, the arguments against it are clearly in the ascendancy.

First, the government already engages in substantial redistribution of income. Money income is only one measure of a family's resources, and a significant number of low-income families receive services and in-kind benefits as well as cash transfers. In fiscal 1976, according to a study by the Congressional Budget Office (Rivlin, 1977), 25.5 percent of all families fell below the poverty level, using the Census Bureau definition of poverty which is based largely on money income. But when public *cash* transfers were counted, families in poverty fell to 11.4 percent of all families. Further, when in-kind transfers were included and taxes taken out, only 6.9 percent of families were under the official poverty line—a total of 5.4 million families. Looking at income after taxes and after total transfers, then, demonstrates that the incidence of poverty among families has fallen by approximately 60 percent since 1965. Morton Paglin (1979), a professor of economics at Portland State University, comes up with an even lower estimate of the portion of our population in poverty. In addition to the kinds of adjustments made by the Congressional Budget Office report, Paglin also looks at household groupings to take into account the economies of scale that exist in real life, and adjusts for the underreporting of income (including over a million people whose taxable income was under $1,000 because of accounting reasons, but who nonetheless had positive cash flow). His results are startlingly low—some 3.6 percent of all citizens in 1975 fell below the poverty level, a total of 7.8 million individuals. Paglin estimated that an additional $4 billion would be sufficient to raise them above the poverty level.

Obviously any consideration of these statistics is going to evoke disputes. Those who want to increase the share of the budget going to help the needy will tend to overstate the number of families and individuals needing help. Similarly, those who want to cut such spending will try to minimize the number in need. None, however, can dispute the tremendous increase in federal expenditures on social programs. Between 1965 and 1975, public expenditures for social welfare programs quadrupled—from $77 billion to $286 billion. During the same time, official poverty statistics showed only a 30 percent drop in the number of poor people. Something is obviously wrong either with the way we measure poverty or with the target efficiency of our programs—or both. In any event, arguments are now made that we already devote enough of the budget to welfare, and resistance is growing to the idea of doing much more than we now are.

A second argument against massive redistribution of income is that taxes are already scheduled to reach a record percentage of gross national product by fiscal 1981. As a result, the American public appears unwilling to pay more. Thirty states of the required 34 have already petitioned Congress to call a Constitutional Convention that would require a balanced federal budget. Perhaps such a convention and the resulting Constitutional amendment are still unlikely. But these calls are symptomatic of the feeling that the government is already spending too much for what it is getting. Economists point out that if taxes get high enough, they become a disincentive for work and begin to exert a drag on the economy. Further, as times become harder, the number of people in need increases.

Advocates of redistribution sometimes argue that redistribution would not necessarily cost any more than the present hodgepodge of in-kind and cash transfers. Congress has indicated that it does not believe this. First, as we learned from Carter's welfare reform effort in the last Congress, advocates of redistribution would probably balk at supporting a program that did not yield greater benefits than the existing system. Second, many believe that it would be only a matter of time before various in-kind services reappeared to address situations where income redistribution left gaps or where the redistributed income was not wisely spent.

As the Carnegie Council (Keniston, 1977) candidly points out, its recommendation would indeed raise taxes for families with incomes higher than the median level—those over $18,000. Although families with incomes between $18,000 and, say, $35,000 are not in poverty, many of them are feeling the pinch of trying to maintain middle-class standards in today's economy. Over half of these middle-class families have two workers, and to put it mildly, they are less than sympathetic to paying any more taxes than they already do.

The third reason that a massive income redistribution program is unlikely to be enacted is that redistribution of income is not viewed as a legitimate goal by most Americans. A recent article by Marc Plattner (1979) in *The Public Interest* correctly points out that although some of our policies, such as income taxes and social insurance, have a redistributive impact, they were not adopted with a redistributive rationale. Instead, they were structured on a progressive basis so they would be financed by those best able to bear the burden. It is important to remember this distinction when thinking about any enlargement of the government's redistributive function. Plattner quotes Christopher Jencks's (1972) conclusions:

> The crucial problem today is that relatively few people view income inequality as a serious problem ... Americans now tend to assume that incomes are determined by private decisions in a largely unregulated economy and that there is no realistic way to alter the resulting distribution. Until they come to believe that the distribution of income is a political issue, subject to popular regulation and control, very little is likely to change (p. 30).

Of course, Jencks believes this viewpoint needs to be changed—an opinion with which Plattner and most public officials seem to disagree.

CONCLUSIONS

Summing up, the chances are very low for enactment of income redistribution as a key component of a national program to address the needs of families with children. There is no room in the budget for massive new expenditures; there is some question as to the need for them; people are unwilling to pay more taxes; and there is virtually no political support for a policy of income redistribution.

This may sound like a bleak, downbeat analysis of the political landscape, but it is not totally without hope. It will not be possible in the future simply to bulldoze programs through the legislative process as has been done for the past ten years. Considerable skill and finesse will be needed. And it will be necessary to use strategies which do not depend on any—or much—further leveling of income.

My guess is that the kinds of initiatives with the most chance for success in the future will combine some or all of the following elements:

—Preventive services that can be demonstrated to save government expenditures later on. Lazar's (Lazar *et al.*, 1977; Chapter 3) work showing that early intervention programs appear to reduce the incidence of special education assignments or repeating a grade once children enter the public schools, and the current emphasis on providing family services or permanent placement via adoption in order to avoid the personal catastrophes that so often accompany foster care are two examples of such preventive programs.

—Government will probably use the regulatory process to force the private sector to undertake some activities that ten years ago would have been considered government responsibility. Health insurance may turn out to be a series of regulations prescribing what types of health insurance programs employers must offer their employees while the government limits itself to supporting people who are not covered by one program or another. Schools are already requiring that children be immunized before they can begin first grade. The government is taking an active role in instituting flexitime and permanent part-time positions, and this may soon extend to private employers—much in the same way that Congress has mandated the provision of pregnancy disability coverage in company-wide disability plans.

—In the matter of child care particularly, there is likely to be a great deal of encouragement of individual initiative. Adoption of good parenting techniques will continue to be encouraged through government support of media and school programs. Advice on how to choose child-care services, how to provide for sound health practices in the home, how to ensure appropriate prenatal care, and so forth, may be subsidized in hope that government intervention will not be necessary.

—Existing programs addressed to the needs of children and of families in poverty will continue, but there will probably be continuing efforts to target them more exclusively on those in need. I mentioned several instances of this attempt earlier.

—Finally, we may see a continuation of the current trend toward coordinating and consolidating existing programs, particularly at the delivery level. At the very least, programs should not cancel out one another. With luck, they might be made to work together in ways that address local needs and priorities and which make sense for children and their families.

Looking ahead, some items on the legislative agenda do not appear likely to be enacted. Any version of a comprehensive child development program funded and sponsored by the federal government has a very dim future. The same is true, as I mentioned earlier, of a massive, comprehensive system of income redistribution, and probably also of a more modest blending of existing in-kind services into an income transfer system of the sort that was contemplated in the 95th Congress. Tax incentives or vouchers for things like day care, school tuition, and possibly other services might have some appeal, but it appears likely that their cost rules out any substantial expansion in the near future.

If there is a silver lining in this cloudy picture, it is the discipline that tight budgets and lowered expectations will impose. The clear impossibility of blitzing a problem with federal funds means that other strategies must be pursued. Ways must be found to target funds effectively, use them to leverage results, coodinate them to maximize impact. Possibly, if the current austerity yields more effective strategies and techniques, we shall be better able to argue for more generous funding in the future.

REFERENCES

Jencks, C. *Inequality.* New York: Basic Books, 1972.

Keniston, K. *All our children: The American family under pressure.* New York: Harcourt Brace Jovanovich, 1977.

Lazar, I., Hubbell, V., Murray, H., Rosche, M., & Royce, J. *The persistence of preschool effects: A long-term follow-up of fourteen infant and preschool experiments.* (Final report for ACYF Grant No. 18-76-07843). Ithaca, N.Y.: Cornell University, Community Service Laboratory, September 1977.

National Academy of Sciences. *Toward a national policy for children and families.* Washington, D.C.: Author, 1976.

Paglin, M. Poverty in the United States: A reevaluation. *Policy Review,* 1979, *8,* 7-24.

Plattner, M. F. The welfare state vs. the redistributive state. *Public Interest,* 1979, *55,* 28-48.

Rivlin, A. *Poverty status of families under alternative defintions of income* (Congressional Budget Office *Background Paper* No. 17). Washington, D.C.: U.S. Government Printing Office, 1977.

Comments on Phillips's Paper

ELI A. RUBINSTEIN is Adjunct Research Professor of Psychology at the University of North Carolina at Chapel Hill. Dr. Rubinstein is also a faculty member of the Bush Institute for Child and Family Policy at UNC.

My wife and I recently moved to Chapel Hill because we had heard it was a marvelously hospitable and stimulating place to live. For us, it has certainly lived up to its reputation. There is a quality of life here which seems to reinforce itself. You almost expect the environment to be supportive and that expectation subtly helps to produce its own fulfillment. It's just the opposite of a vicious cycle. I'm not sure what to call it, but I see it working in many ways. People smile more here, they seem to want to help, they want good things to happen, and they commit themselves to doing good things.

I say all this not just as a comment on Chapel Hill, but as a preliminary comment on Martha Phillips's paper. As someone who was in Washington in the "good old days" when budgets for federal social programs were most forthcoming, I am saddened that the Washington environment is no longer as encouraging a place to be as it once was. Effective public policy needs a supportive environment just as you and I do.

But wishing won't make it so, and as Martha Phillips points out, one cannot look toward the Washington scene with optimism insofar as supporting new social programs is concerned. The practical question is: What policy choices are there and how are they best made?

I would begin with a basic conceptual approach that may seem heretical to many readers of this book; namely, do not talk about programs for "families and children." On the one hand, it seems most important to structure public policy in its broadest terms. Certainly, no one could be opposed to programs that strengthen the family and support and protect children. We were all children once and most of us grew up in families. How could we be opposed to any public program in these areas? Easy. Less by being opposed than by not actively supporting a *particular* program. Children and families as public issues are, paradoxically, so large, so central, and so basic to the fabric of our society that one cannot really identify with so broad an issue. Support for retarded children? Yes, if I have a retarded child. Support for low-income families? Yes, if I live in a low-income family. Support for anything that I feel touches me directly. It may sound selfish, but it is political reality. Overstated perhaps, but basically valid.

Let me give you an example from an area I know best; the federal mental health program. Here, in its essence—improving the mental health of the nation—is another large, central, basic goal. It, like the family and the child, is of great general interest. But effective program development came from dealing with mental health as a series of related special interests—schizophrenia, juvenile delinquency, suicide, mental retardation, psychopharmacology. Those were some of the specifically identified areas for which program funding was obtained. And I might add, it didn't hurt at all if one of the key senators or congressmen on the appropriations subcommittees had a schizophrenic or retarded child. As you all know, the entire mental retardation program was expanded and removed from the National Institute of Mental Health (NIMH) in the early 1960s because President Kennedy, with a mentally retarded sister, was personally interested in the development of a major program in mental retardation.

It is the specific program and not the larger conceptual framework that received support even in the good old days. True, the success rate—at least as measured by increasing budgets—was much higher then, but the process of seeking support was not that dissimilar. What is so discouraging now, despite the silver lining Martha Phillips sees in these dark clouds, is that even the best efforts are now meeting only limited success.

Aside from focusing on specific issues, what are some other approaches that worked in the past and can still work even in an era of tight budgeting? Show how the program will actually save money. They call it cost-effectiveness now, but it is not new at all. From the late 1950s through the early 1970s, the one most persuasive argument in the annual budget presentation of the director of NIMH was a chart showing the decline in total number of public psychiatric hospital inpatients. In 1955, there were 559,000 inpatients as a result of a continuing rise since the end of World War II. In 1970, this figure had declined to 339,000 instead of rising to 755,000 as the earlier curve had projected. As the NIMH budget went up, the inpatient population went down. Although it is naive to see a direct causal relation between NIMH budget increase and psychiatric inpatient decreases, that inverse ratio was a powerful budget argument each year.

A third approach beyond proposing specific programs and demonstrating cost-effectiveness is also important. You must actively involve a vocal public constituency. And this gets back to the special-interest approach. If the budgetary process is largely a political phenomenon—and it is—an active constituency is important. Not to make invidious comparisons, the National Rifle Association is as successful as it is because its members can be counted on when the association wants a demonstrated response to a proposed piece of legislation. Many times in the late 1960s when small clouds were beginning to gather on the Mental Health fiscal horizon, professional groups made no concerted effort to support national program needs. In fact, psychiatrists, psychologists, social workers, and psychiatric nurses were unable to find a common platform on which to argue their common budgetary needs. It is a happy accident that Mrs.

Carter came along with her strong interest in mental health. For the first time in recent years, some increases in mental health funding seem likely. But even these will dissipate in the present general climate without continued effort.

And that's a fourth important part of generating support for new policies— continued effort. You have to keep working at it year after year, budget after budget. And you have to build on a series of powerful arguments to support those budgetary needs. Another example is apropos. In 1955, the Joint Commission on Mental Health was formed. By 1960, it had published eight major monographs and a comprehensive call for action on a large mental health program. In 1963, the Community Mental Health legislation was passed. That's eight years from the initial development of an argument for budgetary increases to their first major implementation. It takes time and continued effort to get program support.

And, finally, you can't get discouraged no matter how bad things look. You have to keep working at it. I like the way Martha Phillips ends her paper. I'm not sure she believes that fiscal austerity yields more effective strategies and techniques. But that is a necessary attitude to present if you are to continue producing new ideas and get others to believe in those ideas. And getting other people to believe your good ideas is how policy ultimately gets implemented.

And so, I would say to Martha Phillips and all her colleagues in Washington, it can be done. Funding for social programs—for specific programs ultimately beneficial to families and children—can be found by using the same old strategies and techniques even though you call them something new. I must end as I began—on a personal note. With sympathy and good wishes to Mrs. Phillips, right now I'd rather be in Chapel Hill believing in what she is doing and helping her do it, than be in Washington doing it.

Comments on Phillips's Paper

FRANK A. LODA is a Professor of Pediatrics at the University of North Carolina at Chapel Hill. Dr. Loda is also a faculty member of the Bush Institute for Child and Family Policy at UNC.

I agree with Martha Phillips that the United States has serious economic problems. There are no villains to eliminate and no magic cures to be effected. Sacrifice is required and waste should not be tolerated. But admitting that things are bad hardly seems an ideal justification for maintaining the *status quo*. Particularly in the area of my own concern—child health—many positive changes could be achieved if we attended more to priorities and less to expensive new programs.

It probably reflects my own Populist background, but I find it difficult to accept the inequities of our society as they effect children without fighting for change. I am reminded of one of the great Populist heroes, Mary Ellen Lease, who once said that Kansans needed "to raise less corn and more hell." The time has come for those of us who are concerned about children to be less willing to accept the old excuses for inaction and begin to raise more hell.

We can no longer depend on table scraps for children. They need a place at the dinner table, but under current conditions, they're lucky to eat in the kitchen. This situation is especially distressing because, at least in the case of health expenditures, the problem is not simply a lack of funds, but the way available health money is actually spent. Let me give examples.

I am responsible for running the general pediatric clinics at North Carolina Memorial Hospital. One out of eight children who comes to our clinic is medically indigent but has no Medicaid coverage, primarily because the child comes from an intact family that does not meet the guidelines established for Aid to Families with Dependent Children in North Carolina. One out of every four children who comes to our clinic has income that, by federal standards, is in the 40 percent pay category. Again, for such children, there is no available third-party coverage. Leaving aside the question of adequacy of Medicaid payments, it is difficult to provide good care when 25 percent of all patients cannot begin to meet the cost of service and those 25 percent frequently require the greatest amount of help.

Think for a moment what these data mean for a young physician who wants to serve the entire patient population in a small rural community in the South. Pediatricians in private practice have an overhead that amounts to about 50 percent of their fees. If 25 percent of their pediatric patients cannot meet the expenses of care, how can young doctors begin to earn a living? Pediatric ambulatory fees are marginal to begin with, and heavy volume is required. Thus, pediatricians and family doctors can't afford simply to write off 25 percent of their time—especially when their colleagues in other specialty areas can take advantage of federal funds in adult Medicaid and Medicare programs.

Students and house staff learn in medical school which specialties are able to generate adequate funding. Except for idealistic reasons, medical students are foolish to go into the child-caring profession when the whole basis of federal funding is to support expensive in-hospital procedures and the care of the elderly, with little attention to children's health needs. Thus, current federal policies discourage the development of an adequate pool of primary child health care providers.

Another example of the impact of federal policy on children's health concerns the coordination of health care at the local level. In North Carolina, for example, two state task forces, one on primary care and another on child health, recently reported to the governor. Both of these task forces urged local planning involving the public and private sectors to develop coordinated services for the total population. I believe such planning efforts, which are currently being attempted in a number of states, are doomed unless the emphasis on funding for health services by the federal government is radically reversed.

In the area of newborn care, for example, we have seen controversy in North Carolina and elsewhere over where perinatal monies will go. It is painful to see the argument over whether the money should go into intensive care nurseries or outreach services divide professionals who must work together to develop a coordinated perinatal program. Both are desperately needed. Further, quality care for the newborn means potentially 70 years of productive, healthy life. Yet we are told that there isn't enough money for both intensive care nurseries and outreach programs for mothers and children. Why not? Federal expenditures for health care continue to increase as billions of dollars are devoted to expensive and highly complicated—but questionably effective—treatment for the chronically and terminally ill.

The federal government must assume the major share of blame for this imbalance between child health services and adult care. Only 8 percent of federal spending on health care goes to children. Less than 15 percent of all spending for health care goes to children, even though private sources contribute a significantly greater percentage of their health spending to children. But the trend of disproportionate federal spending on health care for adults continues. In fact, recent proposals of catastrophic medical care for adults would be a catastrophe for health expenditures on children.

Let me reiterate that the problem is not simply lack of money for health care. Much of the recent talk of fiscal restraint that Phillips emphasizes has not affected health care expenditures. The benefits of this spending are simply being unevenly distributed to the adult population. Indeed health care costs now account for 8.8 percent of the GNP, up from 5.5 percent only a few years ago. By 1983, health care costs are projected to rise to 10 percent of the gross national product. The question is how this money is to be spent. We must argue for more effective child health care programs as part of any federal health program. It is the federal government that, in large measure, is fueling the inflation in health care costs and is directing the flow of health care dollars increasingly away from children to the elderly and chronically ill. Thus, at least in the case of child health programs, significant progress should not be impeded by the trends toward fiscal conservation and resentment of federal regulation that Phillips views as obstructions to new initiatives on behalf of children. What I have argued is that a larger proportion of the federal health dollar should be spent on children—precisely where it will do the most good.

Many years ago Edmund Burke, the great English statesman, set forth a conservative view of the social contract that can still guide our actions on behalf of children:

> Society is indeed a contract. Society is a partnership in all science, a partnership in all art, a partnership in every virtue, and in all perfection. As the ends of such a partnership can not be obtained in many generations it becomes a partnership not only between those that are living but between those who are living, those who are dead and those who are to be born.

We are violating that contract every day and every hour as we allow future generations to be born without access to the basic health care that our riches and technology can provide.

JAMES J. GALLAGHER, William Rand Kenan Professor of Education, is Director of the Frank Porter Graham Child Development Center and the Bush Institute for Child and Family Policy at the University of North Carolina at Chapel Hill. A former Chief of the Bureau of Education for the Handicapped and Deputy Assistant Secretary for Planning, Research, and Evaluation of the Office of Education, he has consulted with numerous state, federal, and private agencies on programs for handicapped and programs for gifted children. Dr. Gallagher is also the author of over 70 books and articles on education, handicapped and gifted children, and policy analysis. He has also been chairman of the North Carolina Competency Test Commission and chairman of the Social Policy Committee of the Society for Research in Child Development.

9

Some Final Thoughts—
Social Policy and
the Academic Community

The seven presentations in this book show the range and depth of interest within the academic community on public issues. Though two of the papers (Hoffman's and Phillips's) speak from the decision makers' viewpoint, each gives its perception of the academicians' attempts to help the decision process. This interest of academia in policy is not a new phenomenon, but it is a growing one. In the three and a half decades since World War II, fundamental changes have taken place in the United States academic community. Many professors were employed in the war effort on a wide variety of policy issues and were loathe to go back to the splendid isolation of the ivy-covered walls that were the universities of the '20s and '30s.

After World War II, more and more professors were called upon by business and government to apply their academic knowledge to practical problems and issues in the real worlds of business, economics, education, and social problems. Coincident with that change was a new attitude on the part of government itself. It was concluded that the government could not stand by and ignore the social problems of poverty, discrimination, lack of health care, and protection against the ravages of old age.

So there developed an increased traffic between the halls of academe and the legislative and executive branches of government at state and federal levels. Academicians soon found that what they thought to be desirable policy often didn't get implemented, that their knowledge was ignored, and that policies they considered foolish or ill-advised were adopted. All this experience was a prelude to academician's searching for a better understanding of the process by which the world of knowledge and the world of power intersected.

THE NEED FOR MODELS

The papers in this book reflect a continuing search for models of policy analysis. This is a quest for a process by which academic knowledge and public action can be placed into a more systematic context. Each analysis is conducted from the author's unique view about the policy problem itself. Thus, no single model or system of predetermined policy analysis was applied. Although the varied approaches show creativity, they do little to strengthen the systematic nature of policy analysis. Until we can provide some general guidance through a model or system, we shall continue to rely too much upon the creative insights of individual analysts.

In dealing with policy analysis, it is in everyone's interest to move procedures as quickly as possible from the stage of creative art to that of systematic science. Haskins, in the introductory chapter, points out some stages by which some system can be brought to bear on policy issues.

Recognition of the different factors that are important in moving from the world of knowledge to the world of power is one of those first prerequisites. In academia, the world of knowledge and science, the search for truth is presumed to be predominant. There facts are valued; and theories which explain facts are valued even more highly. It is something of a shock and requires a major adaptation for academicians to realize that their reverence for facts is not necessarily shared by those in the political arena.

Facts, as the comment by Lazar clearly indicates, sometimes merely operate to reduce the options available to the policymaker. If the fact is that our health needs are not being met, then the pressure becomes great upon the politician to take action. If the fact is that our educational system is not as efficient as it might be, or that large numbers of children in the country suffer varying states of malnutrition, each set of facts evokes pressures for remedial action that require the politician to respond and, in that sense, reduce his opportunities to temporize—a situation the public decision maker may not relish.

Politicians seem to hold a rather similar viewpoint toward program evaluation. If as a politician you have risked becoming the initiator of a new program designed to meet some important health or educational objective, you do not want to hear that your program is not working. On the contrary, you have a great desire for good news, proof that the action you took was wise and prudent and brought substantial benefits to your constituencies. News that the program is not working or has failed in some fundamental fashion is an embarrassment—information to be suppressed or ignored. It has even been suggested that legislators provide rather limited sums for program evaluation because they do not wish to hear that their attractive ideas have been translated or implemented in a way that has not borne out the effective rhetoric needed to get the laws passed in the first place.

Is Rational Analysis Possible?

The contributors to this book have raised enough issues to discourage any thought that some new methodology, such as social policy analysis, will, by itself, build a sturdier bridge between knowledge and its public application. There are even those who call it a waste of time to try to apply a rational system to an irrational world, a world of politics where passions, prejudices, and biases hold sway. As Lazar and Silver point out, the work of professionals can be diverted into support for naked advocacy of a predetermined political goal or position, much as expert professional witnesses can be manipulated by the legal system into a single-minded advocacy position over some complex issue in psychiatry or sociology.

In addition, there are forces at work in the society that prevent the easy application of knowledge to social action. In the past decade we have seen rapidly expanding service programs for children and families that do not match a much more slowly growing economy. In this era of severe competition for limited resources, advocates for special services for children and families have proved, as Hoffman points out, to have little effective political power. Phillips also notes that many Americans have become increasingly resistant to the re-distribution of funds to meet social needs and have seriously questioned the effectiveness of those programs that have been tried.

To these difficulties, one can add the issue raised by Silver: we have no national plan for health, or education either for that matter, because of long-standing belief that basic decisions in these areas should arise from the states and local communities, rather than from a comprehensive national level, as is the tradition in European countries.

Given all these forces that seem to act against accurate or adequate knowl-edge translation, does the process of social policy analysis have inherent merit? Obviously, we believe it does. The policy advocate must still make a case and that case cannot be based merely on naked political force. More and more, it must marshal facts and evidence in order to provide a rationale that can be supported against challenge.

Policy analyst as technician. In this role the policy analyst primarily collects information in order that the decision maker can more appropriately make proper choices. The policy analyst tries to avoid showing personal policy prefer-ence on the grounds that this would extend beyond his given mandate, and such advocacy might cast doubt on the objectivity of his reports.

This role would generally be played by an aide or lower-echelon official to a policymaker. Information on child-care options or different modes of financ-ing, for example, would be presented with no judgment offered by the analyst himself, clearly fixing the responsibility for the decision upon the policymaker. Many decision makers prefer this model and resent the analyst who attempts to present his own choice of the most desirable option.

Policy analyst as counselor. In this role the policy analyst has an obligation to display the full range of options and alternatives to the decision maker and, of course, to point out what might be likely unintended consequences or externali-ties of each alternative. In addition, the policy analyst is expected to make value judgments about which proposal or strategy seems to be the best. Such judgments seem to be well received when there is substantial agreement between the value systems of analyst and decision maker.

In this instance, for example, child-care options are presented with their advantages and disadvantages, but the analyst feels free to recommend the option that seems to have come off best in the analysis, always leaving room for the decision maker to weigh all options and reach a different choice.

Policy analyst as advocate. In this role, policy analysts are seen as having a responsibility for enhancing desirable social goals. Their intimate knowledge of the problem and possible strategies should obligate analysts to step into the policy field as vigorous supporters of the "best" way.

For such an analysis to be effective, the biases of the policy analyst should be apparent from the beginning so that no one will be surprised at the slanted interpretation of the data. Sometimes, for example, the analyst has had a great deal of professional experience in advocating an increase in day-care funds or increased employment opportunities for women. Since everyone knows the bias, the analyst has a special responsibility to make sure the data and other information are not distorted by that personal bias; otherwise, the analysis is likely to convince only those who already support the position advocated.

One can see all three of these approaches on the current scene, and the consumer of such reports needs to be alert to the role played by the analyst in order to evaluate the report itself. The public impression of the objectivity of scientists is quite mistaken. There are few more passionate advocates than scientists for their own convictions—the objectivity comes from the process, the scientific method, not from some superhuman attempt by scientists to ignore their own biases. We need similar methodology in policy analysis to bring the objectivity that cannot be provided by policy analysts themselves.

Finally, we should not despair over Lazar's point that there are few direct linkages between research and action. Only a research study deserves direct translation into action. It is the synthesis of a wide variety of information, research, and knowledge that can lead to effective public policy. Those who contributed to this book hope that by exploring alternatives, by testing criteria for decision making, by providing facts about the effectiveness of programs, we can progressively aid our society to achieve a greater conjunction between what is, and what ought to be, in programs for children and families.

Numbers in *italics* indicate where complete references are listed.

Author Index

Subject Index